B. F. Van Meter,
Author of this Book.

# GENEALOGIES

## AND SKETCHES

OF SOME

# OLD FAMILIES

WHO HAVE TAKEN PROMINENT PART
IN THE DEVELOPMENT OF VIRGINIA AND KENTUCKY
ESPECIALLY, AND LATER OF MANY OTHER
STATES OF THIS UNION.

BY

BENJAMIN F. VAN METER.

Southern Historical Press, Inc.
Greenville, South Carolina

Please direct all correspondence and book orders to:
**SOUTHERN HISTORICAL PRESS, Inc.**
**PO Box 1267**
**Greenville, SC    29602-1267**

ISBN #978-1-63914-151-7
*Printed in the United States of America*

# INDEX.

| | PAGE |
|---|---|
| LEWIS FAMILY | 5 |
| John Lewis | 5 |
| Thomas Lewis | 13 |
| Andrew Lewis | 15 |
| Colonel William Lewis | 17 |
| Colonel Charles Lewis | 19 |
| Colonel Thomas Lewis | 20 |
| Nancy Lewis Garrard | 22 |
| General James Garrard | 22 |
| Sallie Lewis Clay | 22 |
| General Green Clay | 22 |
| Elizabeth Clay Smith | 22 |
| Colonel John Speed Smith | 22 |
| Pauline Clay Rodes | 22 |
| Sidney Payne Clay | 23 |
| Brutus J. Clay | 24 |
| Clays | 26 |
| Henry Clay | 27 |
| Hector P. Lewis | 28 |
| Asa K. Lewis | 31 |
| Edward Lewis | 32 |
| Kitty Lewis Payne | 32 |
| Colonel Henry C. Payne | 32 |
| Stephen D. Lewis | 33 |
| Thornton Lewis | 34 |
| Captain Thomas Wright | 34 |
| Sophia Lewis Johnson | 38 |
| Hon. John T. Johnson | 38 |
| Alpheus Lewis | 38 |
| Theodosia Ann Turner Lewis | 38 |
| Douglass Payne Lewis | 40 |
| Samuel Lewis | 43 |
| John Lewis | 43 |
| William Lewis | 43 |
| Stephen Lewis (son of General Robert Lewis) | 43 |
| PHILLIPS FAMILY | 44 |
| MOSS FAMILY | 45 |

PAGE

Van Meter Family...................................... 47
Isaac Van Metre, or Van Meter .................... 49
Garrett Van Meter.................................. 50
Isaac Van Meter.... .............................. 53
Jacob Van Meter ................................... 53
Isaac Van Meter ( "Big Ike" ) .................... 59
Hon. John I. Van Meter............................ 61
Colonel Jacob Van Meter's Children............... 62
Isaac Van Meter (of Clark County, Kentucky)...... 65
Solomon Van Meter................................. 65
Captain William D. Nicholas ...................... 69
James Stonestreet ................................ 72
Irvine Hockaday .................................. 73
Nelson Prewitt.................................... 74
Thomas Moore Field................................ 76
Dr. S. W. Willis ................................. 78
George W. Swoope.................................. 79
Evaline Swoope Van Meter.......................... 80
Isaac C. Van Meter (of Fayette Co., Ky.)......... 81
Henry Hull........................................ 81
Jacob Van Meter .................................. 83
Sarah Ann Van Meter Hall ......................... 83
Susan T. Van Meter Allan ......................... 83
Dr. Algernon Sidney Allan ........................ 83
Benjamin F. Van Meter ............................ 88
Archie L. Hamilton, Sr............................ 91
Henry Clay Bigelow ............................... 92
William Pettit ................................... 93
Colonel James H. Holloway......................... 94
General John Stuart Williams ..................... 95
Patton D. Harrison ............................... 97
Captain Alex. Macomb Wetherill...................100
Paper read by Emma Van Meter Hamilton before D. A. R. Society .....102
Thos. C. Van Meter ...............................111
W. H. Campbell....................................111
Eliza Caroline Van Meter .........................111
Abram Van Meter ..................................112
Jonas Marks Kleiser ..............................112
Louis Marshall Van Meter .........................113
Horatio W. Bruce .................................123
Thomas H. Moore ..................................124
Colonel John H. Moore.............................130
James M. West ....................................131

PAGE

John S. Hanna.................................................132
John Milton Van Meter .......................................133
Rev. Stephen Yerkes, D. D....................................137
Abram Van Meter (of Fayette Co., Ky.) .......................138
Garrett Van Meter (West Virginia) ...........................140
Solomon Van Meter (son of Garrett)...........................141
William C. Van Meter ........................................144
Charles W. Van Meter ........................................145
Sarah Inskeep Van Meter......................................147
Van Meters, as given by Mrs. Anna Louise Thompson, of Clinton, Iowa .149
Van Meter family in reunion..................................156
Memorandum from Emanuel Van Meteren, author of old history .......159

CUNNINGHAM FAMILY............................................166
Joseph Helm Clay ...........................................168
Captain Isaac Cunningham ...................................169

HARNESS FAMILY..............................................171
Captain J. Hanson McNeill...................................173
McNeill's capture of Crook and Kelley ......................176
Roll of McNeill's Command ..................................181
Mary Johnston ..............................................182

# PREFACE.

In this book I have gleaned and collected from every authentic source within my reach such genealogical, biographical, and historical facts as I consider entirely reliable concerning the prominent old families of which I treat, and, as a general rule, have endeavored to show the connection by marriage of the different families.

While genealogies and biographical sketches are the principal aim of this book, I have not hesitated to add historical sketches when of sufficient importance to justify recording ; and by way of adding interest and entertainment, amusing incidents and anecdotes have not been rejected.

It can not be denied that to our forefathers we owe much of the happiness and prosperity we now enjoy, and every worthy descendant of those gallant and adventurous spirits must feel the desire to become acquainted with their history and characters as well as their lineage, as far back as it can be authenticated. In undertaking to establish this lineage before it is entirely lost, and to gather up many interesting and valuable facts and incidents which, in their present disconnected and much scattered condition, are already obscure and would soon be entirely covered up by the "sands of time and the clods of the valley," I have made free use of various authors, and only confine myself to such sources of information as I consider reliable. Among the authors from whom I have drawn are : Churches and Families of Virginia, by Bishop Mead ; Annals of Augusta County, Virginia, by Joseph A. Waddell ; Genealogy of Virginians, by Horace P. Hayden ; Foot's History of Virginia ; Campbell's History of Virginia ; History of Augusta County, Virginia, by J. Lewis Payton ; Kerchival's History, and others ; as well as from family records when access could be had to them ; and for later facts I rely on the oldest living members of the family and on my own recollections of what I have learned from the older members of these families, whose testimony can not now be had ; on tombstones and recorded wills, and any source from which authentic information can be had.

As to the Lewis family, of which I shall treat first, I had the advantage and enjoyed the pleasure of a personal acquaintance with nearly all the sons of the late Col. Thomas Lewis in the latter part of their lives, and gained from them some valuable information concerning that family.

THE AUTHOR.

# GENEALOGIES AND SKETCHES.

## THE LEWIS FAMILY.

For years before 1700 there lived in Donegal County, Province of Ulster, Ireland, a farmer, John Lewis, and his wife, Margaret, a daughter of Laird Lynn, of Loch Lynn, Scotland. This man belonged to what was known as the middle class of society, although he had descended from a French nobleman, and was an educated, practical business man of his day (of that class which constituted the nerve and sinew of the body politic). Above him in that country the Irish lord reveled in luxury and wealth, which was frequently attended with idleness and vice, while beneath him struggled the peasantry, most generally in ignorance, penury, and want.

John Lewis was the son of Andrew Lewis, Esq., and his mother was Mary Calhoun, and this family was of Protestant-French descent from the Huguenots, who had been driven from France by religious persecution about 1685, directly after the revocation of the Edict of Nantes.

Margaret Lynn descended from a very distinguished old Protestant family of Scotch Highlanders who were quite famous for their bravery and military prowess back in the early history of Scotland, when the clans were so frequently marshalled for bloody contest on the moors and glens of that historic old country, where her ancestry had fought valiantly and successfully for their lands, their leaders, and their religion. She was therefore of a stock that were intelligent, generous, hospitable, and fearless.

John Lewis was born in Donegal County, Ireland, in 1678; was educated in Scotland, where he made the acquaintance of Margaret Lynn, who became his wife and went with him to his native county of Donegal, where they were prospering and rearing a family, having obtained an advantageous land lease under a wealthy Irish Lord who was a Catholic. John Lewis and his wife being Protestants and Presbyterians, and the Catholic Lord preferring a Catholic ten-

ant, undertook to oust Lewis from his lease without regard to law
or justice.    Lewis refused to vacate, and the Lord with his bailiff
and posse undertook to compel him to surrender the house and
lands.    Lewis barred the doors and refused admittance.    His lordship fired a shot through the window, which killed Charles Lewis,
the brother of John, who was lying sick in bed in the house, and
another shot wounded his wife, Margaret Lewis, in the arm.    Thus
outraged, John Lewis attacked the landlord with his shillalah,
cracked his head and scattered his brains.    He also killed the chief
bailiff, and drove the balance of the posse in a panic from the prem-
ises.    John Lewis is described as a man more than six feet tall,
very powerful and active.    After this tragedy he left his wife to
settle up his business affairs in Ireland, while he made his escape to
Portugal; but after three years Margaret Lewis emigrated to Philadelphia with her children, and, according to pre-arrangement, met
her husband there in 1720.    They lived in Pennsylvania for twelve
years, and then removed to the very frontier of Virginia in 1732 and
settled on the west side of the Blue Ridge Mountains, near where
the town of Staunton is now located.    This family, with one or two
others, were the first white people who ever lived in the wilds and
wilderness west of the Blue Ridge when Augusta County comprised
all that territory claimed by the British Government west of this
range of mountains and extending to the Mississippi River, comprising a considerable part of what is now West Virginia, and all of
Kentucky, Ohio, Indiana, and Illinois.

John Lewis and his sons built a substantial stone house on a
small stream called Lewis Creek (about two miles from where the
town of Staunton is now situated), and in this stone house John
Lewis resided for the rest of his life.    It was called Lewis' Fort,
and is still standing, unless it has been recently destroyed.    In it
the sturdy and fearless John Lewis and his worthy family withstood
the opposing Indian savage of the West, while his substantial home
furnished hospitable shelter and protection for the enterprising emigrant who crossed the Blue Ridge in search of a home in this then
wilderness country, until he could select a location and build his
cabin; and here, notwithstanding the apparent adverse surroundings, he, by fearless, determined effort, prospered and accumulated a
large estate, and reared a family of sons, every one of whom became
famous men in their country's service — either military or civil.    At
the time of this settlement this family consisted of John Lewis, his

wife (Margaret), with sons Samuel, Thomas, Andrew, and William, and one daughter named Margaret.

All of these children were born in Ireland except Margaret and the youngest son, Charles — the daughter born in Pennsylvania and Charles in the wilderness. In a book entitled "Annals of Augusta County, Virginia," we find the following :

"John Lewis and his sturdy sons were just the men to battle with the adverse circumstances which surrounded them in this wilderness country ; and, again, John Lewis and his entire family were famous for their military prowess. And the sequel shows that they were quite prominent in civil affairs as well ; for we find that when Governor Gooch, under King George 2d, appointed the first Bench of Magistrates which established civil government in Augusta County, when this county embraced all the territory west of the Blue Ridge, Col. John Lewis and his son Thomas were both appointed, and Col. Lewis served until his death. They were appointed to this responsible position October 30, 1745, and Col. John Lewis died February 1, 1762, at the advanced age of 84 years. (Robert Cunningham, James Patton, and others were appointed at the same time.) Thomas Lewis held this responsible position until the independence of the colonies was established."

Col. John Lewis was noted as the best frontiersman of his time, and was recognized by all as a man of great influence and force of character. He displayed excellent judgment in his selection of land and other practical business affairs, and left a very valuable estate to his family. In Orange County Court of Record there is a deed conveying to John Lewis 2,071 acres of land, dated February 21, 1738, from the Beverly Manor Grant, and he possessed several other valuable tracts of land in other sections of the State. But more important than this, he was one of the most substantial pillars of the church, and did much to plant and foster religion in this wilderness. The first sermon ever preached west of the Blue Ridge was delivered by the Rev. James Anderson, of the Pennsylvania Presbytery, in the year 1738, at the stone house home of Col. John Lewis, and he did his full share along with Col. James Patton, John Preston (the shipmaster of Dublin), and others in building and sustaining Tinkling Spring Church.

Its first pastor was Rev. John Craig, who came to Augusta County in 1740 and preached for that congregation many years, sowing the good seed of the gospel according to the Presbyterian faith and creed, which still flourishes there and brings forth fruit to this day.  This remarkable man was born in Ireland in 1678, during the reign of Charles 2d, William and Mary, Queen Ann, George 1st, George 2d, and two years of George 3d.  He lived first in the north of Ireland, and while yet in the full vigor of his manhood he came to America in time to advance beyond even the front line of civilization in the then struggling colony, and take a very prominent part in public affairs, ever bearing his full share of the trials and hardships of the times, and reared a family of sons worthy of their parentage, and who took even a still greater share in making a glorious history for their adopted country.

Col. John Lewis' will, executed November 28, 1761, after expressing commendable faith and hope for his eternal future, disposes of his large estate to his family, and then names his three sons (Thomas, Andrew, and William) as his executors.  He was buried at Bellefonte, and an enormous uncut limestone slab was placed over his grave, where it yet lies half buried.  In 1850 this was supplemented by a marble slab bearing the following inscription :

HERE LIE THE REMAINS OF

JOHN LEWIS,

Who slew the Irish Lord, settled Augusta County,
Located the town of Staunton,
and furnished five sons to fight the battles of the
American Revolution.
He was the son of Andrew Lewis, Esq., and Mary Calhoun,
and was born in Donegal County, Ireland, 1678,
and died in Virginia, Feb. 1, 1762.
He was a brave man, a true patriot, and a firm
friend of liberty throughout the world.

———

Mortalitate relicta vivit immortalitate inductus.

A quotation from the " History of Augusta County " reads thus : " Irreproachable in his public and private morals ; courteous, affable, and eloquent ; fond of society, and excelling in conversation, he excited the admiration and love of the people, who adhered to him and the policy he pointed out, as well from their attachment to his person as because of their respect for his talents and his character." Had he continued in Europe his abilities and accomplishments, which had already given him a high local reputation and position, could not have remained long unknown and unrewarded by his sovereign.

He was destined, however, for another career—a more appropriate theater for his ardent and restless genius. Providence ordained him to become a pioneer of civilization—to erect the standard of the cross in the wilderness. In the colony which he founded the church anticipated the town and the county. Before either was established the gospel was preached in the houses of the settlers or under the shade of the trees. In Col. Lewis' house the first sermon ever delivered in the county was preached.

The circumstances which led to the emigration of John Lewis and his settlement in Augusta County are related in the Virginia Historical Register for 1851, and were written by John H. Peyton from information obtained of William I. Lewis, a member of Congress from 1817 to 1819, and a grandson of John Lewis, and are no doubt correct. After substantiating what has already been stated, he continues as follows : " He was the holder of a freehold lease for three lives upon a valuable farm in the County of Donegal, Province of Ulster, obtained upon equal terms and equivalents from one of the Irish nobility, who was an upright and honorable man and the owner of the reversion. This leasehold estate, with his wife's marriage portion, enabled the young couple to commence life with flattering prospects.

" They were both remarkable for their industry, piety, and integrity. They prospered and were happy. Before the catastrophe occurred which completely destroyed the hopes of this once happy family in Ireland and made them exiles from their native land, their affection was cemented by the birth of four sons : Samuel, Thomas, Andrew, and William. About the period of the birth of their third son, the Lord from whom he had obtained his lease — a landlord beloved by his tenants and neighbors—suddenly died, and his estates descended to his eldest son, a youth whose principles were directly the reverse of his father's. He was proud, profligate, and extravagant. Anticipating his income, he was always in debt, and to meet his numerous engagements he devised a variety of schemes, and among them one was to claim of his tenants a forfeiture of their leases upon some one of the numerous covenants inserted in instruments of the kind of that day. If they agreed to increase their rents the alleged forfeiture was waived ; if they refused, they were threatened with a long, tedious, and expensive lawsuit. Many of his tenants submitted to this injustice and raised their rents rather than be involved, even with justice on their side, in a legal controversy with a rich and powerful adversary, who could in this country, under these circumstances, devise ways and means to harass, persecute, and impoverish one in moderate circumstances.  Lewis, however, was different from any man who thus tamely submitted to wrong.  By industry and skill he had greatly improved his property ; his rent had been punctually paid, and all the covenants of his lease had been complied with faithfully.  To him, after seeing all the others, the agent of the young Lord came with his unjust demands. Lewis peremptorily dismissed him from his presence, and determined to make an effort to rescue his family from this threatened injustice by a personal interview with the young Lord, who, Lewis imagined, would scarcely have the hardihood to insist before his face upon the iniquitous terms proposed by his agent.  Accordingly he visited the castle of the young Lord.  A porter announced his name.  At the time the young Lord was engaged in his revels over the bottle with some of his companions of similar tastes and habits.  As soon as the name of Lewis was announced he recognized the only one of his tenants who had resisted his demands, and directed the porter to order him off.  When the porter delivered his Lord's order, Lewis resolved at every hazard to see him.  Accordingly he walked into the presence of the company—the porter not having the temerity to stand in his way.  Flushed with wine, the whole company rose to resent the insult and expel the intruder from the room.  But there was something in Lewis' manner that sobered them in a moment, and instead of advancing they seemed fixed in their places, and for a moment there was perfect silence, when Lewis calmly observed : 'I came here with no design to insult or injure any one, but to remonstrate in person to your Lordship against threatened injustice, and thus to avert from my family ruin.  In such a cause I have not regarded ordinary forms or ceremonies, and I warn you, gentlemen, to be cautious how you deal with a desperate man.'  This short address apparently stupefied the company.  Silence ensuing, Lewis embraced it to address himself particularly, in the following words, to the young Lord :  'Your much-respected father granted me the leasehold estate I now possess.  I have regularly paid my rents, and have faithfully complied with all the covenants of the lease.  I have a wife and three infant children whose happiness, comfort, and support depend, in a great degree, upon the enjoyment of this property, and yet I am told by your agent that I can no longer hold it without a base surrender of my rights to your rapacity.  Sir, I wish to learn from your lips whether or not you meditate such injustice, such cruelty as the terms mentioned by your agent indicate ; and I beg you before pursuing such a course to consider this matter coolly and dispassionately, or you will ruin me and disgrace yourself.' By the time this address was closed, the young Lord seemed to have recovered partially (in which he was greatly assisted by several heavy libations of wine) from the effects produced by the sudden, solemn, and impressive manner of his injured tenant. He began to ejaculate : 'Leave me, leave me, you rebel, you villain !' To this abuse Lewis replied calmly, as follows : 'Sir, you may save yourself this useless ebullition of passion. It is extremely silly and ridiculous. I have effected the object of my visit ; I have satisfied my mind, and have nothing more to say. I shall no longer disturb you with my presence.' Upon which he retired from the room apparently unmoved by the volly of abuse that broke forth from the young Lord and his drunken comrades as soon as he had turned his back. After they had recovered from the magical effect which the calm resolution and stern countenance of Lewis produced, they descanted upon what they called the insolence of his manner and the mock defiance of his speech with all the false views aristocratic pride, excited by the fumes of wine, in a monarchical government were so well calculated to inspire. During the evening the rash purpose was formed of dispossessing Lewis by force.

"Accordingly, on the next day, the young Lord, without any legal authority whatever, proceeded at the head of his guests and domestics to oust Lewis by force. Lewis saw the approach of the hostile array and conjectured the object of the demonstration. He had no arms but a shillalah, a weapon in possession of every Irish farmer at that period ; nor was there any one at his house but a brother, confined to bed by disease, his wife and three infant children ; yet he resolved to resist the lawless band, and closed the door. The young Lord on reaching the house demanded admittance, which, not being granted, the posse attacked the house, and after being foiled in several attempts to break down the door or in other ways to effect an entrance, one of the party introduced the muzzle of a musket through an aperture in the wall and discharged its contents — a bullet and three buckshot — upon those within. Lewis' sick brother was mortally wounded, and one of the shot passed through his wife's hand. Lewis, who had up to this time acted on the defensive, seeing the blood stream from the hand of his wife and his expiring brother weltering in his blood, became enraged, furious, and, seizing his shillalah, he rushed from the cottage, determined to avenge the wrong and sell his life as dearly as possible.

"The first person he encountered was the young Lord, whom he dispatched at a single blow, cleaving in twain his skull and scattering his brains upon himself and the posse. The next person he met was the steward, who shared the fate of his master ; rushing then upon the posse, stupefied at the ungovernable ardor and fury of Lewis' manner and the death of two of their party, they had scarcely time to save themselves, as they did by throwing away their arms and taking to flight. This awful occurrence brought the affairs of Lewis in Ireland to a crisis. Though he had violated no law, human or divine ; though he had acted strictly in self-defense against lawless power and oppression, yet the occurrence took place in a monarchical government, whose policy it is to preserve a difference in the ranks of society. One of the nobility* had been slain by one of his tenants. The connections of the young Lord were rich and powerful, those of Lewis poor and humble. With such fearful odds, it was deemed rash and unwise that Lewis should, even with law and justice on his side, surrender himself to the officers of the law. It was consequently determined that he should proceed, on that evening, disguised in a friend's dress, to the nearest seaport and take shipping for Oporto, in Portugal, where a brother of his wife was established in merchandise. Luckily he met a vessel just ready to sail from the bay of Donegal, in which he took passage. After various adventures — for the ship was not bound for Portugal — in different countries, he arrived at Oporto in the year 1729. Upon his arrival there he was advised by his brother-in-law, in order to elude the vigilance of his enemies, to proceed to Philadelphia, in Pennsylvania, and there to await the arrival of his family, which he learned was in good health, and which his brother-in-law undertook to remove to America. Lewis, following this advice, proceeded at once to Philadelphia. In a year his family joined him, and, learning from them that the most industrious efforts were being made by the friends of the young Lord to discover the country to which he had fled, he determined to penetrate deep into the American forest. He moved then immediately from Philadelphia to Lancaster, and there spent the winter of 1731 and 1732, and in the summer of 1732 he removed to the place near Staunton, in the

---

*The man killed was Sir Mungo Campbell, Lord of the Manor.

county of Augusta, Virginia, now called 'Bellefonte,' where he settled, brought up his family, conquered the country from the Indians, and amassed a large fortune."

After the Rev. John Craig's pastorate of Tinkling Spring Church, Rev. John A. Van Lear was pastor for many years. John Lewis emigrated to Virginia with Isaac and John Van Meter, who had obtained a grant of 40,000 acres of land from Governor Gooch, under King George 2d, and were on their way to that country to locate it. (See p. 25, History of Augusta County.) Samuel Lewis was captain of a company at Braddock's defeat, in which were Andrew, William, and Charles. This company cut their way through the enemy's lines and made their escape. Three of the brothers were wounded, and Samuel mortally. He died leaving no wife or children.

## THOMAS LEWIS.

The second son of Colonel John Lewis, Honorable Thomas Lewis, was born in Donegal County, Ireland, April 27, 1718, and removed with his parents to Philadelphia about the year 1729, and thence with them to Augusta County, Virginia, in 1734. He received a liberal education, first in this county from the teaching of Rev. John Craig, pastor of Tinkling Spring Church, and after this at the best school at that time in Eastern Virginia. He entered the public service at an early age, having been appointed along with his father and others, by Governor Gooch, as a member of the first Bench of Magistrates for Augusta County, when that county comprised all of the British claims west of the Blue Ridge Mountains and extending to the Mississippi River. He was appointed to this then responsible and honorable office at the age of twenty-seven years, and it should be borne in mind that this Bench of Magistrates constituted the entire civil government over that country at that time. This appointment was made October 30, 1745, and he held this office until the colonies declared their independence — about thirty years. Meantime he filled other very honorable positions. He was appointed County Surveyor, and held that office for many years. The town of Staunton, the county seat, was laid off by him, and the survey and plot were very neatly executed by his hand in 1748. He had the reputation of being the best mathematician in the State of Virginia in his day. He surveyed many tracts of land in that wilderness country, and he and General George Washington held large tracts of land in partnership until after the close of the Revolutionary War. General Washington spent many days at Mr. Lewis' house settling up their business and closing up their partnership. He was, for several terms, one of the members of the House of Burgesses from his country. He held this honorable position from 1761 to 1768, and was a member again during the trying times which immediately preceded the Declaration of Independence, as well as when that important document was framed in 1776. He and Captain Samuel McDowell, being at the time the representatives of their district in the House of Burgesses, were requested by a public meeting of their constituents to write a letter to Virginia's representatives in the Continental Congress, then in session, to commend them for the stand which they had taken and to sustain them in their position.

These Congressional representatives were : Peyton Randolph, Richard Henry Lee, George Washington, Patrick Henry, Richard Bland, Benjamin Harrison, and Edmund Randolph. The letter which they wrote to those very distinguished men on that very eventful occasion could have been dictated only by intelligent, cultivated, and patriotic minds, and was fully worthy of the occasion. (It can be found on page 150, Annals of Augusta County, Virginia.) Thomas Lewis was also one of the commissioners of the thirteen colonies to treat with the Indian tribes of the West in 1777. This treaty settled for the time all of the Indian wars, and enabled Washington to concentrate all of the colonial army against the British and compel them to acknowledge the Independence of the Colonies. In 1775, while he was a representative in the House of Burgesses, he was unanimously elected a delegate to the Colonial Congress, and was among the first to enroll his name among the "Sons of Liberty." He was a member of the convention that ratified the Constitution of the United States. He urged with eloquence and ability the adoption of the Constitution, and voted for its ratification. Thus we find that this distinguished man rendered very valuable services to his country in civil and political affairs during the most trying ordeal in its early history. His very defective eyesight rendered him unfit to join with his famous brothers in military affairs, but we find that his services were not less important nor less faithfully rendered. In a letter written by one of his grandsons, General Samuel H. Lewis, to Honorable Samuel Price, of Lewisburg, West Virginia, and dated April 15, 1885, he is described as a handsome man, fully six feet tall, with dark hair and eyes, but fair complexion, and though not inclined to corpulency, was robust and finely formed.

On the 26th of January, 1749, being then thirty-one years of age, he married Jane, daughter of William Strother, Esq., the bride being seventeen years of age. She was born and reared on an adjoining farm to that of the father of General George Washington ; was about the same age as General Washington, and went to school with him when young. Thomas Lewis and his wife, Jane, raised a family of thirteen children, a list of whom will be found on the concluding pages of these sketches. He was a man of very considerable literary attainments, was an eloquent speaker, and owned an extensive library. He died of a cancer in the face, at the age of seventy-two years. His widow died in 1820, at the age of eighty-eight years. Many distinguished men are among the descendants of this couple : Judges of Courts of Appeal, Congressmen, etc.


## ANDREW LEWIS.

General Andrew Lewis, the third son of Colonel John Lewis, was born in Donegal County, Ireland, in 1720, and removed with his parents and brothers first to Pennsylvania and thence to Augusta County, Virginia, in 1734, where he grew up to manhood, taking an active part along with his father and elder brothers even in his boyhood days, and doing his full share to bring the frontier wilderness of Virginia to civilization. He secured a liberal education along with his brothers, first taught in the wilderness by Rev. John Craig, and afterward at the best school at that time in Eastern Virginia, taught by the Rev. James Waddell. He entered the military service of his country while a mere boy, and displayed great talent for it quite early in life, which was recognized by all, but especially by the Governors of the Colony of Virginia. He advanced rapidly in rank from Captain to General. Nearly half of his life was spent in active military service of his country, and he was scarred with many wounds. Perhaps the first wound received in battle was at Braddock's defeat. In the French and Indian War he endured very severe and dangerous military service. But the most desperate battle he ever fought was against the great Indian chief, Cornstalk, who commanded the Five Tribes, numbering more than 1,300 warriors, against his 1,100 Virginia militia, at the bloody battle of Point Pleasant, October 10, 1774, which was waged with great fury from sunrise to sunset, and finally resulted in driving the Indians across the Ohio River, leaving General Lewis' army in possession of the field, but with a loss of seventy-five killed, including the youngest brother of the General, Colonel Charles Lewis, and more than 150 wounded. The Indians' loss was great, but could never be definitely known, as they carried their wounded and many of their dead across the river.

Away back in 1754 he commanded as Captain a company of Augusta County volunteers at the capitulation of Fort Necessity with Major George Washington, and "although wounded and hobbling on a staff, by his coolness probably prevented a general massacre of the Virginia troops." He commanded the American forces at Williamsburg in 1776, and in July of that year drove Lord Dunmore with his British from Gwyn's Island after a severe conflict. He had not a fair opportunity to display the extraordinary military skill which was universally attributed to him. It is said that "Washington recommended him for the post of Commander-in-Chief of the Continental armies."

He died of fever during the war in 1781. He had resigned his commission in the army and was on his way home, and when about twenty miles from his destination he was taken so severely ill that he was compelled to stop, and died. His will is recorded in the County Court of Botetourt, dated in 1780, and admitted to record in 1782. His remains were buried "on an eminence overlooking the beautiful valley of the Roanoke River, spreading out for six miles above and below the spot where the grave is now marked." His will is an interesting document. Notwithstanding the fact that nearly or quite half of his life was spent in military service, he devised by his will fully 30,000 acres of fine lands in Virginia and Kentucky to his children and grandchildren, and then the will closed thus: "It's my desire that my brother Thomas, Colonel William Preston, and my three sons, Samuel, Thomas, and Andrew, be and I hereby appoint them executors of this, my last will and testament, and that each of them, with my brother William and sister Margaret, as well as my other children, wear a mourning ring, to be purchased at the expense of my estate before a division."

LEO LOGAN LEWIS,
Of Fayette County, Kentucky.

By the devise made to his eldest son, John—among others—of 1,000 acres on Sinking Creek in Kentucky County, being a part of a 5,000 acre tract, and to his grandsons, Andrew, Samuel, and Charles (sons of his John above mentioned), he gives all of his part of the Pocotalico tract of land, which part he thinks is 2,100 acres, and the whole patented in the name of John Fry, Adam Stephen, Andrew Lewis, and others, and from these paragraphs in this will, in connection with the records of the Fayette County (Kentucky) Court, we find that Samuel Lewis and his wife (a daughter of Colonel Whitley) were parents of Jesse Lewis, and he with his wife, Jane Logan, were the parents of Margaret, Samuel Higgins, Leo Logan, Catherine, Mary Ann, and Rebecca, who have quite a numerous connection now living in Fayette County, Kentucky, and other sections of the country. Other grandsons of General Andrew Lewis settled on 9,000 acres of land which he owned at the mouth of the Kanawha, between it and the Ohio River, being the very ground over which he fought that memorable and bloody battle of Point Pleasant, which virtually drove the Indians to the west side of the Mississippi River, and gave to the white settlers the immense territory of Ohio, Kentucky, Indiana, and Illinois, and his descendants are scattered throughout that country, as well as the South and Southwest. Mrs. W. Scott Van Meter (*nee* Miss Anna Farra), through her connection with the Lewis family of Fayette County, is a lineal descendant from this branch of the Lewis family.

## COLONEL WILLIAM LEWIS.

The fourth son of the famous pioneer was born in Donegal County, Ireland, in 1724, and, like his brothers, came to America with his parents, and was brought up in Augusta County, Virginia. Being of a retiring and studious disposition, he obtained an excellent education from the two Presbyterian ministers, Rev. John Craig and Rev. James Waddell, and he then went to Philadelphia and graduated in medicine. While there he made the acquaintance and won the heart of Ann Montgomery, of Delaware, who afterward became his wife. Returning to Virginia he would gladly have spent his life in the quiet pursuits of his profession, but the war of 1753–4 coming on, he volunteered for service, and was severely wounded at the battle of Braddock's defeat. Returning to Augusta he resumed the practice of medicine, and soon became conspicuous for his medical skill and large intelligence, and his influence in the community.   He urged the erection of schools and churches, and was remarkable for his high regard for all things relating to education and religion.   He was an elder in the Presbyterian Church. In the practice of his profession, and in his high moral and religious influence as a private citizen, he would have gladly spent his life but for the Revolutionary War; but he, being embued with a sense of our wrongs and a determination to resist the tyranny of Great Britain, abandoned a second time his peaceful employments in 1776 and accepted a commission as colonel in the old Continental line. He served in the army until 1781, when, after the death of his brother Andrew, he resigned his commission and returned to his private life.   He was known and spoken of as the "Civilizer of the Border."   Governor Gilmer, in his sketches, thus speaks of him : "William Lewis, though as powerful in person and brave in spirit as either of his brothers, was less disposed to seek fame by sacrifice of human life.  He was a man of lofty character and indomitable spirit."

His sons gained distinction as officers in the Revolutionary War. On one occasion, away back at the time of the French and Indian War against the settlers, when Dr. William Lewis' eldest sons were already in the army, the report came to Staunton that the enemy were advancing upon them in force.   The doctor was sick in bed and not able to get out, but his wife called her three youngest sons — one seventeen, one fifteen, one thirteen — and said to them : "Go, my sons ; go to the front and do your duty for your country ; it is better to die like men in battle than to be scalped by the savage brutes at home."

Colonel William Lewis removed to the Sweet Springs, where he resided for many years, and died in 1811, revered by all as patriarch.   His wife died in 1808.   They raised five sons and three daughters, who have many descendants in Virginia and throughout the South.   Solomon L. Van Meter's wife, of Lexington, Kentucky (*nee* Miss Evaline Swoope), daughter of the late Colonel G. W. Swoope, of Virginia, was a lineal descendant of this Colonel (Dr.) William Lewis from her father's mother, who was Eliza Trent, and married Honorable Washington Swoope, of Augusta County.

Eliza Trent was a daughter of Elizabeth Montgomery Lewis, daughter of Colonel (Dr.) William Lewis and his wife, who was Miss Ann Montgomery.   Colonel G. W. Swoope married Margaret Baylor, daughter of Jacob Baylor and his wife, Evaline Hanger, daughter of Peter Hanger. Washington Swoope's father, Jacob Swoope, came from Germany and settled in Staunton in 1750; married Mary McDowell, daughter of Ephraim McDowell, who came from the north of Ireland and settled near Staunton in 1737. Honorable Jacob Swoope was a member of Congress in 1809–11. He was a man of great influence and a leader of the Federalist party in his day. He could speak German as well as English, and carried the entire German vote in his district. The Swoopes, Baylors, and Hangers were all gallant and distinguished officers of the Confederate army of Virginia in the late war, and fought under Jackson and Lee.

## COLONEL CHARLES LEWIS.

The youngest child of the famous pioneer was born in Augusta County, Virginia, in 1736, and was inured from his very cradle to the hardships and excitements of frontier life and border warfare. He had the same advantages of education as the other children, and grew up to manhood the most brilliant and promising man of the family. Especially gifted as to military talent, and possessing great magnetism of person and extraordinary social qualities and conversational powers, he was what would now be styled a fine mixer with great military talent; but it was decreed that he should go to an "untimely grave" at the bloody battle of Point Pleasant. He had made many narrow escapes in frequent conflicts with Indians; was reckless and void of fear. When he led his regiment out at sunrise that morning to bring on the engagement he was dressed in a red jacket and other gorgeous apparel, and when his brother Andrew remonstrated with him for attiring so as to make himself a special target for the enemy, he made a jocular reply and went on, only to return to his tent about two hours after with a mortal wound received in the very front line of battle.

His brother met him as he returned and asked him if he was seriously wounded. He replied: "Yes, I am, and such is the fate of war." He died a few hours after.

Colonel Charles Lewis married Sarah Murrey, of Bath County, Virginia, and left four sons and three daughters, some of whom came to Kentucky, some to West Virginia, and other descendants are in the South and West. Honorable Peter Lewis, of Point Pleasant, West Virginia, is a lineal descendant of this Colonel Charles Lewis, and owns land near where he was killed.

## COLONEL THOMAS LEWIS.

Colonel Thomas Lewis and wife removed with their family to Fayette County, Kentucky, in 1780, and settled on a large farm three miles west of Lexington, where they lived for the balance of their lives and raised thirteen children, viz :

Nancy, born in Fairfax County, Virginia, August 18, 1774.

Sally, born in Virginia, December 14, 1776.

Hector P., born in Virginia, December 28, 1778.

Asa K., born in Fayette County, Kentucky, January 3, 1781.

Betsy, born December 16, 1782.

Edward, born October 27, 1785, and died August 31, 1803.

Kitty, born December 2, 1787.

Stephen D., born December 27, 1789.

Polly, born January 27, 1792, and died December 7, 1792.

Thornton, born June 7, 1794.

Sophia, born October 13, 1796.

Alphius, born March 28, 1799.

Douglas P., born August 4, 1804.

Thomas Lewis was possessed of considerable means when he came to Kentucky, consisting of money, slaves, and live stock. He made extensive investments in lands, and soon became one of the influential and wealthy men of this region of the country. His brother-in-law, Henry Payne, and his family removed from Virginia with him and settled on an adjoining farm, and were life-long neighbors. Thomas Lewis was a very intelligent, enterprising, old-fashioned Kentucky gentleman, who kept his well-trained body-servant close at hand wherever he went ; was noted, like most of the gentlemen of this region and of Virginia in that day, for hospitality and high living. While he possessed no overweaning thirst for political honors, but rather preferred the ease and comfort of a private citizen and the independent self-reliance of a Kentucky gentleman of that day, yet he served his district in the convention which met in Danville and framed the first Constitution of Kentucky, in 1792, and was a member of the first State Senate of Kentucky, which met the same year. He filled other positions of honor and trust. He was fond of fine stock, especially of blooded horses, bringing some good ones from Virginia with him when he came to Kentucky, and bred to the very first imported horses that came to the latter State. Among the most judicious investments in land which he made in Kentucky was a purchase of 3,000 acres, one half of a military claim and survey of 6,000 acres in Clark County, Kentucky, on Prettyrun and Stoner Creek, the purchase made of Mr. Gest not many years after he came to Kentucky. A considerable part of this land is still in the possession of his descendants and heirs-at-law.

He died in September, 1809, at the age of sixty years. At the Olympian Springs, in what is now Bath County, Kentucky, having gone that far on his intended journey to Virginia on horseback, attended only by his body-servant, he was taken sick, and after a short illness died there. His body was returned to his home and buried in the family graveyard on his farm, and the grave is still marked by a monument with an appropriate inscription. For his military career see " Historical Register of Officers of Continental Army " (page 263), viz: Second Lieutenant of Fifteenth Virginia, November 21, 1776, and First Lieutenant March 20, 1777. Regiment designated Eleventh Virginia, September 14, 1778. Retired February, 1781, a Colonel.

Although he was a Colonel in the Revolutionary War, there is very little left of record as to his military career. He was a consistent member of the Old Baptist Church (the " Ironside "), and was one of the pillars of a church and congregation, the " meeting-house " (Old Sacra) having been located on the line between his farm and that of his brother-in-law, Mr. Payne, and on the public road, where it remained for years after the death of both of the original families and the dispersion of their children from these farms. All of the children of Thomas Lewis adhered to this denomination, although from the most reliable information the ancestry, before the Revolutionary War, were prominent in the Established Church of England. No doubt but the antipathy and hatred for the British Government drove them from that Episcopal form of worship, and as the Old Baptist was the pioneer religion in Kentucky in their day, they readily adhered to it. The widow of Thomas Lewis survived him some eighteen years, and lived to see all of their children well educated and raised to years of discretion, and most of them married and in possession of the ample estates which their father had left them. She was a devout, pious Christian woman, who was held in the highest esteem by all of her acquaintances, and had the unbounded and tenderest love of all her children. When her sons were very old men they delighted to rehearse over and over again the superior excellencies of their mother. She died March 24, 1827, and was buried by the side of her late husband in the family graveyard.

Nancy, the eldest daughter of Thomas and Elizabeth Lewis, married, December 18, 1793, General James Garrard, of Bourbon County, a very distinguished man in the early history of Kentucky, being a son of the Hon. and Rev. James Garrard, second Governor of Kentucky, and a Baptist minister — a man of great force of character, who took a very prominent part in public affairs in his day, and his name figures extensively in the early history of Kentucky.

Mrs. Nancy Garrard died November 17, 1835, and General James Garrard died September 8, 1838. They raised thirteen children, viz : Thomas Lewis Garrard, of Pendleton County, Kentucky ; James, of Todd County, Kentucky ; Stephen L., of Harrison County, Kentucky ; Masina, of Hannibal, Missouri ; Jeptha D., of Cincinnati, Ohio, married Sarah B. Ludlow, of Ohio ; William (died young and unmarried) ; Elizabeth L., married Volney Bedford, of Bourbon County, Kentucky ; Edward P. (died young and unmarried) ; Sallie L., married Colonel Thomas A. Russell, of Fayette County, Kentucky ; Charles T., married Miss Kennedy, of Bourbon County, Kentucky ; Ann Maria, married Ben C. Bedford, of Bourbon County, Kentucky ; Margaret T., married Edwin G. Bedford, of Bourbon County, Kentucky ; Mary, died unmarried.

Many descendants from the above are scattered throughout Kentucky, the West and South.

Sallie, the second child of Thomas and Elizabeth Lewis, was born in Virginia, December 14, 1776. Married, first, General Green Clay, Madison County, Kentucky, who figured extensively in both military and political affairs of Kentucky in his day, and was a man of more than local fame and distinction. They raised a family of six children (three sons and three daughters), who when taken as a family have been very seldom equaled for high character and reputation by any of the old families of Kentucky.

Elizabeth Clay, the eldest daughter, married Colonel John Speed Smith, of Madison County, a man of very estimable character, a lawyer of ability and learning, and of extensive influence in his day. He held places of trust and honor.

Pauline married Colonel William Rodes, of Madison County, Kentucky, who was a man of education, cultivation, and very marked ability and great popularity in his community ; a high type of a Kentucky gentleman.

Pauline Green Clay, born 7th of September, 1802, married William Rodes, November 3, 1819. He a son of Robert Rodes and Eliza Delaney, his wife, who were married May 30, 1782. Robert Rodes was a captain of a company from Albemarle County, Virginia, during the Revolutionary War. He was a son of John Rodes, who married, September 9, 1754, Sarah Harris. John Rodes was a son of John Rodes, Sr., who married Miss Crawford. Sarah (Harris) Rodes was the daughter of Robert Harris, of Albemarle County, Virginia, whose will was recorded August 8, 1768. He was the son of William Harris, and he a son of the emigrant, Robert Harris.

Sidney Payne Clay, born in 1800; graduated at Princeton College; married, first, Miss Nancy Keen, by whom he had one child, Sallie W. After the death of this wife he married Miss Isabella Reed, by whom he raised three children, viz: Sidney, born December 20, 1828, who graduated at Center College; married Miss Warfield, of Lexington, Ky., and was the only living child of his father; a gentleman of culture and high standing in his community. He owned until recently the farm on which his father lived and died, and which had been handed down to the third generation from the ancestor who redeemed it from the primeval forest. He died at his residence in Lexington, Ky., November 12, 1899. Second child, E. Davidson; born November 29, 1831; graduated at Center College, and died December 6, 1851, while attending the law lectures in the city of Lexington. Third child, Green; born December 14, 1833; graduated at Center College in 1854; removed to Texas; died May 24, 1860.

Sidney Payne Clay died at the early age of thirty-four years. While at Princeton College he joined the Presbyterian Church, and ever afterward lived a consistent and influential member, being an elder, and, in fact, one of the main pillars of that denomination in Bourbon County. Very few men at so early an age attain to such high standing for piety and render such earnest, influential labor in behalf of religion. He was the executor of his father's will, and settled up his large estate. He was in no wise inferior to his illustrious brothers who survived him, and but for his very early death he would, no doubt, have established a reputation and a name which would have reached far beyond the confines of his native State. In his character, to high order of educated and cultivated intellect was added the adornment of a regenerated Christian spirit.

Brutus J. Clay, of Bourbon County, Kentucky, was a man of national reputation as a farmer, a breeder of blooded stock, with extraordinary good judgment and practical sense ; President of the Agricultural Fair of Bourbon County for many years ; the Representative of his district in Congress, and held other positions of high honor. He commanded the unbounded confidence of all in his integrity, high sense of honor, and practical sense.   He married, first, Miss Amelia Field, by whom he raised children, and after her death he married her sister, Miss Anna Field, both of Madison County, Kentucky. By the second marriage he raised one child, viz : Hon. Cassius M. Clay, Jr., of Bourbon County, who is yet in his zenith and resides upon his father's old homestead, one of the finest farms in the State, and he is one of the most prominent men in Kentucky ; has represented his native county and district in both branches of the legislature.   He presided over the last Consiitutional Convention of Kentucky, and has held other positions of honor and trust.   Colonel Ezekiel F. Clay, a son of the first wife, is a very prominent man, although less inclined than his younger brother to participate in political affairs.   He took quite an active part in military affairs during the late great unpleasantness between the two sections of this Union, and had an eye shot out in one of the many battles in which he participated while in the Southern army, and received other less serious wounds at different times.   He is largely engaged in breeding thoroughbred horses, and is universally recognized as one of the most prominent turfmen of America, not only on account of the many valuable horses which by his skill, judgment, and enterprise he has produced, but also because of his reputation for honor and integrity in all things pertaining to this exciting and alluring avocation, as well as to all of his affairs of life.   Colonel Clay spent quite a large part of his military service under General Humphrey Marshall in defending the salt works and an important gap or gateway to the South near the line between Kentucky, Virginia, and Tennessee — a rugged mountain pass — a long way from a railroad with no means for transportation except by wagons over a rugged mountain road ; therefore rations, clothing, and provisions became very scarce.   There were intervals when no enemy was near except '' General Starvation,'' and nothing to break the monotony except the devising of ways and means to obtain rations and clothing for the army.   There were, no doubt, very many amusing occurrences which took place there and are now lost, but one has been handed

GENERAL GREEN CLAY.

HONORABLE BRUTUS J. CLAY.

GENERAL CASSIUS MARCELLUS CLAY.

SIDNEY CLAY.

down to date and shall be recorded.  To get at the full force of the joke one must know that General Marshall weighed four hundred pounds and was as high around as he was high up and down, and rode a sorrel mare which was made a good deal on the same style. More than once General Marshall's army was reduced to all the parched corn they could eat and very little of any thing else, and clothing was as scarce as rations.  On one of these occasions the General called for a dress parade, and all the soldiers were readily drawn up in line with guns and bayonets bright and glistening, but many of them had their hair sticking out above their hat-crowns and their toes smiling out at the ends of their shoes, when General Marshall came along, presenting the appearance of as well-fed and highly kept man as ever was seen.  As soon as he passed beyond ear-shot of a company of mountaineer ragamuffins, a long, lank, lean, raggedy fellow from the head of the company drolled out, " Now, boys, you see what goes with our rations."  The entire company broke into an uproar of laughter, which soon went with the joke throughout the command.  General Marshall was so corpulent that he was incapacitated for campaign work, although he possessed a high order of talent.  He descended from the same family as did Chief Justice Marshall of Virginia, and gained a military reputation in the Mexican War.  The soldiers said during the war that he was too much good material to be wasted, and Jeff Davis stopped up a gap in the mountains with him.  His command did some desperate hard fighting, and were never driven from their post until the latter part of the war when the Federal forces from the East and West got so completely on his flanks and his rear that he was compelled to join the more Southern forces.

One daughter, Miss Martha, married Colonel Davenport, of Virginia, where they now reside.  He is a gentleman of excellent character and reputation, and descends from distinguished lineage.

Green Clay, the second son, is an influential planter of Mississippi, with a residence and farm in Missouri, and has taken quite a prominent part in public affairs in both States ; has represented a constituency in the legislature of  each State ;  was Secretary of Legation at St. Petersburg during President Lincoln's administration, and has held high and responsible positions, both State and Federal.

C. F. Clay, the eldest son, is a prominent and intelligent farmer of Bourbon County.

A list of the children of Brutus J. Clay, taken from a book of "The Clay Family," by Mrs. Mary Rogers Clay:

Martha Clay, born February 1, 1832, married Henry B. Davenport, of Virginia, January 5, 1860; Christopher F. Clay, born November 20, 1835, married, June, 1867, Mary F. Brooks, daughter of Samuel Brooks, of Bourbon County; Green Clay, born February 11, 1839, married, in 1871, Jane Rodes, of New Orleans, after graduating from Cambridge Law School; Ezekiel F. Clay, born December 1, 1840, married, May 8, 1866, Mary L. Woodford; Cassius M. Clay, Jr., born March 26, 1846, has been three times married: first, January 27, 1869, to Susan E. Clay, daughter of Samuel and Susan (Wornall) Clay; after her death, second, November 29, 1882, to Pattie T. Lyman; after her death, third, December 6, 1888, to Mary Blythe Harris.

## CLAYS.

Charles Clay emigrated to Fayette County, Kentucky, at an early day. He married Miss Lewis, probably a sister of Hopkins Lewis, who married Patsy Clay, the daughter of Charles and Martha Green Clay, of Powhattan County, Virginia, and sister of General Green Clay.

On returning to Virginia on business, he was murdered, leaving a wife and several children. Of these, Charles Clay married Elichia Stuart; Temperance Clay married Charles Black, of Maryland.

Elizabeth Lewis Clay married John Speed Smith, for forty years one of the leading lawyers and prominent men of Kentucky. He was born in Jessamine County, Kentucky, July 3, 1792; settled in Richmond when its bar was one of the ablest in Kentucky. He was frequently a member of the Kentucky Legislature, and was a Representative in Congress during President Monroe's administration in 1821 to 1823; was appointed by President John Q. Adams, Secretary of Legation to the United States Minister to the South American Congress, which assembled at Tocubaga; was appointed by President Jackson, United States Attorney for District of Kentucky; was appointed by Kentucky Legislature, January 5, 1839, Joint Commissioner with ex-Governor Morehead to visit Ohio and solicit passage of a law to prevent evil disposed persons in that State from enticing away or assisting slaves to escape from Kentucky, and to provide more efficient means for recapturing fugitive slaves, which mission was eminently successful. In the campaign of 1812 and 1813 Colonel Smith served as aide-de-camp to General Harrison.

## HENRY CLAY.

The fifth of that name in direct descent was born June 4, 1798, and in 1821 he married Olivia, daughter of Major George M. Bedinger, and after her death he married Elizabeth, daughter of Samuel Scott and his wife, Elizabeth Cunningham. Issue : Five children, three of whom lived to be grown.

The three branches of the Clay family who were represented in the early settlers of Kentucky by Henry Clay (the statesman and sage of Ashland), Dr. Henry Clay (the father of Colonel Henry, who lived and died in Bourbon County, near Paris), General Green Clay (the father of Sydney, Brutus J., and Cassius M. Clay), all united on a common ancestor named *Henry*, viz., General Green, son of Charles, grandson of *Henry*, sage of Ashland ; Henry, son of Reverend John, grandson of John, great-grandson of *Henry* ; Colonel Henry, son of Dr. Henry, grandson of *Henry*.

Sallie Ann, youngest daughter of General Green Clay, married, first, Mr. Irvine, of Madison County, Kentucky, who lived only one month after their marriage, and after his death she married Major Madison C. Johnson, of Lexington, Kentucky, but lived only eleven months after her second marriage and left no children. Both of these were men of distinction. Major Madison C. Johnson lived to be an old man, in the city of Lexington, never married again, was for many years the most influential man in the city, and one whom the people delighted to honor. He was one of the most profound jurists of the State and nation, and held many positions of honor and trust, and could have held more if he had been inclined to seek them, or even if he had accepted them when tendered to him.

Cassius Marcellus Clay, the youngest son of this noted family, is now the only survivor of General Green Clay's children, and although in his eighty-fourth year is still active in body and mind — stout and healthy, with flattering prospects of years yet being added to his life. He married quite early in life Miss Mary Jane Warfield, and they reared a family of children. He has written " The Life, Memoirs, Writings, and Speeches of Cassius M. Clay," in two large volumes—quite large books — which give a detailed account of himself from his early youth and of his family, so that whatever I could write concerning him would be but a repetition. Suffice it, therefore, to say that he has had a very eventful career in peace and in war, and has a name and a fame which reach almost to every civilized country.

After the death of General Green Clay, his widow, Mrs. Sallie Clay, married her brother-in-law, Mr. Jeptha Dudley, of Frankfort, Kentucky, who had before married her younger sister, Elizabeth Lewis, and by her raised one child named Edward Ambrose Dudley, and from the second marriage of the above named there was no issue. Elizabeth Lewis, the first wife and the mother of Edward A. Dudley, was born December 16, 1782, and died February 11, 1807, when in the twenty-fifth year of her age. Mrs. Sallie (Clay) Dudley survived her second husband, and died July 7, 1867, when in the ninety-first year of her age. She was an extraordinary woman, possessed of great force of character and practical sense. Mr. Jeptha Dudley, above mentioned, was an influential, intelligent gentleman who had descended from a distinguished old family of Virginia and Kentucky. He was for many years connected with the State Government at Frankfort. Edward A. Dudley, above mentioned, only child of Elizabeth L. and Jeptha Dudley, married Miss Sarah M. Russell, of Fayette County, Kentucky, and removed to Quincy, Illinois.

Hector P. Lewis was educated at Lexington, Kentucky, at Transylvania University, when that institution was quite young. He owned and resided for many years, and to the time of his death, on an excellent farm of about a thousand acres of land some six miles north of Lexington. He told the writer that when he took possession of this land, where his residence was located, buffalo skulls were as abundant, scattered over his land, as stumps were at the time he was relating this fact. (The stumps would then, perhaps, have averaged half a dozen to the acre.)

He married twice : first, Miss Nancy Domigan, and second, Miss Rebecca Ashurst, but raised no children from either. He lived to be seventy-nine years of age, and with his robust, stout constitution and active mind and body he appeared to bid fair to live much longer but for an accident which caused his death. At the laying of the corner-stone of the Clay Monument, when there was a very large crowd in Lexington, he was run over and very seriously injured by a horse and buggy on Main Street, in front of Mr. Payne's residence. He was removed to his home and lived but a few days, having received internal injuries which proved fatal.

HECTOR P. LEWIS,
Of Fayette County, Kentucky.

He died September 29, 1857, and was buried in the Lexington Cemetery. He was a man of striking appearance ; he dressed with scrupulous neatness in the old-style broadcloth, with ruffled shirt, and all of his surroundings comported therewith ; he was an aristocrat "to the manner born." He owned a large number of the best trained servants that could be found in this country. No matter how much company he was entertaining, it was very seldom that he was ever known to speak to one of them, but they almost invariably anticipated his wishes, and when perchance one failed, a glance or a look from "old master" was always sufficient to remind him of just what was needed. He never employed an overseer or slave manager of any kind, but required the father of each family to direct and control all of his children, and held each father responsible for the behavior and labor of each child. No slaves were better clothed and cared for than his.

He possessed great force of character, intelligence, and high sense of honor ; was a very influential member of the Old Baptist Church. He had ample capacity and opportunity to occupy a position in the very front rank of politics if he had been so inclined ; he was an intimate friend and associate of Henry Clay and other statesmen, but never held a political office. Honorable James Beck was a confidential friend of his and his attorney at law from Beck's earliest law practice to the time of Hector Lewis' death.

Hector P. Lewis, as well as several of his brothers, was from his early boyhood very fond of hunting and fishing, and up to the time that he was quite an old man he had his annual hunting and fishing trip to the mountains of Kentucky in October and November of each year.

The letter " P." in his name was generally supposed to stand for his mother's name of Payne, but this is not the fact. It was placed there under rather peculiar circumstances. When he was quite a young man and unmarried he loaded a large flatboat with tobacco, flour, bacon, etc., on the Kentucky River, near the mouth of Tate's Creek, about nine miles from Lexington, and went with the boat to New Orleans to sell his cargo and boat. On his journey, after he had passed the mouth of the Ohio and was going down the Mississippi River along the Kentucky shore, he concluded to tie up his boat and take a day's hunt until night came on. When he concluded to make his way back to the boat he found that he was completely bewildered and lost. After rambling for some time he discovered a dim light in the distance, and, on making his way to it, found there the comfortable home of a very hospitable family, who cheerfully took him in and made his night's stay quite pleasant. In this family he found what he concluded was the most beautiful and lovely girl that he had ever seen. He enjoyed her company during his brief stay next morning, but found his boat next day and made his way to New Orleans. That beautiful girl haunted his waking hours until he determined to see her again. It was several months before he returned to Lexington and shaped his business to go in search of his heart's idol. He finally mounted his horse and rode across the country nearly two hundred miles to find the home in the woods, but the girl had married only a short time before he arrived and he did not see her, and never saw her but the one time. Her family name commenced with P, and he put that letter in his name. He did not marry for several years after this occurrence.

He was on the staff of his brother-in-law, General Green Clay, with the rank of Colonel, in the War of 1812, and participated very efficiently in helping to raise the seige of Fort Meigs. Immediately after the British were driven from that post he was entrusted with the chief command of a strong detachment from this army to go to the rescue of General Dudley, whose army had just been defeated and was in great danger of capture or destruction. In this army his younger brother, Asa K., was at that time participating with the rank of Major. Colonel Hector gave timely and successful assistance to Dudley's defeated army, and rescued them from their perilous situation. He told the writer only a few years before his death that no one had ever held his name to a note ; he never signed his name to a note in his life, but he held many notes against other people, and was a money-lender for many years. He lived in affluence ; he attended only to his own private business, and that in a very systematic way, and to the affairs of his church. He was held in high esteem as a man of integrity and intelligence, with unyielding will and determination.

ASA K. LEWIS,
Of Clark County, Kentucky.

## ASA K. LEWIS.

Asa K. Lewis, the second son and fourth child, was educated at Transylvania University, and afterward graduated at Princeton, also graduating in law there. He was a man of more than ordinary talent and ability, with very refined and polished manners, and was very popular. He practiced law for a few years in Mt. Sterling, Kentucky, and was afterward Judge of the County Court of Clark County for several years, but finally retired to his farm in that county, and could not be induced to hold any political office, contending that he was disgusted with political affairs and professional business. He owned and resided on a large and excellent farm about six miles north of Winchester, in Clark County, being a one-fifth interest in the three thousand acres purchased by his father, Thomas Lewis, from Gest. He was a Major in the War of 1812, and displayed great bravery in the military service, especially at Dudley's defeat, where he took a very active part and gained distinction for courage and skill.

He was very fond of hunting and fishing in the mountains, and spent several months of each year in this enjoyment. He found and made the acquaintance of his wife, Miss Peggy Eilerzley, a beautiful mountain girl, while on one of his mountain excursions. They were married March 2, 1820. She was born June 8, 1799. He was eighteen years her senior. They raised only six children to be grown; although twelve were born to them. Only one of them is now living. They raised to be grown : Elizabeth, who died unmarried ; Hector, who married Miss Jane Moore, daughter of Peter Moore, of Bourbon County ; raised two daughters, viz : Mary M., born September 4, 1856, married C. P. Grimes, Esq., in September, 1878, and has five sons. This family is now residing in Rogers, Arkansas. Anna Belle, born August 28, 1859, married H. Hutchison, Esq., November 15, 1876, and died March 6, 1882, leaving one daughter named Mary C. Hutchison, who is now dead and left no issue. A third daughter, about sixteen years of age, is now living with her father in Phillips County, Arkansas. After the death of Hector Lewis' first wife he married Miss Anna Talbott, with whom he is now living in Phillips County, Arkansas. By this marriage he has only one child now living, named Mattie. She is about twelve years of age. Mary, third daughter of Asa K. Lewis, married Captain Mat. Clay, of Bourbon County, Kentucky, and lived for many years at the old Clay mansion in that county — a highly respectable and honorable couple — but they are both now dead and left no issue. The fourth child, Sarah, married, first, Shelton Oldham, of Fayette County, Kentucky, by whom she raised three daughters, viz : Mary E., married Stephen Lewis, formerly of Bourbon County, Kentucky, but now of Arkansas, a son of Douglas P. Lewis. The other two daughters, Margaret and Sallie, have not married. After the death of Mr. Oldham, Sarah, his widow, married J. G. Lipscomb, Esq., of Arkansas, where she resided until her recent death. The fifth child, Henry, never married ; was a gallant soldier of the Southern army in the late great war, and was killed in a battle near Gallatin, Tennessee, in 1862. He was a generous, noble, fearless man, and very dextrous with fire-arms of any kind. No nobler or better soldier ever bled for his country. He was killed in a charge, many rods in advance of his command. After the war his remains were reinterred at the family mansion near his parents.

Sidney, the sixth child, never married ; served through the war, a brave and gallant soldier of the Southern army. He died some years after the Southern war, in Arkansas.

Asa K. Lewis was one of the highest Masons of Kentucky at the time of his death, and held high offices in that fraternity. He died August 15, 1850, and was buried with imposing Masonic ceremonies. His widow survived him nearly twenty-five years, and died May 25, 1875. They are both buried in the family graveyard, near the old family mansion, on the farm where they lived and died.

Edward Lewis, third son and sixth child of Thomas and Elizabeth Lewis, was born October 27, 1785, and died August 31, 1803, in the eighteenth year of his age.

Kittie Lewis, seventh child of Thomas and Elizabeth Lewis, was born December 2, 1787, and married her cousin, Colonel Henry C. Payne, of Fayette County, Kentucky.

Colonel Henry C. Payne was one of the most prominent farmers and gentlemen of Fayette County, lived on a part of the original Payne homestead adjoining the Lewis homestead, and raised a family of ten children, viz: Romulus Payne, born July 29, 1809, died unmarried; Remus, born July 3, 1811, married Mary Talbott ; Lewis D., born May 11, 1813, married Elizabeth Keene ; Eliza, born May 3, 1815, married Colonel Rodes Estill ; Anna Maria,

STEPHEN D. LEWIS,
Of Clark County, Kentucky.

born April 21, 1817, married Dr. John Jackson; Thomas H., born November 1, 1819, married Maria Viley; Lydia, born February 29, 1822, married B. B. Taylor; Sallie, born March 1, 1824; Benjamin, born February 22, 1826; Kittie, born March 23, 1828.

Kittie L. Payne died August, 1829. Colonel Henry Congers Payne died June 5, 1856. This husband and wife were faithful and consistent members of the Old Baptist Church, and highly respected and esteemed by all of their acquaintances. Many of their descendants are now living in Kentucky and other sections of this Union.

Stephen D. Lewis, fourth son of Thomas and Elizabeth Lewis, was born in Fayette County, Kentucky, at the homestead of his parents, December 27, 1789. He received a good education at Transylvania University, in Lexington, and moved soon after he had attained the age of twenty-one years to his farm in Clark County, Kentucky, being a one-fifth interest in the three thousand acre tract purchased by his father of Gest. On this farm he resided to the day of his death, adding several parcels of land to his original portion, so that he owned of that Gest land one thousand acres at the time of his death. He did not marry until he was nearly sixty years of age, when he married Miss Tincher. They raised no children, but he adopted his wife's niece, Miss Anna Stith, whose name was changed to Lewis, and by the terms of his will she inherited his entire estate. She married Charles Swift, Esq., of Lexington, Kentucky, and they now reside upon that farm.

Stephen D. Lewis was a man of more than ordinary capacity, with a good education; had a fine library of books, and read a great deal of history and scientific literature. He possessed great ingenuity; was very dextrous with the use of tools, and could make nearly any thing of wood, iron, brass, or silver that he wished. His disposition was modest and retiring. He was excessively fond of playing the game of chess, and it was told of him, with more than the shadow of truth, that when there came a rainy day or a bad spell of weather so that he could not get out on his farm with comfort, he would send around to the negro cabins to see if he could not find some one sick enough to furnish an excuse to send for his family physician, who was about an even match for him in a game of chess, and then he would hold him as long as the bad weather lasted. They would play almost continually, day and night, until the weather changed or until some one who needed the medical services of the doctor tracked him up and pressed him into service. Stephen D. Lewis was a very handsome, robust, stout, dressy, and fine-looking man when young, and enjoyed excellent health until he had passed fifty years of age, and until he fell and broke his limb. By this fall he was very severely injured, so that he was compelled afterward to use a crutch, and could only get about with difficulty. He lived to be eighty-one years of age, and died on the 21st of May, 1870. He left a fine estate of land and personalty.

## THORNTON LEWIS.

Thornton Lewis, fifth son of Thomas and Elizabeth Lewis, was born June 7, 1794, at the residence of his parents in Fayette County, Kentucky, and was educated at Transylvania University, in Lexington, and removed when he was quite a young man to his farm in Clark County, it being a one-fifth interest in the Gest tract of land purchased by his father, and on this farm he resided for more than thirty-five years. When his health began to fail he rented his farm and purchased a residence in Winchester, and lived there for the balance of his life. He was a cautious, prudent, and successful business man, and of a retiring and unobtrusive disposition. When about forty years of age he married Miss Emma Wright, a daughter of Captain Thomas Wright, of Clark County, and they raised five children to be grown, viz: Thomas Wright Lewis, born January 11, 1833; Amelia Clay, born May 26, 1836; Frances (Fanny), born March 26, 1841; Mary S., born May 16, 1848; Sidney Allen, born April 17, 1851.

Captain Thomas Wright, above mentioned, removed from Virginia to Clark County about the year 1780, and settled on Pretty-run Creek, on a part of the remaining one half of the Gest land— a part of the military survey of which Thomas Lewis purchased one half from Gest.

And on this farm, about one mile from the residence and farm of Thornton Lewis, he lived and died. He was descended from a very worthy old English ancestry, who were among the very earliest emigrants to America.

He was a native of Virginia, a Captain in the Revolutionary War, a very prominent and highly respected man, and a very influential member of the Old Baptist Church for a number of years. He

THORNTON LEWIS.

married, first, Elizabeth Graves on September 5, 1778, and from this marriage raised five children, viz: Jefferson, Morgan, Dr. Connor, Elizabeth, and Polly. After the death of this wife he married, second, Mary Rice, and from this marriage raised four children, viz: Elizabeth, Pamelia, Emma, and Harrison. Jefferson and Morgan Wright settled in Missouri, and their children are now living there. Dr. Connor married Mary Hall; lived and died in Clark County, Kentucky; was a very prominent physician; left no children. Elizabeth married R. D. Green and raised twelve children, viz: Amelia, LaFayette, Dr. M., Susan, Nanny, Edward, Emma, Dr. Beel, Thomas, Rush, Elizabeth, and Alvius. Polly married Darius Bainbridge and settled in Missouri. Eliza married Robert Smith; lived and died in Clark County, Kentucky; raised two children, viz: Mary and Eliza. Pamelia married Harvey Wilson, of Montgomery County, Kentucky, who finally removed to Winchester, Kentucky, and died there, leaving six children, viz: William, Clay, Thomas, Frelinghuysen, Mary, and Emma. Harrison Wright married Sarah Holley and raised several children, viz: Lewis, Mary, and William, and maybe others.

Thornton Lewis married Miss Emma Wright, March 27, 1832.

Thomas W. Lewis, the eldest son of Thornton and Emma Lewis, as above mentioned, was born and raised on his father's farm in Clark County, Kentucky; was a graduate of Frankfort Military Institute, and at the age of about twenty-two years married Miss Pauline L. Young, second daughter of Johnson Young, Esq., of Bath County, Kentucky. They resided upon the farm of his grandfather, the late Captain Thomas Wright, who had died only a few years before, and his father, Thornton Lewis, had purchased all the remaining interest in the said landed estate which his wife did not inherit.

On this farm Thomas W. Lewis and his young wife were residing happily and prosperously, and he was extensively and successfully engaged in breeding blooded stock, when, in 1861, Fort Sumter was fired upon and the tocsin of war was sounded; then, true to his lineage and education, he was among the first to call together a company of about sixty young men of his native county and commence to drill them. Captain Roy S. Cluke, a gallant and experienced soldier of the Mexican war, was elected captain of this company, and Thomas W. Lewis was chosen first lieutenant; but Captain Cluke, as well as all of the company, soon discovered that

Thomas W. Lewis, being a graduate of a military college, and also naturally endowed with military talent, was much the better drilled officer, and by unanimous consent he did most of the drilling of the company. He had been chosen captain of a military company which had been organized in Bourbon County several years before, immediately after he returned from college. This company he had drilled for dress parade on public occasions, and they had quite a reputation for efficiency ; but the company he drilled in 1861 was for a bloody war. On the 15th of August, 1861, while drilling the company on horseback as cavalry, by the accidental discharge of a pistol in the hands of one of his best friends, he received a bullet in the back of his head where the neck joins, causing his instantaneous death. This shocking accident caused such consternation and grief throughout the company that it disbanded at once. Very soon after this sad occurrence Captain Cluke received a colonel's commission from the Confederate Government at Richmond, and raised a regiment in Clark and surrounding counties, in which a large majority of the men who composed this original first company joined some one or other company in this regiment. Thomas W. Lewis was about six feet two inches in height, rather spare made, stood very erect, and presented a commanding appearance.

He was a generous, honorable man, and very popular with all his acquaintances. He left no living issue. After his death his widow married Mr. Steigall and raised a son and daughter, but the son died recently about the time he was grown, and since the mother has died, leaving the daughter and her father still living in Shelby County, Kentucky.

Amelia C., second child and eldest daughter of Thornton and Emma Lewis, was educated at Walnut Hill Seminary, in Fayette County, Kentucky, when that institution was in its zenith of usefulness under the management of Rev. Dr. J. J. Bullock. When in the nineteenth year of her age she married B. F. Van Meter (the author of this book), and for further particulars see Van Meter family.

Frances, or Fanny, second daughter, married James Van Meter, and for further particulars see Van Meter family. She died June 27, 1880. Mary S., third daughter, married Theodore F. Phillips, of Jessamine County, Kentucky, and they now have a residence in Winchester, Kentucky, and one in Clear Water Harbor, Florida. They have raised three sons, viz : Henry, Thornton L., and James

S. Henry married Jane Milam. Thornton L. married Annette Kidd, daughter of Bird Kidd, of Clark County, Kentucky. (For Phillips family see page 44.)

Sidney Allen Lewis, youngest son of Thornton Lewis, was educated at Millersburg College, Kentucky, and before he was twenty years old married Emma J., daughter of Frank Fisher, of Bourbon County, Kentucky. They were married November 30, 1870. She was a beautiful and accomplished young woman ; died very young after only four years of married life, leaving two daughters, named Emma and Minnie. Emma married William H. James, of Colorado, and he now owns a large ranch at Axail in that State, but he resides in Chicago, where he deals largely in coal. The younger daughter, Minnie, makes her home with her sister in Chicago, although they both own a fine landed estate in Kentucky, left to them by their father.

S. A. Lewis survived his wife only a few years, and died August 23, 1883, leaving his two daughters above named to the care and nurture of their grandmother. Sidney Allen Lewis very early in life received the nickname of "Dock" when a lad, and carried it with him to his grave ; he was a tall, slender man of rather delicate frame and constitution, but he possessed the prominent characteristics of the Lewis family in quite a marked degree ; and it can be well illustrated by relating an occurrence which took place about the first time that he ever exercised the right of suffrage, directly after the war, when the negoes had just received the right to vote and a few unscrupulous Radical white men were trying to stir up as much prejudice and ill-feeling as possible in the negroes against their recent masters. One influential fellow had succeeded in getting up quite a disturbance at the voting-place in the Courthouse, and, having been very roughly handled before he made his escape, had gone off to get his reinforcement of negroes. He had succeeded in collecting seventy-five to one hundred negroes, armed with guns, pistols, axes, clubs, and such like weapons as could be hurriedly collected —all the while haranguing them and making great threats of vengeance. There was very much excitement, and, to all appearances, a battle of no small proportions was impending. The white men had entire possession of the Courthouse ; some armed, and others unarmed, had taken refuge there as the safest place. S. A. Lewis had taken his position alone out on the pavement in front of the Court-house, calmly watching the movements of the mob, which was coming up with great noise and excitement on the other side of the street. Just then an old soldier hurried from the Court-house, and, rushing past, tapped Lewis on the shoulder and exclaimed : " ' Dock,' what are you doing here by yourself ? " With a significant smile he replied : "I am just waiting for that scoundrel to leave that pavement to come this way, and then I am going to kill him." Then turning again to face the leader of the mob, he called him loudly by name, saying : "Whenever you leave that pavement and start this way I'll kill you." The leader heeded the warning and did not come. The old soldier that related this circumstance a short time after it occurred, wound up thus : " ' Dock ' Lewis is as game a man as ever I saw." S. A. Lewis died at the early age of thirty-two years, leaving his two orphan children quite a handsome estate in Clark County, Kentucky.

Sophia Lewis, fifth daughter of Thomas and Elizabeth Lewis, was born October 13, 1796. She married Honorable John T. Johnson, of Scott County, Kentucky. He was descended from one of the most distinguished old families of Kentucky, being a near relative of Richard M. Johnson, one of the Vice-Presidents of the United States ; also of General Albert Sidney Johnston, one of the most famous men of America, besides other distinguished men. Honorable John T. Johnson represented his district in the United States Congress, and afterward became quite a noted minister of the Reformed or Church of the Disciples. They raised six children, viz : Elizabeth Lewis, who married Victor M. Flournoy ; Sallie Lewis, who married Broaddus W. Twyman ; Alpheus Lewis, married Miss Virginia Herring ; Mary, married Colonel John T. Viley ; Laura, married D. W. Standeford ; Victor Flournoy Johnson never married. From the above quite numerous descendants are now living in this and other States, and among them are distinguished men.

Alpheus, the sixth son of Thomas and Elizabeth Lewis, was born in Fayette County, Kentucky. He married Miss Theodosia Ann Turner, of Fayette County, and resided the remainder of his life on his farm on Stoner Creek, in Clark County, being the eastern end of the three thousand acre tract of land purchased by his father of Gest, and a part of the same tract which Stephen D. and Thornton inherited and lived upon. As Alpheus' land was considered inferior to the other, he received two hundred acres more than either of the other heirs. Theodosia Ann Turner, his wife, was

ALPHEUS LEWIS.

born June 3, 1810, and married Alpheus Lewis June 2, 1824. He was a sedate, quiet, intelligent farmer, honorable in all of his dealings ; a strict member of the Old Baptist Church. He was, like several of his brothers, very fond of fishing and hunting in the mountains, and derived most of his recreation in that way. He spent his entire life quietly on his farm, and was held in high esteem by all his acquaintances as an honest Christian man. He died April 6, 1865. His wife survived him more than twenty years, and died March 6, 1888.

Thirteen children were born to them, four of whom died in infancy and nine lived to be grown, viz : Sallie Ellis, born August 24, 1825 ; Thomas, born in 1826, and died unmarried at the age of twenty-five years ; Alpheus, Jr., born January 2, 1828 ; William, born December 20, 1834 ; Elizabeth Payne (Bettie), born February 13, 1836 ; Theodosia Ann, born December 4, 1837 ; Nancy Turner, born May 11, 1840 ; Sophia Johnson, born July 5, 1842 ; Lucian Tupper, born April 15, 1853.

The eldest child, Sallie E., married Mr. Isaac Miller, of Clark County, Kentucky, September 21, 1845, and they removed to Missouri. To them were born five children, viz : Sallie, Junius, Alpheus, Isaac, and Willie. Mrs. Sallie E. L. Miller died September 19, 1854. Alpheus, Jr., married Elizabeth Scott, of Bourbon County, Kentucky, September 12, 1850, and to them were born four children, viz: Henrietta, Maude, Alpheus, and May. They removed to the far West, and are now living in California or Oregon.

Elizabeth P. married Mr. A. E. McGrath, of Philadelphia, October 14, 1856, and to them were born two children, viz : Katie and Elizabeth P. Mrs. Elizabeth P. McGrath died November 14, 1862.

William L. married Ecca Tracey, of Clark County, Kentucky, September 22, 1858, and to them were born thirteen children, viz : Edward, Buford, Mattie, Theodosia, Willie, Thomas, Tracey, John, Tupper, Alpheus, James, Asa K., and Minnie May.

Theodosia, third daughter of Alpheus Lewis, married Dr. Frank M. Greene, of Clark County, Kentucky, September 22, 1858. Dr. Greene has heretofore been mentioned as a son of Dr. Greene, who married a daughter of Capt. Thomas Wright, of Clark County, Ky. To them were born eight children (the youngest died in infancy), namely : A. Lewis, Frank M., Cora Lee, Sophia Maude, Nanci Lewis, Willie V., and Elizabeth P. Mrs. Theodosia Ann L. Greene died May 15, 1881. Dr. Frank M. Greene is a prominent physician, and with his interesting family of children resides in the city of Lexington, Kentucky. His third daughter, Miss Nanci Lewis, even at her present early age has developed quite a literary talent. Some of the best papers and periodicals of our country have published productions from her pen with high commendations. She graduated with honor at Sayre Institute, Lexington, Kentucky.

Nannie Turner, fourth daughter of Alpheus and Theodosia Ann Lewis, married Charles B. Duke, of Nashville, Tennessee, May 1, 1866. To them were born three children, viz: May, Charles B., Jr., and Sophia Lewis. They reside in Nashville, Tennessee.

Sophia Johnson, fifth daughter of Alpheus Lewis, married Elder J. Taylor Moore, of Scott County, July 25, 1876, and to them was born one child, named Alpheus Lewis. Mr. Moore is a minister of the gospel according to the faith of the Old Baptist Church, and resides in Georgetown, Kentucky.

Lucian Tupper, youngest child of Alpheus Lewis, married Sophia Maude Grant, July 25, 1876. After her death he married, October 13, 1887, Mollie McDonald, of Clark County, Kentucky. By the first marriage he had no children ; by the second marriage three children, viz: Mollie Miles, John Stuart, and Lucian Tupper, Jr. Dr. L. T. Lewis is a veterinary surgeon, and resides in Winchester, Clark County, Kentucky.

Douglas Payne Lewis, youngest child of Thomas and Elizabeth P. Lewis, was born August 4, 1804. His father died when he was only five years of age, and he was nurtured and reared by his widowed mother, his oldest brother, Hector, acting as his guardian. He inherited his portion of land in Clark County, being a part of the Gest tract, but he sold this land—a part of it to his brother Stephen, and the remainder to Mr. Bean. He then purchased a tract of fine land on Cane Ridge, in Bourbon County, Kentucky, adjoining the lands which his wife had inherited from her father, and they removed to Cane Ridge estate, where he spent the remainder of his life. He married Rachel Elizabeth, daughter of Colonel Henry Clay, of Bourbon County. Colonel Clay was also the father of Captain Matt. Clay, who married Mary, the daughter of Major Asa K. Lewis, heretofore give. Douglas P. Lewis was a well educated, cultivated gentleman, fond of congenial society, and very highly esteemed by all of his acquaintances. Although he preferred the quiet life of a private citizen on his large and excellent farm, he served one term as Representative of Bourbon County in

DOUGLAS P. LEWIS,
Of Bourbon County, Kentucky.

the Kentucky Legislature in 1847. He owned a large and valuable cotton plantation in Arkansas. He was a strong Clay Whig until the war came on, when he espoused the Southern cause, and was an ultra and uncompromising Southern man during the conflict. All of his sons who were of sufficient age and able to bear arms were in the Southern army. They had ten children born to them. One of them died in infancy, and eight of them are now living, viz : Elizabeth P. L. (Bettie), the eldest child, was born December 16, 1831. She married Henry C. Howard, of Mt. Sterling, Kentucky. They resided in that town until July 1, 1883, when Mr. Howard died, and soon after this his widow removed to Paris, Kentucky.

To H. C. Howard and his wife were born eight children. Three of them died in infancy, five lived to be grown, and four are now living, viz : Mary B., who married Rev. William Dudley Powers, of the Episcopal Church, of Richmond, Virginia, and who is now Rector of St. Paul's Church in Henderson, Kentucky, where they reside ; Ann M., who married Joseph O. Embry, of Mt. Sterling, where at present they reside. Douglas L. Howard, eldest son, was a very popular young physician of great promise, who graduated at the Louisville Medical College at nineteen years of age, winning the highest honors in his class and thereby the first place at the City Hospital, where he practiced for one year. He then located in Paris, where he was fast gaining a reputation and an increasing practice. He died April 30, 1889, at twenty-seven years of age. George Howard is in business in Cincinnati, Ohio. Henry C. Howard is an attorney at law in Paris. He graduated with honor at the head of his law class at the Columbian University of Washington City with degree of B. L., and afterward took the degree of M. L. at the same college.

Stephen D., eldest son of Douglas P. Lewis, was born July 12, 1833. He married, first, Helen, daughter of General William Johnson, of Scott County, Kentucky, and lived on his father's Arkansas plantation for some years, and afterward in Helena, Arkansas, where his first wife died. From this marriage he had two children, a son named William J., who lives in New York, and a daughter named Helen, who is married to Henry Y. King, of Rogers, Arkansas. After the death of this wife, Stephen D. married, next, Emily Burton, by whom he had no children. His third wife was Mary E. Oldham, and they are now living in Rogers, Arkansas. During the war he was a quartermaster in the Southern army, and was stationed at Little Rock.

Thomas H., second son of Douglas P. Lewis, was born **January** 8, 1835. He married Lucy B., daughter of Jacob Spears, a prominent merchant of Paris, Kentucky. By this marriage he raised one son, named Thomas Spears, who is now living in Lexington, and is a clerk in the Second National Bank of that city. The wife of Thomas H. died several years before, and he died September 19, 1881. Thomas H. was a gallant soldier in the Southern Army, and First Lieutenant in the First Kentucky Mounted Rifles when he entered the service, and was in Colonel E. F. Clay's regiment in General Humphrey Marshall's command. While cutting his way through the enemy's line in an engagement at Jim's Creek in Eastern Kentucky he was severely wounded and taken a prisoner, and after a long and severe imprisonment at Fort Delaware he was exchanged. Not a great while after this, in a severe engagement, he was again captured and held for a long while at Camp Morton prison, where he suffered great hardships, from which he never fully recovered. He was one of nature's noblemen and a Christian gentleman.

Margaret Helen, second daughter of Douglas P. Lewis, was born October 15, 1836. She married Moses C. Chaplin, of Wheeling, West Virginia, who died October 20, 1889, and from this marriage there were three children, named Lewis Loring, Lizzie Lewis, and Mary Loring. After the death of Mr. Chaplin his widow removed to Cincinnati, where she now resides with her children.

Douglas P., Jr., third son of Douglas Lewis, was born January 24, 1839. He married Miss Lucy B. John, daughter of S. P. John, of Greenville, Ohio, and from this marriage he had one son, named Douglas, now about fourteen years of age. The wife died December 18, 1883. She was a descendant from an old Welch family of nobility.

Douglas P., Jr., with his two younger brothers, is extensively engaged in the grate and mantel business at 552 and 554 West Sixth Street, Cincinnati. He is the inventor of a patent grate or base-burner which is likely to supersede all of the older styles of grates.

Asa K., Jr., fourth son of Douglas P. Lewis, was born June 7, 1842. He married Ann Elizabeth Lindsey, of Bourbon County, Kentucky, and they have two living children. He is a partner with Douglas P., Jr., and lives in Cincinnati.

Howard, another son of Douglas P. Lewis, was born August 15, 1851. He is unmarried, and is also in business and in partnership with his two above named brothers.

The youngest daughter of Douglas P. Lewis, Mary Laetitia, was born October 29, 1844. She married Frank R. Armstrong, Esq., of Wheeling, West Virginia, and they reside in Paris. They have six children, viz: Joseph DuBois, their eldest son, married Lillian Metcalfe, of Lexington. Douglas, Frank, and Cassius are younger sons; Bessie and Isabella the two daughters.

Frank C. Lewis, youngest son of Douglas P. Lewis, married Viva Mudge, of St. Louis, and he lives and is in business in St. Louis.

Samuel Lewis, John Lewis, and William Lewis, three brothers, fled from France to England after the revocation of the Edict of Nantes in 1685, to escape persecution. (See Smile's History of the Huguenots.) William removed to the north of Ireland and married a Miss McClelland. They raised one son named Andrew, who married Miss Calhoun, and from these parents came the great Pioneer John and his numerous descendants, as we have already given. Samuel settled in Wales, and two of his sons, John and General Robert, came to America about the year 1700. John located in Hanover County, Virginia, where he spent the balance of his life.

General Robert's son Stephen* married a Miss Offutt, of Fairfax County, Virginia. He died quite young, having only one child, named Thomas Lewis, who came to Kentucky, as we have already given. General Robert Lewis' son, Colonel Robert, lived and died on his father's estate in Gloucester County; raised three sons, named Fielding, John, and Charles.

Colonel Fielding Lewis, the eldest son, was twice married; first, to Miss Washington, a cousin of General George Washington, and

* NOTE—Why do we know that Stephen Lewis was the son of General Robert Lewis, of Gloucester County, Virginia? First, it is a well-known fact, authenticated by the sons and daughters of Colonel Thomas Lewis, that his father's family was closely allied by marriage with the Washington family. Colonel Fielding Lewis was the only Lewis that ever married into the Washington family in that day, or before or for many years after the day and generation of Stephen Lewis' lifetime. Colonel Fielding married, first, Mary Washington, a cousin of General George, and after her death he married Bettie, sister of General George. Colonel Fielding was a son of Colonel Robert, the brother of Stephen. By reference to the ages of each and all of these men it will be conclusively known that Stephen could not have been related in any other way by marriage to the family of Fielding Lewis, and the only family of this name which intermarried with the Washington family. See First and Second Volumes of "Churches and Families of Virginia," by Bishop Meade; "The Life of General Washington," and other histories which refer to his lineage and connections.

his second wife was Miss Bettie, a sister of General George Washington. By the first marriage there was one son, named John Lewis, who came to Kentucky with his sons Joseph and William, and who lived in Mercer County, Kentucky. Joseph married, first, Miss Williamson, and by this marriage there was one son, named Richard. After the death of this wife he married Mrs. Sampson, a widow, who was a Miss Porter, and was descended from French Huguenot ancestry, who were among the early settlers on James River above Richmond, Virginia. From this second marriage Joseph Lewis raised five sons, named Robert, Charles, Joseph, Andrew, and John. Many descendants of these sons are now living in Kentucky and other States of this Union. John, the last named, who resided in Barren County, Kentucky, was the father of our present distinguished Judge Joseph H. Lewis, of the Court of Appeals.

John, the immigrant brother of General Robert, and who settled in Hanover County, Virginia, raised a son named David Lewis David Lewis married a Miss Terrell, and their daughter, Hannah Lewis, married James Hickman, of Culpeper County, Virginia, and removed to Clark County, Kentucky, where they spent the remainder of their lives. From them quite numerous descendants are now living in Kentucky and other States. The Kincaids, Hansons, Taliaferros, Stones and many other families are blood relatives of this branch of the Lewis family. James Hickman was of distinguished lineage.

From an old French history of the Huguenots it is learned that these three French Protestant brothers, Samuel, John, and William, who were banished from France, were sons of Lord John Louis, a French nobleman, and no doubt a French scholar could trace this lineage back many generations further.

## PHILLIPS FAMILY.

William Phillips came from England and first settled in Maryland, but afterward moved to Kentucky. He raised six children, viz : William, Ezekiel, Thomas, James, Rachel, and Nancy. William (his son) was born August 18, 1775, and died in Kentucky, February 11, 1815. He was married to Elizabeth Moss, and raised five children, viz : Buford, William M., Lorenzo Dow, Lucinda M., and Henry Harrison. The last named was born in 1812 and died in 1892. He was married to Matilda Pickrell, of Fleming County, Kentucky, in 1833, and raised six children, viz :

Sarah, who married Dr. S. D. Welch.

Martha, who married Dr. George S. Brother.

Delila, who married H. Clay Megee.

Judge William H., who married, first, Polina V. Spears ; second, Alice Shook.

Theodore Frelinghisen, who married Mary S. Lewis.

Thomas, who has not married.

Theodore Frelinghisen, who married Mary S. Lewis, raised three children—sons—viz :

Henry H., who married Jeane Milam.

Thornton L., who married Annette Kidd.

James S., who has not married.

Matilda Pickrell was a daughter of Henry Pickrell, who was born in Loudon County, Virginia, on March 17, 1782, and emigrated to Kentucky and married Sallie Gilkerson, of Kentucky, who was of Irish descent. Henry Pickrell's parents came from Yorkshire, England, and settled in Loudon County, Virginia. Henry Pickrell settled in Montgomery County, Kentucky, near Aaron's Run, and very near where the post-office of Side View is now located, but afterward removed to Shelby County, Kentucky, and finally settled in what is now Sangamon County, Illinois, with several of his grown sons and most of his family, and died there. His grandson, Hon. Henry Pickrell, now lives in Springfield, Illinois, a very prominent man, and one among the most prominent shorthorn breeders of that State. (Now dead since this was written.)

## THE MOSS FAMILY OF JESSAMINE COUNTY.

It appears from the records of Goochland County, Virginia, that Hugh Moss, the ancestor of the Moss family in Jessamine County, was commissioned Captain of the Goochland County Militia in 1760, and was commissioned in 1770. He served in the Revolutionary War, and died from wounds received in battle in 1780. The father of Hugh Moss was James Moss, who was born in England in 1719, where he married Elizabeth Henderson, whose forefathers came from Scotland. Hugh Moss married Jane Ford, daughter of Thomas and Keturah Wynne Ford. Hugh Moss left six sons and three daughters. William Moss was one of the sons, and it is said was born in 1759. Dr. James Moss, the eldest son of Hugh Moss, was a Major in the Revolutionary War, and settled in Kentucky, where he died in 1817. Keturah L. Moss, a daughter of Dr. James Moss, married General James Taylor, of Newport, Kentucky. William Moss married Louise Le Compte, who was of French descent. They had twelve children, all born in Virginia, viz :

Polly, who married Jerry Dickerson.

Judith, who married John Taylor.

Patsey, who married Charles McCabe.

Elizabeth, who married William Phillips, was the mother of Henry Harrison Phillips, and was born in Virginia in 1782, and died in Kentucky in 1867.

Jennie, who married John Garner.

Tabitha, who married —— Kersey.

Nancy, who married Charles Myers.

Ray ——, who married Jane McKinney.

James, killed at the battle of River Raisin.

William Moss.

Peyton Moss.

# THE VAN METER FAMILY.

The Van Meters of the United States have, so far as I have been able to learn, all sprung from two men, a father and son, who came from Bommell, in South Holland, and landed at New Amsterdam in 1663, when that village belonged to the Dutch. The father was a widower, and the son was then about ten years of age. It is well known in Holland the prefix "Van" to a name signifies of, and was originally spelled without a capital letter V. Thus the emigrant father's name was Jans Gysbertsin van Meteren, and his son's name was Kryn Jansen van Materen. Now these two names brought to our language would be: the father's name, John Gisbertson of Metren, and the son's name was Kryn Johnson of Metren. This father and son located in Ultricht, in King's County, and afterwards removed from there to Monmouth County, New Jersey. The above facts are all on record in Bergen's Kings County, pages 345, 346, and also the following facts, viz: The son married Neltje (Nellie) Van Cleef, of New Ultricht, September 9, 1683.

He is on assessment roll of New Ultricht from 1675 to 1709; was a member of the Dutch Protestant Church in 1677, and was a deacon of that church in 1699. He is on Dongan's patent of 1686, and took the oath of allegiance to the British Crown in that town in 1687. He is assessed for forty-six acres of land in New Ultricht in 1701. In 1709 he removed to Middletown, Monmouth County, New Jersey. His children were: Jan, baptized April 24, 1687 (it was the custom of that church to baptize infants on or before the time that they were one month old); Engeltje, Gysbert, Kryn, Benjamin, Eyda, Joseph, Cyrinius, and Janitje. The time of the baptism of each of the above named children is recorded in the old church records of New Ultricht and Middletown. The father of this family signed his name finally Kryn Van Meteren, and sometimes Kryn Jansen Van Meteren, for all of which see Bergen's Kings County, pages 345 and 346, and church records as above stated.

Jan Van Metren, this eldest son, as above shown, was the afterward noted Indian trader who went in command of a band of Caugh Indians, a friendly tribe, on a trading expedition to Virginia in 1739. He had meantime moved his family from New Jersey to

New York.  On this expedition in 1739 he explored the country then almost unknown to the white people, the valley of the south branch of the Potomac (known then by the Indian name of the Wapatonica).  This man soon became sufficiently Americanized to spell his name John instead of Jan, and finally dropped the "n" off, thus leaving the name Van Metre.  My father frequently received letters with his name spelled in that way when I was a boy, and said that was the old style way to spell it.

When John Van Metre returned to his home in New York from the beautiful valley of the Wapatonica he urged his sons to lose no time in possessing that land, declaring that it was the most beautiful and fertile country he had ever seen.  Four of his sons emigrated to Virginia about the year 1740, viz: Abraham, Isaac, Jacob, and John.

Abraham and John settled in Berkeley County, on the east side of the Alleghany Mountains.  Jacob settled at the lower end of the South Branch Valley, and Isaac on the beautiful valley of the South Branch, known as the Indian Old Fields, in what is now Hardy County, and there he constructed his fort, as this was then a frontier and much exposed to Indian depredations.  John and Isaac had procured a grant of forty thousand acres of land through Governor Gooch, of the British Crown.  They sold one half of this grant to Joist Hite, which left them about ten thousand acres each, which they located and settled upon, as above stated.

Before we confine ourselves exclusively to one branch of this family, we will go back to state that the emigrant father, Janse Gisbertsin Van Metren, also married a Miss Van Cleef, who was, no doubt, an aunt of the son's wife, and raised a family of children in New Jersey, some of the descendants of whom are still in that State, as well as in New York and other States; many of them bearing the names of Van Metren and Van Matren.  These New York and New Jersey families intermarried with the early Vanderbilts, Bennetts, Hendricksons, Schencks, and other families, some of which have become quite noted for wealth and influence.

Some of the sons of John and Abraham, and perhaps Jacob, were among the very early emigrants from Virginia to Kentucky, as far back as 1780 to 1790.  Some of them settled in the southwestern part of the State, and quite a number of their descendants are there now. Two or three sons of John settled at that time in what is now Harrison County, Kentucky, but after a sojourn there of some ten or twelve years they all removed to Ohio, and one of them, named Morgan Van Metre, lived and died there, and founded Morgantown, which was located on his farm and named for him. Many of the descendants of these brothers went further west and are living in Indiana, Illinois, Iowa, and other Western States. Some of the descendants of the early emigrants to the southwestern part of Kentucky are now in Missouri, Illinois, and other Western and Southwestern States.

We will now deal more exclusively with Isaac Van Metre, or Van Meter (as the name was spelled sometimes one way and then the other), and his family and descendants : Isaac, the son of John Van Metre, the enterprising Indian trader, this same Jan, the eldest son of Krine Jansen Van Meteren, the juvenile emigrant from Bommell, in South Holland, with his father, Jans Gisbertsin Van Meteren, Isaac Van Metre and his family, consisting of a wife and four children, viz : Henry, Garret, Mary, and another daughter, whose name is not known, but who married Jacob Hite, and died leaving no children. These parents and four children took up their permanent abode at Fort Pleasant, in the Indian Old Fields, now Hardy County, West Virginia, in 1744.

The father had come out four years previous and laid what was called a "tomahawk claim" on these lands, but built his fort and residence and took possession in 1744. These facts as to removal of these Van Metre brothers to Virginia, their locations, their settlement, and their adventures with Indians, the protection their forts furnished to the families of the surrounding settlers, can be found in Kerchival's History of the Valley, Foote's Sketches of Virginia, and other histories of the early settlement of Virginia. Jacob Van Meter's fort at the lower end of the valley, near the mouth of the south branch of the Potomac, was quite a strategic point, and was frequently attacked by the savages, but was never taken. One of his sons built a residence some distance outside of the fort and ventured to live unprotected out there, but he and his wife and all of his children were killed and scalped by the Indians. Isaac Van Meter, the founder and owner of Fort Pleasant, when quite an old man was killed and scalped by the savages only a short distance outside of his fort in the year 1757, leaving a widow and four children.

Isaac's daughter, Mary, married a gentleman whose name I can not with certainty give, and she raised only one child, a daughter, who married Vincent Williams, of Williamsport, on Patterson's Creek.

Henry married four times, his last wife being Mary La Felton, daughter of a French Huguenot, Erasmus La Felton. His children were Joseph, Ephraim, John, David, Elizabeth, Rebecca, Jacob, Benjamin, Solomon, and Abraham. Five of these sons lived to raise families. Solomon and David moved to the Shenandoah Valley. Abraham lived on Patterson's Creek, near Williamsport. Joseph and Jacob are buried in the Old Fields Cemetery, not far from Old Fort Pleasant.

And now as to this son Garret (who I think was the oldest child), from whom I directly descend, by the aid of authentic family records I can be more specific and give ages and dates. Garret Van Meter was born in the State of New York, February, 1732, and came with his parents and the balance of their family to Fort Pleasant in 1744. He married Mrs. Ann Sibley, whose maiden name was Ann Markee, in 1756, about one year before his father was killed by the Indians. He inherited from his father's estate Fort Pleasant and a large tract of the surrounding lands. He was a Colonel in the Revolutionary War, and commanded a regiment of militia in General Washington's army. I have heard my father and my uncle Abraham tell several anecdotes of this ancestor's army experience under Washington. He always referred to Washington as General George. I will relate one of them, which made a lasting impression on my boyhood mind. In one of the most severe battles in which he ever participated, General Washington galloped up to him, and, pointing with his sword to a hill only a short distance away, said : "Colonel, take possession of the top of that hill and hold it," and then he started to ride away, but went only a short distance, then turned half around and said, "Colonel, hold the top of that hill at all hazards ; I will support you." He galloped away and was soon out of sight. "We went to the top of that hill, and the Redcoats got there at the same time, but the boys went at them and drove them back. They were not gone long before they came back with double their number, but the boys gave them hot lead and drove them back again, and then they came again in greater force in front, and I looked to our left and the Redcoats were coming on that side, and I looked to our right, and they were coming on that side, and then I thought our time had come. I looked behind us to see if any Redcoats were coming from that way, and who should I see but General George come galloping up on his old sorrel. Then I knew we could whip them, so I hallooed, 'Give them hot lead, boys ; General George is coming.'"

The children of Colonel Garret and Ann, his wife, were: Isaac, born December 10, 1757 ; Jacob, born May 18, 1764 ; Ann, born April 15, 1767. There were other children born to them, but only these lived to be grown. Isaac married Bettie Inskeep and Jacob married Tabitha Inskeep, both daughters of Joseph Inskeep and his wife, Hannah McCullock, who was a daughter of the most famous Indian fighter and scout of his day, whom the Indians finally killed and cut his heart out to eat it while it was warm, saying they ate it so that they could be brave like "Cullock." Ann married Abel Seymour. Colonel Garret and his wife were among the very first supporters of religion among the pioneers of their day in that country.

They lived and died at old Fort Pleasant as full of honor as of years.

### DOCUMENTARY EVIDENCE.

Documentary evidence that Garret Van Meter commanded the militia of Hampshire during the Revolutionary War : " Wherever a county in Virginia bears the name of Shire, it was originally a division of land—generally comprising a large district of country, which had been allotted under colonial government—and soon after the successful close of the Revolution the State government commenced to cut counties from the old Shires, until now there is left only a small portion of the original Shires to bear the name, with several counties surrounding which have been detached. Thus Hampshire comprised all of the valley of the South Branch of the Potomac from its mouth up to Petersburg, together with quite a region of country extending for miles away on either side of the river."

Very soon after the close of the Revolutionary War Hardy County was cut off from Hampshire. Fort Pleasant, the home of Colonel Garret Van Meter and of his father, Isaac, who located the land grant and built the fort, is in Hardy County.

From Kirchival's History of the Valley, pages 129 and 130, we extract the following : "In 1781 Cornwallis entered Virginia at the head of a large army, and in the month of June a party of Tories raised the British standard on Lost River, then in the county of Hampshire (now Hardy). John Claypole, a Scotchman by birth, and his two sons were at the head of the insurrection. Claypole had the address to draw over to his party a considerable majority of the people on Lost River, and a number on the South Fork of the Wapatonica (Potomac). They first manifested symptoms of rebellion by refusing to pay their taxes and refusing to furnish their quota of men to serve in the militia. The sheriffs or collectors of the revenue complained to Colonel Van Meter, of the county of Hampshire, that they were resisted in their attempts to discharge their official duties, when the colonel ordered a captain and thirty men to their aid."

By a (*) star near to Claypole's name in this extract, reference is made to a footnote at the bottom of page 130, which is as follows : "Isaac Van Meter, Esquire, then about twenty-four years of age, was one of the posse and related these facts to the author." This Isaac was the oldest son of Colonel Garret and the oldest brother of Colonel Jacob, the grandfather of the author of this book. The above shows that this Isaac was a private soldier in the militia of Virginia under his father.

From an old book, entitled "Debates and Other Proceedings of the Convention of Virginia, convened at Richmond on Monday, the 2d day of June, 1788, for the purpose of deliberating on the Constitution recommended by the grand Federal Convention, to which is prefixed the Federal Constitution," we learn that this Isaac Van Meter was the accredited delegate from Hampshire to this convention and participated in its proceedings. This old book above referred to was printed in Petersburg, Virginia, by Hunter & Prentis in 1788, immediately after the close of the convention, and bound in leather in an old style, substantial way. This Isaac Van Meter lived to be eighty years of age, and the following is an obituary notice of him :

"The righteous shall be in everlasting remembrance."—Psalm cxii, 6.

"Departed this life at Oldfields, Hardy County, Virginia, December 13, 1837, that truly patriarchal man, Isaac Van Meter, Esq., aged eighty years and three days."

ISAAC VAN METER,

At about Eighty Years of Age, Older Brother of Colonel Jacob; were Sons of Colonel Garrett, and Grandsons of Isaac, who Built Fort Pleasant in 1744.

Born December 10, 1757, at Fort Pleasant, a few rods from the place where he lies buried, he spent his long life in that valley of surpassing beauty and fertility through which the south branch of the Potomac winds its course. His ancestors, descended from emigrants from Holland, emigrating from New Jersey, were among the first settlers of Western Virginia, and took up their abode on the branch before the great Valley of Virginia was abandoned by the Indians. They were directed to this spot by some friendly Indians strongly attached to the family. The grandfather of Mr. Van Meter took his abode on the beautiful tract of land now in possession of his descendants. Fort Pleasant, the birthplace of Mr. Van Meter, now the residence of Abraham Van Meter, was the rendezvous of the families in the neighborhood, and during Braddock's War was, for a time, the place of encampment of Washington.

In consequence of the jealousies attending the encroachments of the whites, the inhabitants of the branch were subjected to all the vexations and pressures of Indian warfare until Virginia ceased to be a frontier. Mr. Van Meter has repeatedly shown the writer the spot where his grandfather was tomahawked by a scouting party from Ohio. To that river the Indians of the branch had reluctantly retreated, leaving in the valleys and mountains of Hardy all that Indians could desire—fertile cornfields, abundance of fish, and herds of buffalo and deer.

No man ever commanded more respect and exerted a greater influence over the entire South Branch Valley than did Colonel Garret Van Meter.

His sons, Isaac and Jacob, inherited the large landed estate around Fort Pleasant. Colonel Jacob inherited and lived at the old fort and homestead, and Isaac lived about a mile away.

Isaac, the eldest child of Colonel Garret, was about seven years older than his brother Jacob. He lived all his life on the estate which had descended to him from his father and grandfather. He was a very exemplary, unassuming man of the very highest standing in the community as a just, upright, practical man, whose opinion as to what should be done in regard to any heated controversy or dispute in his day would invariably settle it at once as he advised in the community in which he spent his life. He lived to be more than eighty years of age, and we have a copy of the obituary notice published in his county papers, written by the Presbyterian pastor of the church of which he was one of the chief pillars, which gives a succinct narrative of and eulogy upon his character and life such as any just and good man can but covet, as follows :

"Mr. Van Meter died in the exercise of a good hope and a cheerful confidence in Jesus Christ. He had not been in connection with the Church many years. Ever since the writer's acquaintance with him, now about fifteen years, he appeared a proper subject for the ordinance of the Church, yet his distrust in himself deterred him from a profession of religion. Some sixteen (16) years ago he, with an old friend, neighbor, and connection about his age, William Cunningham, now at rest with his Lord, united with some now living in efforts to obtain the services of a Presbyterian minister. There was at that time but two or three members of the Presbyterian Church in the county. There had been a church which engaged the early labors of Moses Hoge, D. D., afterward President of Hampden Sydney College and Professor of Theology for the Synod of Virginia, but it now lived only in the recollection of the few. They induced the present minister, Rev. William N. Scott, to take his abode with them, and during the fifteen years of his labors have had cause to bless God for His direction to a pastor. Mr. Cunningham lived to see many of his descendants gathered into a Church of which he was an elder. Mr. Van Meter, always a friend of the cause, always ready to aid by his counsel and to give of his substance, saw with tears and unutterable emotion his children and grandchildren enter the Church of Christ. But while ready to discover traits of Christian character in others, though faintly drawn, and to palliate their errors and cover with the mantle of charity their failings, he was exceedingly slow to believe that he was himself a fitting subject for the ordinances of the Church.

"The writer well remembers the solemnity, the interest, the effect of that occasion, when the old man, with streaming eyes and trembling form, sat down for the first time with his children and friends at the table of the Lord.

"Inheriting a handsome fortune and prospered in his labors upon his farm, he was a man of abundant possessions ; and in the midst of wealth maintained the simplicity of manners, of dress, of living, and of purpose which characterized former days. It may be said of him, as it was once said of the inhabitants of 'Old Virginny'—'the doors of his hall were nailed wide open from dawn of day to shades of night,' and the stranger might find 'rest and food and fire, and a hearty welcome.'

"The infirmities of age acting upon his tall, athletic frame but rendered the mild old man more venerable. And if veneration, affection, attachment, deference of opinion and judgment, obedience to wishes and commands from children, grandchildren, great-grand-children, and numerous connections—if attention to religion and generosity to the various charitable institution of the Church; if the faithful performance of duty as a magistrate and kindness to the poor render a man worthy of the name of 'patriarch,' we heartily accord it to *Isaac Van Meter.*

"Some time before his death, admonished by his infirmities of his approaching end, he made a final settlement of his worldly affairs. I say *final,* because of his abundance he had always given liberally to his children on their marriage and settlement in life, and though still wealthy, he had not reserved a hoarded treasure to make needy children cease to sorrow for a parent's death. He appropriated a liberal sum of money, putting which into his pastor's hands, he said: 'I wish this divided among the charitable institu-tions,' and proceeded to make the proportions. 'I wish to give it before I die; perhaps it may be my last; I give it as a thank-offering.'

"He had not reserved his various acts of charity till he should die; neither would he leave the disbursement of this to be made after his departure; he would enjoy the giving himself. His last days were full of infirmities but full of peace. The writer had full opportunity of conversing with him a short time before his death, and would say (Psalm xxxvii, 37), 'Mark the perfect man, and behold the upright; for the end of that man is peace.'

"Mr. Van Meter for many years filled the office of magistrate, frequently represented his county in the State Legislature, and was a member of the State Convention that adopted the Federal Con-stitution. The scenes of thrilling interest that passed in that body were retained in lively recollection. He has often been heard to relate the circumstances of Patrick Henry's famous replication, 'bowing to the majesty of the people.' And an aged friend, who had been intimate with him for forty years, said to me to-day : 'He was a man who filled his station in society well; my respect and attachment for him increased as our intimacy was ripened by increasing years.'

F. H. W."

Isaac's children were : Garret, who married Sallie Cunningham ; David, who married Hannah Cunningham ; Jacob, who married Louise Frazier ; John I., who married Polly Harness ; Betsey, who married Joseph Inskeep ; Sallie, who married William Cunningham ; and Ann, who married David Gibson.

David, second child and eldest son of Isaac Van Meter, Esq., was born September 1, 1784 ; married Hannah Cunningham, daughter of William Cunningham 3d.

Their children were :

First child, Elizabeth Ann (Betsy Ann), who was born February 19, 1810, married Abram Van Meter, son of Colonel Jacob, of Fort Pleasant.

Second child, William C., born March 13, 1811, married Martha Ann Pierce, of Hampshire County, West Virginia, April 21, 1841.

Third child, Isaac Inskeep, born July 14, 1812, and died June 21, 1814.

Fourth child, Jemima Harness, born January 31, 1814, and married John Inskeep, of Hardy County, West Virginia, December 4, 1832.

Fifth child, Sarah, was born July 15, 1816 ; married William Miller, December 26, 1831.

Sixth child, George, was born March 26, 1818; married Elizabeth Gamble, October 15, 1840.

Seventh child, Garret S., born October 28, 1819, and died June 6, 1836.

Eighth child, Solomon, was born March 11, 1822 ; married Mariah E. Cox.

Ninth child, Hannah C., was born August 18, 1824 ; married John T. Peirce, June 3, 18—.

Tenth child, Isaac, was born April 9, 1827 ; married Sallie Innskeep, May 4, 1852.

Eleventh child, Joseph, was born October 25, 1828 ; married Teressa Cox.

Twelfth child, David C., was born September 10, 1831 ; married Belle M. Henderson, of Pennsylvania, January 22, 1856. David was killed in battle in the Southern army at Sangster Station, December 17, 1863.

Thirteenth child, Jesse, was born August 10, 1834, and died July 20, 1855.

David, first son of Isaac here above mentioned, lived on a part of the old Fort Pleasant estate to the age of eighty-seven years, and raised to be grown this above named large family of children, and saw many of his great grand-children. He died May 12, 1871, as full of honor as of years He was for many years magistrate, and filled other places of honor and trust, and was for many years a ruling elder in the Presbyterian Church at Moorefield. He retained his mental and physical capacity, to a very remarkable degree, up to a few months before his death. When he was past eighty-five years of age he could mount his saddle-horse from the ground with apparent ease, and rode around over his large landed estate on horse-back, just as he had done when a much younger man.

Hannah C., the wife of David Van Meter, survived her husband, and died August 21, 1878, at the advanced age of eighty-five years, "a mother in Israel," noted for practical good sense and Christian character.

Elizabeth Ann, the oldest child here above mentioned, who married Abram Van Meter, has further mention elsewhere in this book.

William C., who married Martha Ann Pierce, lived and raised a family on a part of the old Fort Pleasant tract of land, and died, at the age of about seventy-eight years, December 7, 1889. He was an honored Christian gentleman and a practical, energetic business man. His worthy and devoted wife survived him, and died in the sure hope of eternal life, April 13, 1895.

Fifth child, Sarah, who married William Miller, lived for many years with her husband in Virginia, and afterwards they removed to Coles County, Illinois, where they spent the remainder of their lives and raised a family of children. She died July 31, 1893.

Sixth child, George, who married Elizabeth Gamble, lived in Hardy County, West Virginia ; had two children born to him, and he died at the age of thirty-seven years, while his children were yet quite young ; but his son, David G., was in the Southern army from start to close.

Eighth child, Solomon, who married Maria H. Cox, lived for many years in Hardy County, 'West Virginia ; raised a family of children, and after the war he removed with his family to Baltimore, Maryland, where he and his wife still reside. During the war he took an active part in the Confederate service, although he was too old to bear the hardships of a regular soldier ; but he had two sons in the army, viz : Reson Bell and Edwin P.

Hannah C., who married John T. Peirce, raised no children; lived with her husband in Virginia all of her life, and died September 10, 1882, and John T. Peirce died after a very eventful life, August, 1896. He acted the part of a Scout in the Confederate service, and made some very narrow escapes.

Tenth child, Isaac Van Meter, who married Sally Inskeep, resided on a farm in Hardy County, West Virginia, and raised a family there. He lived the retiring and quiet life of a farmer, and died February, 1890, and his widow is still living at the homestead.

Eleventh child, Joseph, who married Teressa Cox, inherited and lived for many years on the homestead of his father, David, and raised a family of children there, but afterwards removed to Utah, where they now reside. This Joseph was a graduate of college at Cannonsburg, Pennsylvania, and also in law at the University of Virginia; was a captain in command of a battery of artillery in the Confederate army, but was compelled to quit the military service on account of failure of his eyesight. After the war closed he came within two votes of receiving the nomination of the Democratic party for Governor of West Virginia, which was at that time equivalent to an election. He was one of the most prominent and influential men of his State when he left West Virginia.

Twelfth child, David C. After his death his widow married Mr. Tucker, and is now living in Pennsylvania.

Garret, second son of Isaac Van Meter, Esq., was born November 11, 1793; married Sallie Cunningham, daughter of William Cunningham, and resided all his life in Hardy County, West Virginia, on a fine farm a few miles up the valley from Moorefield, where he reared his family, highly esteemed and respected by all of his acquaintances.

Some of his children and descendants are now living in Texas, but so far as we could learn none are now living in West Virginia.

To distinguish him from others of his name he was known as "One-eyed" Garret, as he lost an eye when quite young. Some of his sons were soldiers in the Southern army, but we have not been able to obtain particulars concerning them.

Jacob Van Meter, third son of Isaac Van Meter, Esq,, of the Old Fields, and his wife, Bettie Inskeep, married Louisa Frazier, of Hardy County (now), West Virginia, and owned and lived all of his life on a part of the old original Fort Pleasant tract of land, which he inherited from his ancestry, handed down since the building of the fort in 1744, and he owned besides surrounding lands to the extent of about 14,000 acres. His children were : Catherine and Bettie, who are still living, and Annie and Virginia, who died young and unmarried ; two sons, John T. and Isaac. The last named owns the homestead, comprising the location of the old Fort Pleasant and a fine farm surrounding it. Isaac, the owner of this estate, married Martha E. Peer, of Hampshire County, West Virginia, and they have raised to be grown three children, viz: Sadie, who married George McNeill; Jacob and James, who live with their parents.

John T., the oldest son here above named, is a bachelor, and makes his home with his brother Isaac, at the old homestead of their father.

This Isaac Van Meter here above mentioned, son of the late Jacob Van Meter, who owned this land, is known as "Big Ike." He is well named, for there is nothing little about him—a generous, noble, large-hearted, gallant fellow that weighs about 250 pounds, and is one of nature's noblemen.

He gives the following war experience : "I joined Company F of the Seventh Virginia Cavalry in August or September, 1862. The company was made up nearly all from Hampshire and Hardy County (now), West Virginia, and was commanded by Captain George Sheitz until he was killed in battle at Buckton Station (he was a gallant, brave man), and after his death the company was commanded by Captain Isaac Kuykendall, and our First Lieutenant was Charles Vandiver. Our Colonels were Turner Ashby until he was killed at Fort Republic, and then Richard Delaney until his arm was shot off at Greenland Gap, and then we were commanded by Thomas Marshall until he was killed at Cedar Creek, and then we were commanded by Captain Dan Hatcher until the surrender of General Lee.

"All of these officers under whom our regiment served were gallant, brave men, and we were in nearly all of the battles in which Lee and Jackson were engaged, wherever cavalry was used by them.

"General R. L. Rosser commanded our brigade, which was composed of the Seventh, Eleventh, and Twelfth regiments, and Elicha White's battalion.

"In our company were seven Van Meters and one Cunningham, all as closely related as first cousins, viz : David Pierce Van Meter, R. Beall Van Meter, Edward Van Meter, David Van Meter (son of George), Milton Van Meter (a brother of David P. V. above named), and myself ("Big Ike"), making seven Van Meters and James Cunningham, whose mother was a Van Meter.

"All of the above named were severely wounded during the war except myself.   Milton Van Meter was the only one of the name who was killed from our company.   He was a son of William C. Van Meter, of the Old Fields.   He was killed in the fall of 1864, when General Wade Hampton, in command of three brigades of cavalry, made his famous raid in the rear of the Federal army and captured and brought out 2,484 fine beef cattle, which were estimated to average 800 pounds net, and which proved a great treat for Lee's army at that time.

"In that expedition the loss from our company was Milton Van Meter killed, and two other men had each a leg shot off.   Our company was with Lee's army until its surrender, but we did not surrender at Appomattox, but came home, giving Grant's army leg bail to save our horses and private effects, and then surrendered in squads at New Creek or elsewhere, when more convenient.

"I suppose Joe V. Williams and myself did on our trip home what was never done before or since.   Joe had a good horse, but he had been shot in the stifle joint and could not climb the steep mountain road.   He could not be reconciled to abandon his horse, so I proposed that we ride through the railroad tunnel under the Blue Ridge Mountains, and thus get his horse home, which we did safely.   The road was torn up on both sides of the tunnel so that no cars could run.

"I have never been ashamed of the part I took in that war.   I have always been thankful that I was neither wounded nor confined in prison.   I have always felt sure that confinement in prison would have killed me.

"There never was but one Robert E. Lee.   His equal never lived."

At the home of this Isaac Van Meter, which is the nearest residence to where the old Fort Pleasant was located, there is a large iron kettle which was brought there in 1774 by the Isaac Van Meter who built the fort.   It will weigh several hundred pounds, of an odd shape, very deep, but not broad across the top, about two feet

HON. JOHN I. VAN METER,
Of Chillicothe, Ohio.

# HONORABLE JOHN I. VAN METER.

The Honorable John I. Van Meter, youngest son of Isaac Van Meter, Esq., herein named, and who married Polly Harness, represented his native county of Hardy in the Virginia General Assembly while yet so young as to be barely eligible to the office according to the laws of Virginia, and then removed to a fine farm on the Scioto River in Ohio, where he lived until quite an old man, and then removed to Chillicothe, Ohio, where he spent the remainder of his life. He reared a family of children, only two of whom are now living, viz., Judge John Marshall Van Meter, who is a very prominent lawyer as well as a large and successful farmer, and has served a term as Circuit Judge in the Chillicothe Judicial District, and resides in that city, although he still retains his large and excellent farm on the Scioto River. His sister Mary, who has never married, resides in the excellent homestead of her parents and immediately adjoining the residence of her brother. Judge John M. Van Meter married, first, Miss Sisson, of Ohio, by which marriage he has two children now living, viz., John I. and Eliza. After the death of his first wife he married Miss Susan Cunningham, oldest daughter of William Streit Cunningham, of Moorefield, West Virginia, and of whom more is written in this book. From this marriage they have raised two daughters, who are now living, viz., Mary and Sallie. The Honorable John I. Van Meter represented his district in the United States Congress from Ohio for two or more terms. He lived to be more than seventy years of age, and was a very influential and prominent man. His wife died many years before he did, and more can be learned of her under the head of the Harness Family in this book.

NOTE.—The above sketch having been mislaid and not discovered until after the book was printed, we are compelled to insert it thus. The defect will be remedied in the next edition.

broad at the top and three feet deep, shaped something like an egg-shell with one-third of the sharp end cut off. It is not more than half an inch thick at the top edge, but perhaps three to four inches thick at the bottom, gradually growing thicker from top to bottom. It was used by Colonel George Washington (afterwards our great General George) to make powder in at the old fort when he rendezvoused there for a week or more in about 1750, or the year in which he made his campaign against the French and Indians, under the Colonial government, when he was quite a young man. Our ancestor, Isaac Van Meter, used this kettle, no doubt, for that purpose both before and after Washington did. It is a sound and useful kettle now. The above facts are well authenticated.

Colonel Jacob Van Meter, the younger son of Colonel Garret, inherited the old Fort Pleasant homestead, where he and his wife, Tabitha, spent their lives and reared quite a large family of children. He was a colonel and commanded a regiment, and took an active part in the war against Great Britain in 1812-13. He built a residence about two hundred yards outside of the old fort, where he and his wife spent the balance of their lives. He also built the finest flour mill that had ever been erected up to that time in the South Branch Valley, which was constructed to run by water power, and it is still standing, although now in a very dilapidated condition. He was an enterprising business man, and for many years a partner with Chief Justice Marshall in the breeding of thoroughbred horses.

Judge Marshall lived over in what is now old Virginia, and owned quite a thin and ill-adapted farm for grass and grain, but was a very enthusiastic admirer of the thoroughbred or race horse. Colonel Jacob owned then one of the finest grass and grain farms in the United States. Judge Marshall proposed to furnish Colonel Jacob a lot of fine mares and fine horses if he would take charge of them, be at all expense and care of them, and deliver to Judge Marshall one half of the colts each spring, at two years old. Colonel Jacob accepted the proposition, and delivered to the Judge principally colts for a good many years, and retained the fillies, until finally he sent to the Chief Justice one spring as many or more colts than the entire number of mares which he had originally received, when Colonel Jacob received a letter from the Chief

Justice saying that he was now more overstocked with horses than he was before he made the deal with him, and he would please never send him another horse.   This dissolved the partnership and left Colonel Jacob with a stock of horses which finally improved and bred up the horse stock of the entire South Branch Valley so that it became noted for its excellent horse stock, and held this reputation until the war between the North and the South swept the entire stock away.   At the commencement of that war the horses from this valley were eagerly sought after for cavalry purposes, but before the war closed there were none to be found.   Colonel Jacob was for many years an elder in the Presbyterian Church, and one of the chief pillars of that church in the valley.   His house was headquarters for ministers of the gospel who passed through this valley, whether Presbyterian or Methodist (no other denominations were represented in the valley then).

Colonel Jacob Van Meter and his wife, Tabitha, had born to them the following named children : Hannah, born in Fort Pleasant, November 8, 1791 ; married Mr. John Hopewell, of Hardy County ; lived there to be quite old, and died without children.   The second child, Ann, was born April 1, 1793 ; was never married, but lived with two of her younger sisters, neither of whom ever married, viz : Rebecca, born May 2, 1799, and Susan, born December 12, 1807. These three maiden sisters lived with their parents at the old homestead near Fort Pleasant until the death of both parents, when they built a neat and comfortable brick mansion about a mile distant from the homestead and on a part of the same estate.

There these three maiden sisters spent the remainder of their lives, holding their property as a joint estate, and for many years with a mutual agreement that the survivor should hold the entire estate and dispose of it as she might choose.   The youngest sister, Susan, died first ; after the two elder had lived together for several years longer, the next younger, Rebecca, died, leaving the oldest sister, Ann, to survive for many years.   She died in October, 1892, lacking less than six months of being ninety-nine years of age.

Of the above named Hannah Van Meter, who married John Hopewell, an incident has been related which gives a clear insight of her character.   She was a tall, rather lean person, very erect, with dignified and graceful bearing, full of practical sense, and withal the most prominent feature of her character was her devout piety. She therefore commanded respect at any and all times.

After the death of her husband, who, by the way, was a very intelligent, honorable Christian gentleman, of excellent family, and she was his second wife, during her widowhood, which was for the balance of her life, she resided in the town of Moorefield, Hardy County, West Virginia.

When the Federal army took possession of that town she was very soon singled out as a prominent rebel, and a Federal Captain came very early one morning and ordered breakfast for five. When he knocked she met him at the door and received his order, and in her dignified manner invited the five officers in and to have seats, and as they walked in she added, "the Bible teaches us to feed our enemies," and then asked to be excused that she might give the cook directions for breakfast. After a short absence she returned, and, picking up her well-worn Bible, she remarked: "It is our custom to engage in family worship before we breakfast; I hope you gentlemen will join us," at the same time opening the book; her eye fell at once on the twenty-seventh Psalm:

"The Lord is my light and my salvation; whom shall I fear? the Lord is the strength of my life; of whom shall I be afraid? When the wicked, even mine enemies and my foes, came upon me to eat up my flesh, they stumbled and fell. Though a host should encamp against me, my heart shall not fear: though war should rise against me, in this will I be confident. One thing have I desired of the Lord, that will I seek after; that I may dwell in the house of the Lord all the days of my life, to behold the beauty of the Lord, and to inquire in his temple. For in the time of trouble he shall hide me in his pavilion; in the secret of his tabernacle shall he hide me: he shall set me up upon a rock. And now shall mine head be lifted up above mine enemies round about me; therefore will I offer in his tabernacle sacrifices of joy; I will sing, yea, I will sing praises unto the Lord. Hear, O Lord, when I cry with my voice: have mercy also upon me and answer me. When thou saidst, Seek ye my face; my heart said unto thee, thy face, Lord, will I seek. Hide not thy face from me; put not thy servant away in anger: thou hast been my help; leave me not, neither forsake me, O God of my salvation. When my father and my mother forsake me, then the Lord will take me up. Teach me thy way, O Lord, and lead me in a plain path, because of mine enemies. Deliver me not over unto the will of mine enemies; for false witnesses are risen up against me, and such as breathe out cruelty. I had fainted unless I had believed to see the goodness of the Lord in the land of the living. Wait on the Lord ; be of good courage, and he shall strengthen thine heart : wait, I say, on the Lord," which she read, and, kneeling down, commenced at once with a very fervent prayer, such as few can equal ; and when she arose from her supplications and looked around the room she was surprised to find not a '' Yankee '' in the room. She immediately concluded that they had slipped out into the hall or adjoining room to make fun and ridicule, so went in search, and not finding them, on into the yard and out to the street, looking up and down, but not a sinner of them could she see, and never saw one of them after that morning to recognize him. This is what the town folks of Moorefield and the friends generally refer to as "Aunt Hannah praying the Yankees out of the house."

Miss Ann Van Meter was one of the most remarkable ladies of modern times. All of her life, up to less than one year previous to her death, her mind was as clear, active, and vigorous as it had been when she was only forty to fifty years of age. She possessed a high order of intellect, and was all her life long a constant reader of history and the best current literature. When she was more than ninety years of age she kept thoroughly posted on all important political and public affairs, both American and foreign. All three of these ladies were active and faithful workers in the church, and their residence was—as their ancestors' had been for three generations before them, on the same estate—a welcome rendezvous for all ministers of the gospel who visited the valley, and for many years they furnished almost the entire support to a small country church which was located less than a mile from their residence.

Isaac, the father of the writer of this, was the third child and eldest son of Colonel Jacob and his wife, Tabitha, and was born in old Fort Pleasant, Hardy County, in what is now West Virginia, September 24, 1794. He received a good English education from the best teachers that could be obtained in that country at that time, and received a thorough training from his father in the best mode of farming and the care and attention of live stock.

Even at this early day this valley was producing the finest beer and pork, which supplied the Philadelphia and Baltimore markets. This fertile valley produced enormous crops of corn and wheat, and the very finest of clover and bluegrass pasture, nearly all of which grain and grass was consumed by the best of live stock that could be had at that time, and they were driven to one or the other of these markets and yielded very remunerative profits.

ISAAC VAN METER,
Of Clark County, Kentucky.

My father was very early initiated into the Philadelphia and Baltimore markets with fat cattle and hogs of such stock as commanded the top of the market.

But when about twenty-three years of age he came to Kentucky, married Rebecca, the only daughter of Captain Isaac Cunningham, of Clark County, took up his abode with him on his farm about four miles northwest of Winchester, and in this county he spent the remainder of his life.

Rebecca, daughter of Captain Isaac Cunningham and his wife, Sarah, was born in Hardy County, Virginia, October 14, 1800, and removed with her parents to Clark County, Kentucky, in 1802, where she was reared to the age of seventeen years, when she was married to Isaac Van Meter, of Hardy County, Virginia, by the Rev. William W. Martin, on June 17, 1817. It will be observed by the readers of this article that three of the children of Colonel Jacob Van Meter married Cunninghams.

Isaac Van Meter brought with him to Kentucky about seven thousand dollars' worth of property, consisting chiefly of negro slaves, horse stock, and money. He and Captain Isaac Cunningham were for many years equal partners in their business affairs. They were very successful in business, and accumulated a very large and valuable estate, consisting principally of land and slaves. When they finally dissolved partnership and divided their lands, each owned more than one thousand acres of as valuable lands as were in Clark County. They resided on adjoining farms, with their residences less than one mile apart. Captain Cunningham having only one child (my mother), the grandparents bestowed full as much parental care on the grandchildren as did the father and mother, and it was seldom that all of the children were at one time at either one of the residences.

Isaac Van Meter and his wife, Rebecca, had fifteen children born to them, and raised ten to be grown, six of whom are now living. Solomon, eldest child of Isaac and Rebecca Van Meter, was born July 10, 1818, in Clark County, Kentucky; married, first, Elizabeth, daughter of the Hon. James Stonestreet, of Clark County, and from this marriage a son and daughter, named John S. and Elizabeth. This first wife died March, 1847. After her death he married Lucy Hockaday, of Missouri, and from this marriage one child, named Lucy H. This second wife died in 1849, and in March, 1854, he married Martha C., daughter of Nelson Prewitt, of Montgomery

County, Kentucky, and from this marriage three sons, named Isaac C., Nelson Prewitt, and Solomon Lee.   He lived most of his life in Fayette County, Kentucky, three miles north of Lexington, on a farm called Duncastle.   He was a prominent and successful farmer, and for many years was a consistent member of the Presbyterian Church.   He died September, 1859.   He was chosen as the agent from Clark County (where he was residing at the time and where he was born and reared) to go to England, along with Nelson Dudley, of Fayette County, and Charles T. Garrard, of Bourbon County, to select and import shorthorn cattle and other blooded stock for the Northern Kentucky Importing Company, and they made an importation which paid more than 100 per cent net profit. He was a fine judge of cattle ; a very enterprising and intelligent man ; highly esteemed by all of his acquaintances.

His oldest son, John Stonestreet, who was left an orphan while yet a youth (fell to the charge of the writer as his guardian), is now a prominent and very zealous and successful minister of the Presbyterian Church in Missouri.   He married Elizabeth, daughter of Rev. Stephen Yerkes, D. D., of Danville, Kentucky (of whom we have more elsewhere), and raised one son, named Yerkes.   John S., being a stout, active, and precocious youth, was accepted in General John H. Morgan's command at the age of scarcely seventeen years, without the knowledge or consent of his guardian, and also without consent rode my most excellent saddle-horse away (named Scott), and I never saw the horse afterward.   I was told that it was soon ascertained that no horse in Colonel Cluke's regiment — to which John S. belonged — could run so fast for one fourth of a mile as Scott.   After John S. had been in the army for some time I asked Colonel Cluke, with whom I was very intimately acquainted, what kind of a soldier my ward was making, and in a jocular reply he said forty brigadiers could not command that boy, and then he added, "he is one of the best scouts in my command, and a very reliable soldier."   He was made a prisoner on the Ohio raid, when Morgan and Cluke surrendered their forces, and was in prison for about eighteen months.   He was known throughout the entire brigade as "Street" (an abbreviation of Stonestreet), and quite a large majority of the command knew no other name for him.   After the war closed he graduated at Washington and Lee College, then studied law under Judge John M. Van Meter, of Chillicothe, Ohio ; practiced law in the city of Lexington, Kentucky, for a few years ; meantime

SOLOMON VAN METER, SR.,
Son of Isaac, and Grandson of Colonel Jacob, of Fort Pleasant, Virginia.

became a candidate and was elected County Attorney of Fayette County, Kentucky, and soon after this determined to answer a call to the gospel ministry in the Presbyterian Church; went to Princeton and graduated in theology, and is a very successful minister.

Elizabeth, daughter of Solomon Van Meter and his first wife, Elizabeth Stonestreet, married Captain William D. Nicholas, of Winchester, Kentucky, who after their marriage lived for the balance of his life on a part of the old Duncastle farm, inherited by Elizabeth from her father's estate, and it was that part inherited by her father, Solomon Van Meter, from *his* father and grandfather of lands which they purchased of Henry Clay, of Ashland, and adjoining lands which Solomon Van Meter purchased of Dun and known as Duncastle. A correct estimate of the excellent character and reputation of Captain Nicholas can be had by copying from the public prints, which were written at the time of his death, as follows :

### RESPECT TO THE DEAD

In the passage of these resolutions by the Faculty of State College and the Clearing House in regard to Captain W. D. Nicholas, who died Friday morning — Funeral Arrangements.

The funeral of Captain W. D. Nicholas will be held at 3 P. M. at the First Presbyterian Church this afternoon, as already announced. Following is a list of the pall-bearers who will go to the late residence of the deceased, near the city, and accompany the remains to the church : Ed. Frazer, J. D. Hunt, J. B. Simrall, J. Waller Rodes, John Boyd, G. W. Headley, J. H. Graves, and D. H. James.

At a meeting of the Clearing House, held Friday, resolutions of respect were passed in regard to the memory of the dead.

At a called meeting of the Faculty of the State College, held on Friday, March 11, 1892, Professors Neville, Scoville, and Logan were appointed a committee to prepare resolutions expressive of the feelings of the Faculty upon the death of Captain William D. Nicholas, for many years a trustee of the College and a member of its executive committee. Accordingly the following resolutions were submitted and unanimously adopted :

*Resolved,* That the members of this Faculty, on learning with unfeigned sorrow of the loss sustained by the College and community in the death of Captain Nicholas, desire to testify to his long, faithful, and efficient service as a trustee ; to his extraordinary worth as a man, a citizen, and an official, and particularly to the integrity, the rare modesty, purity, and gentleness that distinguished his character and made it at once so strong and yet so beautiful and attractive. As educators profoundly interested in all that can improve the young, we shall seldom be able to direct our students to so fine a model for their regard and imitation as was Captain Nicholas. Green be his memory.

*Resolved,* That this Faculty in a body attend his funeral.

*Resolved,* That a record of these proceedings be preserved in our book of minutes, and that a copy thereof be sent to his family, and others to the newspapers of Lexington for publication.

### THE SECOND NATIONAL BANK TAKES APPROPRIATE ACTION ON THE DEATH OF CAPTAIN W. D. NICHOLAS.

At a full meeting of the Board of Directors of the Second National Bank of Lexington, held Saturday, March 12, 1892, the following action was taken :

*Resolved,* The Second National Bank was founded by Captain W. D. Nicholas, and he has been its only cashier since its organization in 1883, and the bank owes whatever of success it has attained and whatever of public confidence it has secured, chiefly to his fidelity and devotion to its interests, to his intelligent management of its affairs, to the great purity and integrity of his character, and to the invariable sweetness of his temper and affability of manner, which was the same to all persons and at all times. So gentle and courteous was he in his bearing, and so considerate of all, that the transaction of any affairs with him was ever a pleasure. To the bank, as in every relation of life, whether private or public (and he held many offices of trust), he performed his whole duty faithfully and well, and his death has created a vacancy in the bank which will be difficult indeed to fill, and to his associates is a loss indeed irreparable.

*Resolved,* That these resolutions be spread upon the record of the bank, and that a copy thereof be sent to the family, to whom we, as his late associates, tender our heartfelt sympathy.

## CAPTAIN WILLIAM DOUGLAS NICHOLAS.

Captain William Douglas Nicholas married Elizabeth Stonestreet Van Meter, daughter of Solomon Van Meter and his first wife, Elizabeth Stonestreet, daughter of Hon. James Stonestreet, of Clark County, Kentucky. Captain Nicholas was born February 2, 1836. Graduated in law.

He served in the Confederate army ; was a Captain in Colonel Roy S. Cluke's regiment, General John H. Morgan's brigade. Soon after the close of the war he married, as above stated, and removed to a farm near Lexington, where he lived for the balance of his life. When the Second National Bank of Lexington was organized he was made cashier, and held that position for the balance of his life, and made a most popular, efficient, and successful officer. Captain W. D. Nicholas was a son of Robert Carter Nicholas and his wife, Fannie Jane Massie ; grandparents were Colonel Jona Fry Nicholas and his wife, Patsy McGhee ; and of the third generation was Colonel John Nicholas and his wife, Elizabeth Fry, daughter of General Joshua Fry, who had command of the Revolutionary Army before General Washington took command. The following, taken from a reliable old Virginia newspaper, gives the genealogy of the family for many generations back. It is headed " Genealogy of the Nicholas Family " :

The first of the family in Virginia was Dr. George Nicholas, of Lancashire, England, a surgeon in the British Navy, who settled in the colony early in the eighteenth century, and married, in about 1722, Elizabeth, widow of Nathaniel Burwell and daughter of Colonel Robert Carter, of Corotman ; raised issue, first, Robert Carter Nicholas, of Menotas ; born, 1723 ; died in 1790 ; was vestryman of Bruton Paris ; member of the House of Burgesses from 1756 to 1775 ; Committee of Correspondence in 1773 ; treasurer in 1776-7 ; member of the James City Committee of Safety in 1774 to 1776, and of all committees from James City of the House of Delegates from 1776 to 1779 ; was Judge of the High Court of Chancery and of the Court of Appeals ; was one of the leading men of the Revolutionary period in Virginia. He married, in 1754, Ann, daughter of Colonel Wilson Cary, of Ceeleys. Second was John Nicholas, of " Swim Islands," who was Clerk of Albemarle in 1749 to 1815 ; Burgesses in 1756, 1757, and 1758, and of Conventions of 1774-75 from Buckingham. He married Elizabeth, daughter of Joshua Fry.

Third was George, probably the father of Colonel John Nicholas, long the Clerk of Dinwiddie from 1789, and who died February 22, 1818, and grandfather of the John Nicholas, Jr., who was member of the House of Delegates from Dinwiddie in 1810–11. Of this branch also was Captain John Nicholas, of First Virginia Regiment in the Revolution, who was born in 1758, and was alive in 1824.

Children of Robert Carter Nicholas and his wife, Ann Cary :

First, George, born 1755 ; died 1799 ; Captain of Williamsburg Minute Men in 1775 ; appointed Major of Second Virginia Regiment in 1776 ; served with distinction in the Revolution, and was promoted to the rank of Colone ; was member of the House of Delegates for Albemarle in 1781 to 1787 ; was a member of the Convention of 1788, and of the House of Delegates in 1789 ; removed to Kentucky in 1789, and was a member of the Kentucky Convention of 1792, and helped to frame the Constitution ; was afterwards Governor of Kentucky ; was Attorney General in 1792 ; was Professor of Law in Transylvania University at Lexington in 1789. He married Mary Smith, of Maryland, sister of General Samuel Smith.

Second, Lewis Nicholas, of Albemarle, born 1766 ; died January 17, 1840; married Miss Harris.

Third, Colonel John Nicholas, died December 31, 1819 ; was an officer in the Revolution, and was a member of the House of Delegates from Albemarle from 1784 to 1786 ; was a member of Congress from 1793 to 1801 ; removed to Geneva, New York ; was in that State Senate in 1806 to 1809, and was Judge of Court of Common Pleas for Ontario County from 1806 until his death. He married Anne Rose, of Virginia.

Fourth, Wilson Cary Nicholas, of "Warren," Albemarle, born January 31, 1761 ; died October 10, 1820 ; left William and Mary College and entered the American Army in 1779 ; was Commander of Washington's body guard until 1783 ; was a member of the House of Delegates from Albemarle in 1784, 1785, 1786, and 1787 ; a member of the Convention of 1788 ; was County Lieutenant of Albemarle in 1789 ; was member of the House of Delegates again in 1789 and 1790, and again from 1794 to 1799 ; was United States Senator from 1799 to 1804, when he resigned ; was a member of the United States House of Representatives from 1807 to 1814 ; was Governor of Virginia from 1814 to 1818. He married Margaret, sister of General Samuel Smith, of Maryland.

Fifth, Philip Norbone Nicholas, born 1775; died August 18, 1819; was Attorney General of Virginia; was a member of the Convention of 18— from Richmond, and Judge of the General Court. Married, first, Mary Spear; second, Maria C., daughter of Thomas Taylor Byrd; this second wife died June 26, 1877, aged 83 years.

Sixth, Elizabeth Nicholas; married Governor Edmond Randolph.

Seventh, Sarah Nicholas; married John Hatley Norton.

Children of George Nicholas and his wife, Mary Smith:

First, Robert Nicholas, a Colonel in United States Army.

Second, Cary Nicholas, Lieutenant Seventh (7th) Infantry of United States Army in 1809, Captain in 1811, Major in 1813, retired in 1821.

Third, Samuel S. Nicholas, born in 1796, died November 27, 1869; member of the Kentucky Legislature, Judge of the Court of Appeals, and author of Essays on Constitutional Law. In 1857, married Matilda Prather; second, Mary Smith.

Seventh, Maria Nicholas; married Colonel Owings, of Kentucky.

Eighth, Ann Nicholas; married Lewis Sanders.

Ninth, Georgianna Nicholas, married Joseph L. Hawkins.

Tenth, Margaret Nicholas; married, first, General J. C. Bartlett, of U. S. A., and after his death married General Thomas Fletcher, of Kentucky.

Eleventh, Elizabeth R. Nicholas married James G. Trother, of Lexington, Kentucky.

Twelfth, Henrietta Nicholas; married Judge Richard Hawes, of Paris, Kentucky, and was mother of General Morrison Hawes, C. S. A., and Cary Hawes, C. S. A., who was killed at the battle of Chickamauga.

Thirteenth, Clara Nicholas.

The children of Samuel S. Nicholas by first marriage with Matilda Prather:

First, Mary Jane Nicholas; married Mr. Gravis.

Second, Matilda Nicholas; married Hon. R. Barrett, of Missouri.

Third, Margaret.

Fourth, Thomas.

Fifth, Louisa Nicholas; married Major John Johnson, C. S. A.

Sixth, George Nicholas; married Miss Hawes.

Seventh, John Nicholas, Colonel in U. S. A.

By second wife, Mary Smith :

Eighth, Catherine Nicholas.

Ninth, Cary Ann Nicholas.

Tenth, Sarah Nicholas.

The children of John Nicholas and his wife, Anne Rose :

First, Gavin.

Second, Robert C. Nicholas ; married Susan Rose.

Third, Anne Nicholas ; married John Dox, of New York.

Fourth, John Nicholas ; married Virginia Gallagher, of New York.

Fifth, Margaret Nicholas ; married Dr. Leonard, of Lansingburg, New York State.


## SOLOMON VAN METER, Sr.

Solomon Van Meter married, first, Elizabeth, daughter of James Stonestreet and his wife, Lucy Fishback. Both of these families were prominent in Virginia, and afterwards more so in Kentucky. The Fishback family were originally spelled Fishbrock. Lucy Fishback, who was born in Clark County, Kentucky, November 8, 1789, and died in the forty-ninth year of her age, was a daughter of Jacob Fishback, a very prominent citizen and early settler in Clark County, Kentucky, who was born in Culpeper County, Virginia, April 14, 1749, and married Miss Phoebe Morgan, of Fauquier County, Virginia, February 19, 1771. She was born in Fauquier County, Virginia, September 13, 1751. The names of their children are as follows, viz :

John, born June 9, 1774.

James, born February 4, 1776.

Ann (who married Price), born August 16, 1777.

Betsy (who married Mason), born February 11, 1779.

Jessie, born January 18, 1781.

Charles, born February 11, 1783.

Hannah (who married Taylor), born March 26, 1785.

Sallie (who married Taylor), February 27, 1787.

Lucy (who married Stonestreet), born November 8, 1789.

Samuel, born January 27, 1792.

This Fishback family was very prominent in the early history of the Presbyterian Church of Kentucky, and was one of the founders of old Salem Church, and very prominent mention is made of them in Dr. Davidson's history of the Church in Kentucky. Mrs. Lucy Stonestreet was noted for her piety and zealous, earnest, Christian character.

James Stonestreet was born in Loudon County, Virginia, October 1, 1787, and brought to Jessamine County, Kentucky, by his parents at the age of eight years. He was educated and trained for the bar in the District Clerk's office. He began the practice of law at Glasgow, Kentucky, but soon married and settled in Clark County on a farm near old Salem Church, of which he became an elder, and at the time of his death he was the oldest ruling elder in Kentucky — sixty years, and for many of these years he was clerk of the Synod of Kentucky. For thirty-three years he was Clerk of the House of Representatives of the Kentucky Legislature, and enjoyed the society and commanded the entire confidence and greatest respect of the statesmen of the Commonwealth. "He was able, faithful, and wise ; versed in the doctrines, government, laws, and literature of the Presbyterian Church, and distinguished in all her Church courts and associated with her ablest and greatest men ; " he was accounted "among the Church's best servants ; " thus serving both Church and State with great distinction. He was a son of a sturdy old Scotch Presbyterian emigrant, John Stonestreet, and his wife, Nancy Finley, who came from Scotland and settled in Loudon County, Virginia, but afterward removed to Jessamine County, Kentucky. The maiden name of the mother of Nancy Finley was Elinor Timberlake. In Scotland the Stonestreet family belonged to the Campbell Clan.

## HOCKADAY.

After the death of Elizabeth Stonestreet, Solomon Van Meter married, secondly, Lucy Hockaday, a daughter of Irvine Hockaday and his wife, Emily Mills.

Irvine Hockaday and his wife were both natives of Kentucky, but removed to Missouri and founded the town of Fulton ; was County Judge and one of the most prominent and influential men of that part of the State. He donated sites for churches and public buildings, and manifested a commendable interest in the welfare and prosperity of his country.

Lucy Hockaday Van Meter lived only about one year after her marriage, and left one child, a daughter, named Lucy, who married

Dr. Kerr, of Fulton, Missouri, where she now resides a widow with three living children, named Susan, Elizabeth, and Mary Belle ; a fourth daughter, named Lucy Van Meter, having died March, 1901— a very attractive and lovely young woman called suddenly away from a life of usefulness and great promise. Dr. Kerr was a very prominent physician, but died young.

Irvine Hockaday was a son of Isaac Hockaday and his wife, Amelia Irvine, who were married March 31, 1796, in Virginia, and removed to Kentucky.

Emily Mills, the mother of Lucy Hockaday, was the daughter of Dr. John Mills, and a sister of Dr. Augustus Mills, who was the most prominent and successful physician in Clark County, Kentucky, in his day.

Amelia Irvine, the wife of Isaac Hockaday, was the daughter of David Irvine and his wife, Jane Kyle.

Irvine Hockaday's mother was one of eleven daughters and two sons.

Irvine Hockaday and his wife, Emily Mills, raised three sons and five daughters, viz : Isaac, John, Irvine ; Amelia, who married James Stevens ; Margaret, who married Isaac McGuirk ; Elizabeth, who did not marry ; Evaline, who married Beverly Price, and Martha Ann, who married Dr. Wilkerson.

Isaac Hockaday and his wife, Amelia Irvine, raised three daughters and one son, viz : Evaline, who married Thomas R. Moore ; Martha Ann, who married John H. Field ; Jane, who died unmarried ; son, Irvine, married Emily Mills.

Solomon Van Meter, Sr., married, third, Martha C., daughter of Nelson Prewitt.

Nelson Prewitt, who married Mary Ann Coleman, was the youngest son of Robert Prewitt and his wife, Patsy Chandler, who came from Campbell County, Virginia, to Kentucky, and this Robert Prewitt was a son of Michael Prewitt, whose ancestors emigrated from Ireland to the Virginia Colony many years before the Revolutionary War.

Nelson Prewitt was born August 15, 1806. His wife, Mary Ann Coleman, was born December 24, 1807. They were married April 16, 1829. They lived nearly all their lives on their farm in Montgomery County, Kentucky, about five miles from Mt. Sterling. He was one of the most prominent and influential men of that county, and took a prominent part in all matters of public interest. He represented his county in the legislature, and had quite a potent influence in political affairs for many years of his life — was a "fine mixer," excellent conversationalist, could relate an incident or tell an anecdote with very rare effect, and was very popular with all his acquaintances.

Nelson Prewitt died at his home in Montgomery County, Kentucky, December 9, 1870. His wife preceded him; died May 4, 1867.

Nelson Prewitt and his wife, Mary Ann, raised children as follows: Martha Coleman, born July 6, 1830; married, first, Solomon Van Meter, and after his death married Colonel William R. Estell. Lucy Caroline (Cally), born October 12, 1832; married James D. Gay. John Winston was born January 17, 1835; married Margaret Goff. Anna and Elizabeth (twins) were born July 22, 1838. (Elizabeth, one of the twins, died at less than one year of age.) Anna married Benjamin P. Goff. William Henry was born July 8, 1841; married Bettie Gano Rogers. Henrietta Clay (Nettie) was born February 28, 1844; married Josiah Davis Reed. Chiles Coleman, born September 11, 1846, died by drowning, June 8, 1856.

W. H. Prewitt married, May 4, 1870, Bettie Gano Rogers, born April 6, 1846. Her father was Harvey Addison Rogers, of Bourbon County, Kentucky. Her mother, Elizabeth Jane Moran, daughter of Edward B. Moran and his wife, Letitia Clay, she a daughter of Samuel and Nanny (Winn) Clay. Nancy Winn was a daughter of George and Letitia Winn, of Fayette County, Kentucky. This Samuel Clay was a son of Doctor Henry Clay, and an older brother of Colonel Henry Clay, of Bourbon County.

On a front fly leaf of the old Bible from which most of this Prewitt genealogy was taken is the following, viz: This Bible is given to William C. Prewitt as testimony of the esteem of his father, Robert Prewitt, dated March 8, 1815. In the back part of this book, on a fly leaf, is the following, viz: My grandfather was Michael Prewitt, who married Elizabeth Simpkins, born in the lower part of Virginia, afterwards settled on Staunton River, in Campbell County, Virginia, where he lived for a considerable time and raised a large family, viz: Rachael, who married Robert Shipley; James, Elisha, Judith, Michael, Byrd, Joseph, Joshua, Elizabeth.

Michael Prewitt and his wife, Elizabeth Simpkins, were the ancestors of all the Prewitt families which came from Campbell

County, Virginia, very early in 1800, or maybe just a few years before, and settled in Kentucky. This Michael and his wife were raised in Southern Virginia, no doubt from Irish parents who had come over among the early settlers in the colony. Michael Prewitt's children were : Rachael, who married Robert Shipley ; James, Elisha, Judith, Michael, Byrd, Joseph, Robert, Joshua, and Elizabeth. Of the above named children, Robert married Patsy Chandler and came to Kentucky. Raised ten children, viz : Elizabeth S., who married John Smith ; Vaul, who married, first, Mildred Ellis, second, Elizabeth Kerr, third, Sidney L. Fox ; William C., who married Margaret M. Edmonson ; Henry H., who married Sarah Allen ; Mary H., who married John Cavins ; Robert C., who married, first, Susan Garth, second, Elizabeth Elgin ; Willis, who married Dorothy White ; Levi, who married Margaret Boyce ; James, who married, first, Kizie French, second, Henryetta Dawson ; Nelson, who married Mary Ann Coleman.

Elizabeth, who married John Smith, died July, 1811, and left four children, viz: Patsy C., James H., Winn, and Robert H. Smith.

Vaul Allen, who married three times, left eight children, two sons and six daughters, who were living at his death in February, 1826.

William C. married Margaret Montgomery Edmonson, September 13, 1809. Children, viz : John Edmonson, Robert Henry, Martha Ann, Alexander E., James M., Levi, William H., Robert, Elizabeth S., Vaul Allen. Second wife, Catherine Hickman. By this marriage : Richard Hickman, who married Elizabeth Shafer, and David, who married Elizabeth Tebbs. Both of these last named Prewitts died young, but left children who are prominent in the community where they live.

Isaac C. Van Meter, son of Solomon Van Meter and his wife, Martha C. Prewitt, married Pattie Hockaday Field, of Denver, Colorado, a daughter of Thomas Moore Field and Amanda Young Ellis, and a granddaughter of John Hardin Field and his wife, Martha Ann Hockaday, and a great-granddaughter of Curtis Field (born 1731) and his wife, Rosanna Hardin. Her fourth ancestors were John Field and his wife, Dianna Field. Her fifth ancestors were John Field and his wife, Lucinda Stanton, and her sixth ancestors were Henry Field and his wife, Mary James. Thomas M.

Field and his wife, Amanda Y. Ellis, raised five children, viz : Kate, William, Pattie Hockaday (who married I. C. Van Meter), John Ellis, and Elizabeth Hardin Field. Her grandparents, John Hardin Field and his wife, Martha Ann Hockaday, raised eight children, viz : Amelia, Irvine, Thomas M. (who married Martha Ann Hockaday), Curtis Hardin, Rosanna Hardin, Evaline Moore (who married Colonel Cicero Coleman), Isaac Newton, and Pattie Hockaday Field. Her parents of the third generation, Curtis Field and his wife, Rosanna Hardin, raised nine children, viz : John Hardin Field (who married Martha Ann Hockaday), Dianna, Jane, Mary Ellis, Martin D. Curtis, Rosanna Hardin, Betsy Bryan, Thompson Burnham, and Lucinda Burnham. Her parents of the fourth generation were John Field and his wife, Dianna Field, who raised nine children, viz : Curtis (who was born in 1781 and died in 1863), who married Rosanna Hardin ; Henry, Lucinda, John, Ezekiel, George, Nancy, Sallie, Judy, and Polly. Her parents of the fifth generation were John Field and his wife, Lucinda Stanton, who raised three children, viz : John (who married Dianna Field), Larline, and Elizabeth. Her parents of the sixth generation were Henry Field and his wife, Mary James.

The mother of Pattie H. Field, wife of I. C. Van Meter, was the daughter of John Ellis and his wife, Catherine Doyle, who raised three children, viz : Josephine, William, and Amanda Young Ellis, who married Thomas Moore Field. Her grandmother, Martha Ann Hockaday, who married John Hardin, was the youngest daughter of Isaac Hockaday and his wife, Amelia Irvine, who raised seven children, viz : Irvine, Philip Brandywine, Evaline Walker, Edmond, Jane Kyle, Isaac Newton, and her grandmother, Martha Ann.

Her great-grandmother, Rosanna Hardin, who married Curtis Field, was the daughter of John Hardin and his wife, Jane Davis, who raised four children, viz : Martin D., Mark, Mary, and Rosanna Hardin.

John Hardin was a son of Martin Hardin and his wife, Lydia Waters.

Isaac Hockaday, above named, was a son of Edmund Hockaday and his wife, Martha Otey. Amelia Irvine, wife of Isaac Hockaday, was the daughter of David Irvine and his wife, Jane Kyle. Amelia Irvine had one brother, named William. Amanda Young Ellis, wife of Thomas Moore Field, was a daughter of John Ellis and his wife,

Catherine Doyle, who was a daughter of David Doyle and his wife, Hannah Reaver, who raised seven children, viz : Catherine, Melissa, Lizzie, Burton, Myers, Joseph, and David.

Pattie Hockaday Fields Van Meter, a lovely young woman with many excellent traits of character, went to an early grave, leaving her husband with an infant son named Field, one of a pair of twins, to survive her, the other dying at birth.

Isaac C. Van Meter is a thrifty, intelligent farmer, who was educated at Bethany College, Virginia, and who owns a fine farm in Clark County, Kentucky, which lands were formerly owned by his grandfather and great-grandfather, Isaac Van Meter, and Captain Isaac Cunningham.

## NELSON PREWITT VAN METER.

Nelson Prewitt Van Meter, son of Solomon Van Meter, Sr., and his wife, Martha C. Prewitt, was educated at Bethany College, Virginia; married Elizabeth C., eldest daughter of Dr. Samuel W. Willis, of Clark County, Kentucky, a very prominent physician, land owner, and farmer of that county, and his wife, Anna Coleman, a daughter of Samuel Coleman, of Fayette County, Kentucky, and his wife, Elizabeth Graves, of the same county.

Dr. S. W. Willis was born July 2, 1838, in Madison County, Kentucky, and his wife, Anna Coleman, was born July 31, 1844, in Fayette County, Kentucky. They were married May 25, 1864. Dr. S. W. Willis was a son of John Willis and his wife, Susan Baker. John Willis was born in Madison County, Kentucky, October 29, 1796, and his wife, Susan Baker, was born in the same county, November 21, 1804, and they were married in that county January 10, 1822. John Willis was a son of Drury Willis and his wife, a Miss Phelps. Drury Willis was born in Culpeper County, Virginia, and removed to Madison County, Kentucky, where he married Miss Phelps, a native of that county.

Edward Willis, a native of Culpeper County, Virginia, who removed to Adair County, Kentucky, was not a brother, but certainly a first or second cousin of Drury Willis, here above mentioned, who removed from the same county in Virginia to Madison County, as above stated. This Edward Willis was the father of the great orator and lawyer, Captain William T. Willis, who commanded a company of Mercer County Volunteers in the Mexican

War, and was killed at the bloody battle of Buena Vista in the same engagement where Colonel McKee and the favorite son of the sage of Ashland, Henry Clay, Jr., gave up their life blood for the glory of the United States arms. This Captain Willis was the father of John A. Willis, who is now living in Nicholasville, Kentucky, more than eighty years of age, and for more than forty years a worthy and efficient elder of the Presbyterian Church. No man in that community is more revered or more highly esteemed, and from him much information in regard to this family has been obtained.

Samuel Coleman, the maternal grandfather of N. P. Van Meter's wife, was a son of John W. Coleman and his wife, Lucy Chiles. The wife of Samuel Coleman, Elizabeth Graves, was a daughter of Joseph Graves and his wife, Miss Goodwin.

The children of Dr. S. W. Willis: Elizabeth C., who married Nelson Prewitt Van Meter; Samuel W. Willis, Jr., who married Miss Turney, of Bourbon County, Kentucky; Susan E., who married Beverley Jouett, of Winchester, Kentucky; Benjamin Willis, Annie Willis, Coleman Willis, and Carleton Willis.

Dr. S. W. Willis' father, John, and Susan B. Willis' children: Mary, who married Crutcher; Amos B. Willis, William Willis; Ann, who married Cornelison; Nancy J., who married Arnold; David B. Willis; Susan E., who married March; Dr. Samuel Willis, who married Anna Coleman; John M. Willis, Thomas Willis, Dr. Robert T. Willis, Joseph B. Willis, Richard Willis.

Susan Baker, the wife of John Willis, was a daughter of Michael and Nancy Phelps Baker.

## SOLOMON L. VAN METER.

Solomon L. Van Meter, youngest child of Solomon Van Meter, Sr., and his wife, Martha C. Prewitt, was born at Duncastle, Fayette County, Kentucky, May 11, 1859; was educated at Bethany College, Virginia; married Evaline Trent Swoope, daughter of Captain George W. Swoope, Jr., and his wife, Margaret Jane Baylor (sister of General W. S. H. Baylor of the Southern army). Captain George W. Swoope, Jr., was one of nine children of George Washington Swoope, Sr., and his wife, Eliza M. Trent, both of Augusta County, Virginia. George W. Swoope, Sr., was a son of Hon. Jacob Swoope, member of Congress from 1809 to 1811, and his wife, Mary McDowell, daughter of Ephraim McDowell.

Hon. Jacob Swoope was a son of E. Swoope, who was born in 1744 and died in 1803, spending his life in Virginia.

Margaret J. Baylor was a daughter of Jacob Baylor and his wife, Evaline Hanger. She was born in 1829. Jacob Baylor was a son of George Baylor and his wife, Catherine Argenbright.

Eliza M. Trent was a daughter of Colonel John Trent, of Revolutionary fame, and his wife, Elizabeth Montgomery Lewis, daughter of Colonel Dr. William Lewis and his wife, Ann Montgomery. (For further of these see sons of Emigrant John Lewis, in this book.)

The Swoopes, Trents, Baylors, and Hangers descend from Revolutionary ancestry who had won stars in that famous old struggle for liberty, and these worthy descendants won fresh stars on many bloody fields in the Southern army during the great unpleasantness.

This beautiful, lovely, and devoted young wife died October, 1899, leaving four young children to survive her, viz : Solomon, Jr., Baylor, Margaret, and Evaline. She possessed many charms of person and character, which drew a large circle of acquaintances very near to her with fond admiration ; and best of all was her devoted and faithful Christian character, having lived a devoted and consistent member of the Presbyterian Church from her early girlhood.

She was enabled by the power of grace divine to answer even the inscrutable summons to sever the maternal care of these four young children over which her young mother's heart brooded with overwhelming love, but she could give even them back to the care of her Redeemer with unswerving confidence in His promises, while she fell asleep in the faith and "peace which passeth understanding."

Solomon L. Van Meter is a prominent farmer of Fayette County, Kentucky, and resides less than three miles from the city of Lexington, at "Shenandoah Hall," where he owns a fine landed estate, comprising a part of the "Duncastle" lands, which he inherited from his father's estate, together with other lands which he has purchased.

He was a member of the Kentucky Legislature, elected in the stirring and eventful times of 1899, and has been nominated for re-election from the County of Fayette.

EVALINE S. VAN METER,
Wife of S. L. Van Meter, of Lexington, Kentucky.

ISAAC C. VAN METER,
Of Fayette County, Kentucky.

Isaac C., second child of Isaac and Rebecca Van Meter, was born in Clark County, Kentucky, October 8, 1820. He married Fannie, third daughter of Henry Hull and his wife, Hannah, a daughter of John Harness (of whom more is said on another page). Isaac C. and his wife removed to a farm in Fayette County, five miles west of Lexington, Kentucky, immediately after their marriage, where he lived for the balance of his life. He died suddenly from a stroke of apoplexy April 14, 1898. They had ten children born to them, seven of whom are now living. His widow is still living on a part of the farm where he spent his life from his early manhood.

He represented Fayette County in the Kentucky Legislature and held other responsible positions, and was an elder in the First Presbyterian Church of Lexington for more than thirty years. His children are as follows :

Charles L., married, first, Millie Hurst, and by this marriage had one child, a son, named Allie, who died in his youth. After the death of this wife he married Amanda Barrow, who lived less than two years ; and after her death he married Bettie Redmond, and they are now residing in Clark County, Kentucky. A farmer.

Second child, Sallie C., who married John Steenburgin, of West Virginia, and they raised six children, who survive their mother, viz : William, Peter, Fannie, Isaac, Charles, and John. Their mother, Sallie C. Steenburgin, died October, 1898.

Edwin, who married Ellen Beall, of West Virginia, and died September, 1895, leaving his widow with four children, namely, Rebecca, Charles C., Francis, and Lillian.

William Scott, who married Anna Farra, of Fayette County, Kentucky, and they have eight children, namely, Jesse, Margaret, Sarah, Anna F., Virginia, Gladys, Mary, and James F. They reside in Lexington, Kentucky.

J. Brown, Louis M., Benjamin W., and Jessie have not married, and live on the farm with their mother.

Ann Rebecca died in infancy, and the youngest daughter, Fannie M., married Alfred Savage, of Ashland, Kentucky.

Henry Hull, who married Hannah Harness (twin sister of Sarah, my grandmother), was born February 6, 1780, in Crab Bottom, Pendleton County, Virginia. His father and mother both emigrated from Germany, first to New York, and years afterward settled in Pendleton County, Virginia (now West Virginia). See family of John Harness.

Henry Hull purchased and lived and died on the farm which Mathew Patton sold, which was known as the Bull Pastures, on the North Fork of the South Branch of the Potomac, when Patton removed from there to Clark County, Kentucky, and then Captain Isaac Cunningham (Hull's brother-in-law) purchased and lived and died on Mathew Patton's farm in Kentucky, which he purchased of Patton's executors after his death in 1802.

The children of Henry Hull and his wife, Hannah H., were: William, born January 4, 1802 ; John H., born September 11, 1804 ; Joseph, born August 8, 1806 ; Sarah C., born March 31, 1808 ; Laban, born February 16, 1810 ; Eliza H., born October 8, 1811 ; Jemima C., born March 11, 1813 ; Rebecca Ann, born May 5, 1816 ; Edwin H., born November 26, 1817 ; Jessie C., born September 16, 1819 ; Francis H. (Fannie), born December 1, 1821.

William Hull married Irene Scott, of Virginia ; Peter Hull married Eliza Long, of Woodford County, Kentucky ; John H. Hull married Sally Lacky ; Joseph died unmarried ; Sarah C. Hull married Jacob Palzell ; Laban Hull married Martha Tucker ; Eliza H. died unmarried ; Jemima C. died unmarried, May 5, 1882 ; Rebecca A. died unmarried, August 20, 1892 ; Edwin died unmarried ; Jessie C. married Mahaly Grace ; Francis (Fannie) married Isaac C. Van Meter, of Kentucky. For Isaac C. Van Meter, see Van Meter family. Nearly all of the above named removed from Virginia to the West, and no doubt many descendants from them are now living in the Western States.

Peter Hull removed to Woodford County, Kentucky, and married Eliza, daughter of Nimrod Long, of that county, by which marriage two children were born, viz : Richard H. Hull, born April 27, 1836, and Ann Elizabeth (Bettie), born April 8, 1839. The latter died unmarried, after a useful life among devoted friends, at the age of about fifty-seven years, in Fayette County, Kentucky, where she spent nearly all her life. Richard H. Hull removed to the far Northwest, and at last accounts was a thrifty farmer in that country. These two children were left orphans by the death of their mother on the 21st day of May, 1839, when Bettie was little more than one month old, and the father died not long after, thus leaving these two children to the care of Isaac Van Meter and his wife, their youngest aunt, who reared them up to the years of discretion and usefulness.

Jacob, third child of Isaac and Rebecca, was born February 10, 1822 ; married Florida E. Miles, October 20, 1846, and died October 19, 1849, leaving no living issue.  Although he died at the early age of twenty-seven years, he occupied quite a prominent position in the community in which he lived, and was an influential member of the Presbyterian Church.

Sarah Ann, eldest daughter of Isaac and Rebecca, was born October 26, 1825 ; married Dr. John Hall, son of Rev. Nathan Hall, of Fayette County, Kentucky, July 25, 1843.  They removed to Illinois immediately after their marriage, and returned to Kentucky on a visit about one year afterward, when she was taken sick and died at the residence of the Rev. Nathan Hall, in Fayette County, leaving no issue.

Susan Tabitha, second daughter of Isaac and Rebecca, was born August 1, 1827 ; married Dr. A. S. Allan, a son of Hon. Chilton Allan, of Winchester, Kentucky, April 15, 1846.  They lived in Clark County until about 1866, when they removed to Lexington, Kentucky, where they resided since until the death of Dr. Allan, and where his widow still resides.  Dr. Allan was for many years quite prominent and popular as a skillful physician, and was quite eminent in his profession.  They had no children.  The following will give a correct estimate of him and his family, and was written at the time of his death by the author of this :

### In Memorabilia.

Dr. Algernon Sidney Allan was born in Winchester, Clark County, Kentucky, March 12, 1823, and graduated at Centre College, Danville, Kentucky, in 1842, and at Transylvania University's Medical College in 1846, and a few weeks after he finished his medical course he married Susan T. Van Meter, second daughter of Isaac Van Meter and his wife, Rebecca Cunningham, of Clark County, Kentucky, April 15, 1846.

Dr. A. S. Allan was a son of Hon. Chilton Allan and his wife, Ann Sympson, of Winchester, Kentucky.  Chilton Allan was a very noted lawyer, and for near fifty years a member of the Winchester bar when for talent, oratory, and legal attainments it had a national reputation.  He represented Clark County several times in the

State Legislature, and represented Henry Clay's old district for six years in the United States Congress when Mr. Clay was appointed Secretary of State by John Q. Adams, and he held other positions of honor and trust.

Chilton Allan was a native of Virginia, his parents having emigrated from Ireland to that State many years before the Revolutionary War ; but he removed to Winchester, Kentucky, when he was yet a minor, and by the favor and assistance of Rev. John Lyle and Rev. William Kavanaugh, both eminent ministers of the gospel in Clark County, Kentucky, he was enabled to obtain a good academical education. He then read law under Governor James Clark, who was at that time the Circuit Judge and a resident of Winchester, Kentucky.

Chilton Allan's wife, Ann Sympson, was a daughter of Captain James Sympson, who was also a native of Virginia and removed with his family to Winchester, Kentucky, and was a gallant officer in the War of 1812 under General Harrison at the battle of Thames, and under General McArthur in his memorable Canadian campaign, and received very complimentary notice and honorable mention for his distinguished services and bravery.

Captain James Sympson and his wife were both of Irish parentage, therefore Dr. A. S. Allan was from his paternal and maternal ancestry of Irish descent.

Immediately after his marriage he commenced the practice of medicine in Clark County, residing in Winchester and forming a partnership with Drs. John and Augustus Mills, who were at that time the most prominent and extensive practitioners in the county, and perhaps none more prominent in Central Kentucky.

He was a constant, untiring student with a strong analytical turn of mind, and with refined, gentle, attractive manners, he very soon obtained prominence in his profession and a very extensive practice, which continued to increase until it became more burdensome than he could longer endure, so that he removed in 1866 to the City of Lexington, where he could dispense, in some measure, with the more severe drudgery of country practice, which up to that time had been a great deal on horseback, through gateways and over unpleasant country roads ; but notwithstanding his removal to such a distance from his sphere of practice, whenever a desperate case of sickness occurred in Clark County, where he had been the family physician, as a last resort Dr. Allan must be brought at all hazards, and some of his most severe trials were when he was brought to the bedside of some dying sufferer barely in time to be recognized before the expiring breath ; but then again, not unfrequently, by his tender care and great skill the patient who had been well nigh given up in despair has been restored to health and hundreds of these are now living who grieve for the loss of their great benefactor.

He was throughout his entire life a constant reader, and not only read all of the standard books as well as papers and pamplets of interest on medical science, but many of the best books of fiction and scientific works, taking a great and constant interest in the development of electricity, and just a short time before he was taken sick he attended a course of lectures in New York City on electricity and its application to medical science.

The anxious watchers at the bedside of very ill patients have frequently been much perplexed, if not annoyed, when after much delay and persevering effort they finally succeeded in securing his presence, to have him put question after question to the patient as well as to the attendants, and then after merely arranging as best he could for the temporary comfort of the sufferer, quietly inform the lady of the house or some appropriate person present that he wished to lie down and rest a while, and thus leave the patient and the anxious household to tax their patience and exercise their faith in his consummate skill and judgment for more than an hour before he would return to the room, and then perhaps only to put more questions and make a few comfortable remarks, while he still delayed, sometimes for several hours, before he would come in a very attractive, winning way to the sufferer and assure him that he would try to help him out of his trouble, and proceed finally to give very explicit directions, as well as prescription, while the patient and perhaps no one present could account for the delay ; but that time was well spent in making a careful diagnosis of the case, and most frequently resulted in success, which fully compensated. And he preferred, when at all convenient, to remain with the patient in critical cases for hours, or perhaps for days, until he saw the result of his treatment.

His reputation for extraordinary skill as an obstetrician extended far beyond the circle of his regular practice, and his great success in this especial branch of medical science would compare favorably with that of any man that ever practiced this profession in Kentucky.

Dr. Allan's father had been a life-long Whig, and received all of his political honors and emoluments through that party, and he had been brought up in that school of politics, and in his early manhood voted with that party.

When the war between the North and the South came on he was a strong Union man, and his loyalty to the Northern side was never doubted, although he was ever ready to bestow his medical and surgical skill upon the sick or wounded of either army alike when in reach of him, as was strikingly manifested immediately after the battle of Richmond, Kentucky, when General Kirby Smith made his memorable raid into Kentucky. But his wife had two brothers and a large number of other relations in the Southern army, and all her sympathy and sentiment were for the South and its people, and he could but turn his "blind side and deaf ear" to what she was doing for Southern soldiers in prison or anywhere in distress.

Although he had very little political aspiration, he was very readily elected to the legislature to represent Clark County without opposition during the war while Federal bayonets were quite a potent factor in politics, and the most intense Southern sympathizer was glad to accept him as the best that could be had for the county, placing a high and well-merited estimate upon the sense of justice and equity and conservative moderation by which he could be controlled in those exciting and very trying times.

From his boyhood until quite late in life he was passionately fond of shooting birds on the wing, and was quite an expert shot. On one occasion the writer and he were sitting on the bank of the creek while several of the servants were seining for fish in the early spring, he having his gun lying on the grass within reach of him, when a snipe came flying by, and, just as it was in the act of lighting some forty-five or fifty yards distant, he fired and killed it, when he was immediately accused of taking unfair advantage of the bird ; but he contended that he did not, and after quite a heated controversy no agreement was reached, although he finally admitted that the bird's toes may have been on the ground, but, if so, its wings were certainly not closed.

He was also very fond of the game of chess, and would play for many hours at a time, or derive the greatest pleasure from looking on at a game between two expert players, and during the latter years of his life most of his recreation was obtained in the Chess

Club rooms of the city of Lexington, and many times, in these later years, after he had spent the day from early morning until late afternoon in his office hearing the complaints and woes of a dozen or more afflicted persons and administering to each, he would finally slip away from his office and go to the Chess Club room to escape from this arduous labor, but perhaps to be very soon brought back by urgent request to his office or taken to the bedside of some very sick person.

The greatest source of comfort and consolation to Dr. Allan's many friends and to those who loved him most was the unmistakable evidence that he gave of his preparation for death, and the bright and confident hope which he cherished as he approached daily nearer the great eternity.

He had made a confession of religion in his early manhood, soon after his marriage, and became a member of the Presbyterian Church, in which he was a communicant for more than thirty years, and these years had been spent in ceaseless efforts to alleviate suffering, to heal the sick, and in whatever way he could benefit and bless his fellow-man. His liberality kept him comparatively poor through life, with an income which would have made many a man a millionaire, and this without profligacy, but because he had no love for money, and only estimated it for its use in open-handed generosity.

No one realized more fully than he did that the days of his life were drawing very near to a close, and several months before his death he had occasion to talk with his wife about something which he thought should be done in the autumn, when he remarked, "I will not be here then," but she could attend to it, and to which his devoted wife with tearful eyes chidingly replied, when he assured her with perfect calmness that he would be in a far better country than this, and reminded her that when she learned it was God's will that she should remain here a while longer, then she should submit without murmuring and with resignation to His will. Truly "his last days were his best days," when with full knowledge of his physical condition he approached with steady and unfaltering step the brink of the "dark waters," because he knew in Whom he trusted, and with the eye of faith could plainly see that on the other shore "the lower lights were burning," and when the last trying hour came he lay down upon his couch as if to rest in quiet slumber, with his soul entranced in that "peace which passeth understanding," because it was fixed on Him who has promised "when thou passeth through the deep waters they shall not over-flow thee," and thus he quietly slept to awake with Jesus upon the other shore—"the golden shores of the New Jerusalem."

" Blessed and holy is he that hath part in the first resurrection ; on such the second death hath no power. . . . And there shall be no more death, neither sorrow nor crying, neither shall there be any more pain ; for the former things have passed away."

From Lexington Transcript :

## " DR. ALGERNON SIDNEY ALLAN, WHO DIED ON MONDAY, AUGUST 20, 1894, IN HIS SEVENTY-FIRST YEAR.

"Seldom, if ever, has a death occurred in our midst which has caused more universal sorrow.   The high estimation in which Dr. Allan was held by the community was strikingly evidenced by the concourse which attended the last sad rites, and many bitter tears were shed when the mortal remains of this good man were laid to rest.   In a very wide circle he was known and loved ; not only as the wise physician, where skill brought joy and comfort to many homes, but as the true and tried friend and companion is his loss irreparable.   Into the gloom of the sick-room his bright cheerful-ness brought sunshine, and his well-modulated, sympathetic voice and gentle, magnetic touch always left the sufferer better for having seen him.   In all ranks of life was his influence felt ; in homes of the lowly, as well as those of the rich and prosperous, he was equally loved and reverenced, and none can ever fill the place made vacant by his death.

"Of such a man no more fitting epitaph could be written than 'Well done, thou good and faithful servant, enter thou into the glory of the Lord.' "

## BENJAMIN F. VAN METER.

Benjamin F. Van Meter (the writer of this), fifth son, was born January 30, 1834, and, as has been mentioned in the sketch of Thornton Lewis' family, married Amelia C. Lewis, November 30, 1854.

They have had born to them eleven children, eight of whom are now living, viz : Emma, who married Archie L. Hamilton, of

Bath County, Kentucky ; Everette L., who married Jessie Florence Bigelow, of Ogden, Utah ; Thomas Wright Lewis, who married Mary Holloway, of Clark County, Kentucky ; Annette, who married William Pettit, of Fayette County, Kentucky ; Frank B. ; Mary Belle ; Joseph C., who married Martha Ellen Pettit, of Fayette County, Kentucky ; Benjamin F., Jr., who married Mary Hubbard Wetherell, of Rhode Island. Our youngest, Amelia Ellen, died March 9, 1893. And it was indeed a *dark, dark* cloud which overspread this household when by the Almighty's inscrutable though unerring decree this darling child was taken to dwell with God.

But the lines of a beautiful poem which she repeated while she held the hand of her grief-stricken mother, while she and others surrounded the sick-bed, are appropriate here :

> " Be still, sad heart, and cease repining ;
> Behind the clouds is the sun still shining ;
> Thy fate is the common fate of all,
> Into each life some rain must fall,
> Some days must be dark and dreary."

Ah, yes, and has not the King a perfect right to His own jewel ? Has not the Lord of the vineyard and the garden a right to appropriate the loveliest flower to His own bosom ? What dare the gardener do or say except bare the head and bow in meek submission, while midst flowing tears he whispers mutely from the soul, Amen, Amen ! But will not parental love be pardoned, if the pen is dipped in tears to portray even dimly a few of the beauties of her young, sweet life ? She was not quite thirteen years of age, and yet she was five feet eight inches in height, with perfect form, and features smooth and beautiful. Her mind, her intellect, and her Christian graces were as well advanced in proportion to her age as was her stature. In her classes at Sayre Institute she was on the roll of honor. In her Sunday-school, when a medal was offered to one who would repeat Christ's sermon on the mount without missing a word, she brought the medal to its place among her precious treasures, only to be given as a special legacy of love to her nephew ; and when a prize was offered to one of her class who would answer every question in her catechism, that medal was placed among her treasures to be given from her bed of death to her youngest brother.

But she was as fond of her childish pleasures and received as much joy and gladness from them as any one. It was surprising to see her glide over the brick streets on her bicycle with grace of a gazelle and the speed of the wind. When the snow was deep and the cold would drive other persons to the shelter and fire for comfort, she derived great pleasure from riding on sled through the cold for hours at a time.

On one occasion when she came in from a very exhilarating ride on her sled with her face lit up with glow and smiles and beauty, she said : "I never want to get so grown up that I can not ride on my sled and bicycle. How delightful it is to glide over these nice brick streets on a bicycle ; oh, it is so nice."

When she was little more than five years old she was sitting between her parents in church on a sacramental occasion ; when the emblems were passed around she asked permission to partake, which request was not granted, and when we were returning home in the carriage after the services she appealed to her father to know why she could not partake of the sacrament, contending that she was a member of the church, taken in by baptism when she was a little babe. When it was explained to her that she could have the privilege when she was old enough to understand all about the sacrament, if she would make a public acknowledgment of her love for Christ, she replied: "Well, papa, I know I love Him now." When she was ten years old she made a public confession of her faith, and truly can it be said of her that the evil day never came, nor did the year ever draw nigh when she could say, "I have no pleasure in Thee ;" for she remembered her Creator in the days of her earliest youth and delighted in her Redeemer, and when this dreadful scarlet fever took deep hold upon her body and she was racked with pain, she readily severed all ties to earth and longed for Heaven, saying, "I want to go and be with Jesus." How practically did she verify the words of Christ when He said, "Verily, I say unto you, whosoever shall not receive the Kingdom of God as a little child, he shall not enter therein." Without one doubt or wavering fear she longed to go and dwell with Christ, and with words of tenderest love to all around her bedside and messages for absent ones—"Mother, dear mother, don't you cry ; I am not afraid to go ; Jesus is with me now"—clad in the panoply of Heaven she went like a meteor to the sky, leaving a beacon light to kindred and friends to beckon them on and upward to her abiding-place with God.

Emma, oldest child of B. F. Van Meter and his wife, Amelia C. Lewis, was born January 15, 1857, educated at Sayre Institute, Lexington, and afterward graduated at Staunton, Virginia ; married Archie Logan Hamilton, of Bath County, Kentucky, May 2, 1877 ; raised two children, namely : Amelia May and Archie Logan, Jr.

Archie L. Hamilton, Sr., was born in Bath County, Kentucky, March 22, 1849 ; was educated at the University of Virginia ; died October 19, 1889. He was the oldest child of George Hamilton, Sr., and his wife, Ellen Ashby, who lived in Bath County, Kentucky. George Hamilton, Sr., was a son of Archy W. Hamilton and his wife, Rebecca Berry. Archibald W. Hamilton was a son of John Hamilton and his wife, Mary Stuart, both of whom were reared in Virginia and married there, and removed afterwards to Flat Creek, Bath County, Kentucky, and resided there until his death in 1812, and is buried at Old Springfield Church with his wife. He served in the French and Indian wars, as well as in the War of the Revolution, and quit that war a Major.

He was appointed a commissioner with others to conclude a treaty with the Indians, which commission met and held council with the Indians not far from where Pittsburgh is now situated, where they concluded a treaty of peace with the savages.

He was in the bloody battle of Braddock's defeat, and served in other sanguinary struggles of the two wars. His oldest son, Abner, enlisted as a soldier in the Revolution at the age of sixteen years, and afterward removed to Barren County, Kentucky, where his name is enrolled on the pension list of Revolutionary soldiers.

Mary Stuart descended from a very noted old family of that name with lineage celebrated in Scotch and British history.

The Ashby family, from which the wife of George Hamilton, Sr., sprang, was distinguished in the very early history of this country, and gained fresh stars on sanguinary fields during the late war between the States.

Notably among these was the gallant and daring General Turner Ashby, who shed his life's blood on the sanguinary field at Port Republic, and others of this name might well be mentioned.

Archibald William Hamilton, Sr., who married Rebecca Berry, raised three sons, named James Carrol, Archibald William, Jr., and George, Sr., the last named having already been mentioned above.

James C. married, first, Margaret White, and after her death he married Sarah Gaitwood.

Archibald William married Henrietta Lindsay and died young, leaving two young children, and after his death his widow married General John S. Williams, as is elsewhere stated in this book.

These three Hamilton brothers were full partners in business as long as the three lived, and after the death of Archibald William, the two survivors were partners until the latest years of their lives, when they undertook to dissolve their partnership, but had not fully accomplished the dissolution before the death of James C. They were men of wealth, and had extensive business dealings in live stock and lands in several States.

Emma V. Hamilton resides on her homestead, Kirklevington, Kentucky.

### EVERETT L. VAN METER.

Everett L. Van Meter, eldest son of B. F. Van Meter and his wife, Amelia C. L., was born February 4, 1860 ; was educated at Central University, Richmond, Kentucky, and at the University of Virginia ; married Jessie Florence Bigelow, of Ogden, Utah, February 28, 1899.

Jessie Florence was born August 21, 1871, in Buda, Illinois ; is a daughter of Henry Clay Bigelow, who was born August 5, 1845, in Fulton County, New York, and his wife, Lydia Frances Pierce.

H. C. Bigelow, son of Alfred Bigelow, of New York, and his wife, Eliza Ann Benedict.

Alfred Bigelow, a son of Asabel Bigelow, born February, 1782, and his wife, Phila Barrett, born February 21, 1782, of Norwich, Connecticut.

H. C. Bigelow's mother, Eliza Ann Benedict, daughter of Levi Benedict, who was born April 8, 1806, in New York, and his wife, Desire Moshier, who was born in 1810 in Saratoga, New York. Levi Benedict, a son of James Benedict and his wife, Sallie Jolly, both of New York.

Lydia Frances Pierce, wife of H. C. Bigelow (and mother of J. Florence, wife of E. L. Van Meter), was the daughter of Ephriam Henry Pierce and his wife, Clarissa Slocum.

E. H. Pierce was born February 27, 1815 ; was a son of Abraham Pierce and his wife, Lydia Cummins.

Clarissa Slocum was born May 11, 1828, in Northville, New York. She was the daughter of Caleb Wright Slocum and his wife, Elizabeth Bentley Bass.

C. W. Slocum was born October 22, 1797, in Northville, New York. He was a son of Joseph Slocum, born January 30, 1766, in Bristol County, Massachusetts ; his wife, Elizabeth Wright, born in Sandisfield, Connecticut, March 13, 1772. Joseph Slocum was the son of Eliazer Slocum, born in Bristol County, Massachusetts, May 15, 1744, and his wife, Anstace Vial.

Eliazer Slocum was the son of John Slocum, born August 14, 1717, in Bristol County, Massachusetts, and of his wife, Debora Alma, daughter of John and Debora Alma, of the same place.

John Slocum was the son of Eliazer Slocum, born in Bristol County, Massachusetts, January 20, 1694, and of his wife, Debora Smith.

Eliazer Slocum was the son of Eliazer Slocum, born December 25, 1664, at Newport, Rhode Island, and of his wife, Elephel Phitzgerald.

Eliazer Slocum, Sr., was the son of Giles Slocum and his wife, Joan, who was born in Somersetshire, England, and came to Newport County, Rhode Island, in 1638. He was a son of Anthony Slocum, who was one of the forty-six first ancient purchasers (A. D. 1637) of the territory of Cohannet, which was incorporated March 3, 1639, in New Plymouth, now Massachusetts.

Everett L. Van Meter resides in Chicago, Illinois ; is a member of the firm of Drum Flato Live Stock Commission Company, and is the head cattle salesman of this company at the Union Stock Yards, Chicago.

## ANNETTE VAN METER.

Annette Van Meter, second daughter and third child of B. F. Van Meter and his wife, Amelia C. Lewis, was born January 31, 1862 ; educated at Sayre Institute, Lexington, Kentucky ; married William Pettit, of Fayette County, Kentucky, October 2, 1895 ; resides with Mr. Pettit in the suburbs of the city of Lexington.

William Pettit was a native of Fayette County, Kentucky, a son of Harry Pettit and his wife, Juliet Greenville Atchison. Second generation was Nathaniel Pettit, Sr., and his wife, Rebecca Owens. Third generation was Obedia Pettit, from near Lynchburg, Virginia, who came to Fayette County, Kentucky, about the beginning of the last century with his wife and family—his wife's name not known. Obedia Pettit's brother, named Zedecia, also came from Virginia and settled in Kentucky about the same time.

Obedia's son, Nathaniel, Sr., raised four sons, named Nathaniel, Jr., Harry, John, and William.

The children of Harry Pettit and his wife, Juliet G. Atchison, were: Sarah, who married Daniel Boone Bryan; Mary, who married George Headley, of Lexington, Kentucky; William, who married, first, Miss Jennie Carr, and after her death married Annette Van Meter; Nathaniel, who died in the Southern Army, a soldier, in the hospital; Florence Rebecca, who married J. F. Scott.


## THOMAS WRIGHT LEWIS VAN METER.

Thomas Wright Lewis Van Meter, second son of B. F. Van Meter and his wife, Amelia C. Lewis, was born July 26, 1863; educated at Central University, Richmond, Kentucky; married Mary Holloway, a daughter of Colonel James Hillyer Holloway and his wife, Mary Elliot Williams.

Colonel J. H. Holloway enlisted a company in the Union Army, of which he was Captain, and was mustered into the Federal service at Henderson, Kentucky, in October, 1861; served one year and then resigned, and with Colonel J. M. Shackelford and Ben H. Bristo raised the Eighth Kentucky Regiment of Cavalry, of which regiment he was Major, and later he was Lieutenant-Colonel, and was mustered out in September, 1863.

In 1855 James H. Holloway was chosen deacon of the Presbyterian Church of Henderson, Kentucky, under the pastorate of Rev. John D. Mathews, D. D. In 1865, after he married Miss Williams, he removed to Winchester, Kentucky, and in 1867 he was elected elder of the church there, which office he still retains.

He was elected State Senator from that senatorial district, comprising the counties of Clark, Bourbon, and Montgomery, which term has not yet expired.

Colonel J. H. Holloway was a son of William Starling Holloway and his wife, Mary Hart Hillyer; grandparents were John Holloway and Ann Lyne Starling, both of whom were born in Virginia, and they were married there and removed to Henderson County, Kentucky, in 1797. John Holloway was a Major in the War of the Revolution; was a large land-owner in Henderson County, Kentucky, and was identified with nearly all of the large business enterprises of that county during its early history, and held a very influential place in the estimation of the people of that section of Kentucky.

Mary Hart Hillyer, the mother of J. H. Holloway, was a daughter of James Hillyer, who removed to Henderson, Kentucky, about 1800 from Virginia, and married Susan Hart, a daughter of Captain David Hart, who was a brother of Colonel Nathaniel Hart and Colonel Thomas Hart, each of whom were members of the Transylvania Company and served in the Revolutionary War and in the Indian wars in Kentucky.

James Hillyer was a native of Connecticut and a graduate in law at Harvard College, and was a distinguished lawyer of his day. In the latter part of his life he associated with him in the practice of law his nephew, the late ex-Governor Archibald Dixon.

Ann Lyne Starling was a daughter of Colonel William Starling and Susanna Lyne, both born in Virginia, and after their marriage removed to Henderson, Kentucky, in about 1797.

Mary E. Williams, wife of Colonel J. H. Holloway, was a daughter and only child of General John Stuart Williams and his wife, Ann Harrison. General J. S. Williams served in the war against Mexico, and for gallantry at the battle of Cerro Gordo he was promoted to the rank of Colonel, and received the nickname of "Cerro Gordo Williams," which he carried to the end of his life. At that battle it was said that he was the first man to go over the enemy's fortifications, and his company followed hard after him. When the war between the States began he owned a fine landed estate in Illinois, which he sacrificed at a very low price to withdraw all his interests and effects from the Northern States, and enlisted in the Southern army, where he served to the end of the war as Brigadier General. He was elected and served one term in the United States Senate from Kentucky. He was an orator and a statesman, but more especially a military man.

He never failed to participate among the first in every war of our country during his life, but in time of peace he chose the avocation of agriculture, and made a success of it. When the war between the States came on he was farming on a large scale in Illinois, and left a large crop of wheat growing there to go into the army. His wife had died many years before this, and after the close of the war he married Mrs. Henrietta (Lindsay) Hamilton, widow of William Hamilton, of Bath County, Kentucky, and very soon became one of the most prominent farmers of the State, a breeder of shorthorn cattle, and was the first man to introduce the Burley tobacco into Kentucky. He built large barns and demonstrated to the people the great profit to be obtained from this branch of agriculture, which has rapidly grown to be one of the most profitable crops of the State, and General Williams went from his large live stock and tobacco farm in Bath County, Kentucky, to the United States Senate. He had graduated in law, and was a lawyer of no ordinary attainments, and he had traveled over Europe and over nearly all the civilized world, but adhered to agriculture for the love of it. His parents were General Samuel Williams and his wife, Rebecca Luttrell.

General Sam Williams served in the War of 1812 ; was a Captain in Colonel Lewis' regiment under General Winchester, and was taken prisoner at the battle of River Raisin and sent to Detroit, where he was paroled. General Sam Williams was a State Senator for fourteen years from his district, and was a General of the State Militia. He was born in Culpeper County, Virginia, and died in Montgomery County, Kentucky, at more than ninety years of age.

Some extracts taken from a memorial address delivered by his nephew, Elder John Augustus Williams, at old Somerset Church, where he and his wife had been members, will give a correct estimate of his character, as follows :

"The subject of our address was an old man, very venerable with years. He knew your fathers while they yet slept unconscious in their cradles. He was a guest at your ancestral homes while yet the almost unbroken forest and matted cane closed around their humble but hospitable cabins. Yonder on one spot, almost in sight, he lived for eighty years. For a while he was a subject of George 3d, then a citizen of free America ; first a resident of Virginia, then of Kentucky ; first of Fayette County, then of Bourbon, then of Clark, then of Montgomery counties. Two governments claimed him, two States enrolled him, five counties taxed him, and yet the old patriarch during all these mutations in governmental affairs changed but once the place of his abode. He lived and died at more than four score years and ten among the veritable scenes of his childhood.

"And in all this State there was not a host or hostess whose heart leaped with a more cordial welcome at the approach of friend or stranger than that of the dear old man in whose memory we meet to-day, and the dear old woman whose memory is forever linked with his. And this brings us to the consideration of another phase of his life, from which we may derive the most important lesson that he has left behind. While living in the habitual practice of all the virtues that define a noble man, he was not at peace with himself. There was an undefined and restless want that he long tried in vain to satisfy. He tried every form of life's honorable experience. He grew gray in the vain attempt to satisfy an immortal spirit with the pleasures and honors and service of a life that is earthly and brief, and having tasted every worldly cup, he turned at last to that fountain of which 'if a man drink he shall never thirst again.'

"Dear old man ! We thank thee for all thy sterling virtues ; but we thank thee most and we gratefully bless thee this day that thou hast taught us by thine own experience and thy last best example that true honor and peace can be found only in the acknowledgment and loving service of the 'Lamb that taketh away the sin of the world.' "

General Sam Williams was a son of Raleigh Williams and his wife, Rebecca Luttrell, who were both born in Virginia and died in Kentucky.

Raleigh Williams was born March 20, 1754, and died June 24, 1827. Rebecca Luttrell was born October 24, 1759, and died August 10, 1843. Ann Harrison, wife of General John S. Williams, was the daughter of Patton D. Harrison and his wife, Ann Elgin. The grandparents were Daniel Harrison and his wife, Ann Patton. Ann Patton was the daughter of Matthew Patton, who removed from a place on the south fork of the south branch of the Potomac in Virginia, known as the "Bull Pastures," about 1785, to Clark County, Kentucky, where he resided until his death in 1802, and then Captain Isaac Cunningham purchased the farm in the autumn of that year at his administrator's sale.

Daniel Harrison here mentioned was a grandson of Benjamin Harrison, of "Brandon on the James," who married a niece of Benjamin Harrison, the signer of the Declaration of Independence, and he was a son of Benjamin Harrison, of Berkeley. Therefore Patton Douglas Harrison, of Clark County, Kentucky, was connected more closely to the two ex-Presidents (Benjamin and his grandfather, William Henry) by his maternal ancestry—the wife of Benjamin Harrison, of Brandon—than he was by his paternal ancestry, though no doubt but Benjamin, of Brandon, married his second or third cousin, and this family sprang from a common ancestry within two or three generations from "Benjamin, of Berkeley," and "Benjamin, of Brandon."

Thomas Wright Lewis Van Meter resides in Winchester, Kentucky, and has four children, named Mary Elizabeth, Amelia Clay, Harrison Cunningham, and Thomas W. L., Jr.

Frank B. Van Meter, third son of B. F. Van Meter and his wife, Amelia C. Lewis, was born August 1, 1865; was educated at Morton & Irvine's private school in Winchester, Kentucky, and at the State College of Kentucky in Lexington, and graduated at Smith's Commercial College in Lexington, Kentucky; is a dealer in thoroughbred horses, and has developed some of considerable note, among others Cold Stream, which he now owns; His Eminence, with which he won the Kentucky Derby of $6,000, the Clark Stakes, $3,800, and others of less amounts, and then sold him for about $20,000.

Mary Belle Van Meter, born August 2, 1868, graduated at Sayre Institute in Lexington, Kentucky, and as a trained nurse at Bellevue Hospital, New York City, and practices this profession.

Joseph C. Van Meter, fourth son of B. F. Van Meter and his wife, Amelia C. Lewis, was born September 1, 1870; educated at Morton & Irvine's private school in Winchester, Kentucky, and at the Kentucky State College in Lexington, Kentucky. Married Martha Pettit, of Fayette County, Kentucky, June 1, 1899, a daughter of Benjamin F. Pettit and his wife, Clara Barbee, who was a daughter of George Barbee and his wife, Ellen Poindexter, both of Fayette County, Kentucky. George Barbee's ancestor on the maternal side was John Bradford, who brought the first printing press over the Allegheny Mountains and established the first newspaper (The Gazette) ever published west of these mountains, in Lexington, Kentucky.

B. F. Pettit was a son of Nathaniel Pettit, Jr., and his wife, Martha Clifford.

Nathaniel Pettit, Jr., was a son of Nathaniel Pettit, Sr., and his wife, Rebecca Owens.

Nathaniel, Sr., was a son of Obadiah Pettit and his wife, who came to Fayette County, Kentucky, from Virginia about the beginning of the last century.

MARTHA P. VAN METER,
Wife of Joe C. Van Meter, of Fayette County, Kentucky.

Martha Pettit Van Meter died suddenly, but in the triumphant hope of eternal life, on the 3d day of April, 1899, after a married life of less than one year, leaving an infant daughter only five days old, which she said should bear the mother's name—Martha Pettit Van Meter.

This attractive, lovely young woman had since her early girlhood given her life to the service of Christ as a faithful, earnest worker in the Presbyterian Church and Sabbath-school, and she died as she had lived, with an abiding faith in her Redeemer's love. When she knew that death was rapidly approaching, while her oldest sister was watching at her bedside, she requested that her husband's oldest sister (Mrs. Emma V. Hamilton) should bring the infant to her ; then beckoning for it to be placed upon her arm, she drew it to her bosom and impressed upon its forehead more than one fond kiss, with such demonstrations of tender love as only a fond mother can bestow ; then looking up meekly she said in a calm, clear voice : "Sister Emma, will you take this little darling and raise it tenderly for me, and call it Martha Pettit ?"

Little Martha Pettit is now growing and flourishing at Kirklevington.

Joseph C. Van Meter is a farmer, and resides in Fayette County, Kentucky.

## Dr. B. F. VAN METER.

Dr. B. F. Van Meter, youngest son of B. F. Van Meter and his wife, Amelia C. Lewis, was educated at Morton & Irvine's private school in Winchester, Kentucky, and at the Kentucky State College, in Lexington.   He was graduated in medicine at Bellevue Hospital Medical College, New York City, April, 1897 ; post-graduate course at Mothers' and Babies' Hospital, East Thirty-fifth Street, New York City, and then graduated at the Hospital for the Ruptured and Crippled, corner Forty-second Street and Lexington Avenue, New York City, June, 1898, and August 23d of the same year he signed a contract with the United States Government as Acting Assistant Surgeon in the Army, at Fort Thomas, Kentucky, where he remained in the general hospital, in charge of the surgical ward, until November 16th, at which time he was assigned to the Sixth Infantry and ordered to Fort Sam Houston, Texas, at which post were stationed four troops of the Tenth Cavalry, with Battery K of the First Artillery, besides the

Sixth Infantry. While stationed there he met Miss May H. Wetherill, who, in September, 1900, became his wife. May 17, 1899, he started for San Francisco, en route for Manila, with the Sixth Infantry, General Kellogg commanding, and the regiment sailed from San Francisco, May 22, 1899, on the transport Sherman, and with four days' stop at Honolulu, he arrived in Manila Bay on the night of the 13th of June. Ten days after his arrival there Dr. Van Meter was stationed with the First Battalion of the Sixth Infantry at Jaro, a suburb of Iloilo, on the island of Panay, and for the next eight months thereafter, as surgeon of this battalion, with Captain Z. W. Toney in command, he campaigned over the islands of Negros, Gimery, and Panay. About the 20th of November he was ordered to report to Captain J. S. Culp, Hospital No. 3, Manila, for duty, and there he was assigned to the surgical ward, and for duty also as lecturer to the first class of the Hospital Corps School of Instruction in minor surgery and first aid to the injured. The 19th of June, 1900, he sailed for the States on the transport Hancock. Soon after his arrival at San Francisco he requested an annulment of contract with the Government, which was granted, and on the 29th of September, 1900, he was married to Miss Wetherill, at Jamestown, R. I., and came at once to Lexington, Ky., where he located to practice his profession, and where he now resides.

May Hubbard Wetherill Van Meter (wife of Dr. B. F. Van Meter), born January 13, 1875, is a daughter of Captain Alexander Macomb Wetherill and his wife, May Hubbard, granddaughter of William Wetherill and his wife, Isabella Macomb. Third generation were Samuel Wetherill second and his wife, Rachel Price. The fourth generation were Samuel Wetherill (founder of Society of Free Quakers) and his wife, Sarah Yarnall. The fifth generation were Christopher Wetherill and his wife, Mary Stocton (this last named was a sister of Richard Stocton, a signer of the Declaration of Independence). Her ancestors of the sixth generation were Thomas Wetherill, who was born in Sherburn, county of York, England, September 3, 1674, and removed with his father to Burlington, New Jersey, in 1683, and married Ann Fearon, April 22, 1703.

Ancestors of the seventh generation were Christopher Wetherill and his wife, Mary Hornby. She died in York, England, in 1681, and in 1683 Christopher Wetherill emigrated to Burlington, New Jersey.

Captain A. M. Wetherill.

Ancestry of the eighth generation were Thomas Wetherill, of Parish of All Saints', New Castle on Tyne, England, and his second wife, Jane Hughington, of same parish, whom he married September 12, 1638. (His first wife not known.)

Ancestry of the ninth generation were Christopher Wetherill, of Stocton on Tees, England, and his wife, Mary Watson, sister of Thomas Watson, mayor of Stocton in 1623.

Ancestry of the tenth generation were Gyles Wetherill, of Stocton on Tees, County of Durham, England, and his wife, mentioned but not named in his will dated July 12, 1604.

Maternal ancestry of May Hubbard Wetherill Van Meter's father, Captain A. M. Wetherill: His mother (the wife of William Wetherill), Isabella Macomb, a daughter of John W. Macomb and his wife, Isabella Ramsey. Second was William Macomb and his wife, Sarah Jane Dring. Third was John Macomb and his wife, Jane Gordon. The above taken from Macomb Tree, by Henry Macomb, in 1878.

The Wetherill genealogy, taken from Charles Wetherill's Work on the Descendants of Christopher Wetherill:

Captain Alexander Macomb Wetherill went into the United States service in the Coast Survey at the age of sixteen years, and was in that service two years. He was in a Philadelphia volunteer regiment in the United States Army for about the last six months of the war between the States. Some time after the close of the war between the States he received the appointment of Second Lieutenant in the United States Army in the Sixth Infantry, where he served for the balance of his life — in all of the Indian wars where this regiment participated, and was promoted for gallantry, and was finally made Captain in 1890. He was killed at the Battle of San Juan Hill, in the bloody charge which was made against the Spanish and their barbed-wire fortifications, leading the charge in command of Company A.

May Hubbard Wetherill Van Meter was born in Fort Buford, North Dakota, which was then an out-post in command of General Hazen, in what is known as the "Bad Lands." Some thrilling adventures took place when she was an infant, and her mother, the wife of an army officer, entirely beyond civilization, among wild Indians and buffalo. While May was in her mother's arms — an infant — they were on board of a boat which was suddenly pressed into the military service to transport troops up the Missouri River

to where General Miles, then a Colonel, was engaged in a war with a
hostile band of Indians.   Colonel O. O. Howard was in command of
a regiment on one side of the river, and Colonel Miles on the other,
and it became necessary to combine these forces to capture the
Indians, who were trying to elude both forces and make their way
to Canada, as they said, to get the protection of the " Great White
Mother " (Queen Victoria), but Colonel Miles captured them before
they could cross the line.   Chief Joseph and his band were made
prisoners, and the chief was taken on this boat a prisoner to civilization and to prison, and during this sojourn on the boat a large
herd of buffalo was run into while the herd was crossing this river,
and many of them were killed by the soldiers.

The above facts were obtained from Mrs. May Hubbard
Wetherill.

Children of Captain Wetherill and his wife, May Hubbard, were :

May Hubbard, wife of Dr. B. F. Van Meter.

Alexander Macomb Wetherill, born July 18, 1878.

Samuel Wetherill, born February 22, 1884.

May Hubbard was the daughter of Henry Hubbard and his wife,
Juliet Smith, of Chicago, who built the first brick house in Chicago,
and owned a large and valuable property in that city when it was
only a village.


Line of Ancestry of the Family of B. F. Van Meter and his
    wife, Amelia Clay Lewis, as read by Mrs. Emma Van Meter
    Hamilton Before the Isha Desha Breckinridge Chapter
    of the Daughters of the American Revolution, National
    No. 3281, Lexington, Ky., February 2, 1894.

Our mother, Amelia C. L. Van Meter, is the daughter of Thornton Lewis and his wife, Emma, the daughter of Captain Thomas
Wright, a native of Virginia and a descendant of a worthy old English ancestry, who came to Clark County, Kentucky, with his wife,
Mary Rice, in 1780, and spent the remainder of his life on his farm
in that county, where he reared quite a large family of children.
Emma, our grandmother, was the youngest daughter.   Thornton
Lewis, our grandfather, was born in Fayette County, Kentucky, the
sixth son of Colonel Thomas Lewis and his wife, Elizabeth Payne,
who were both natives of Fairfax County, Virginia, and came to
Fayette County, Kentucky, in 1780.

Elizabeth Payne descended from a very aristocratic family of Welch and Scotch nobility, who wielded quite an influence in Scotland as far back as the year 1500. The motto on the crest of the Payne family when they fought against the Duke of Normandy at the battle of Hastings was "Ready! ah, ready!"

Sir Stephen Payne, of St. Christopher's Island, was of an ancient Devonshire family, and was a member of the Council and a supporter of King Charles 1st during the civil war; fled from England and settled on the island of St. Christopher.

In 1620 Sir Robert Payne's two sons, William and John, emigrated to America. Sir William settled in Maryland near Leonardtown; Sir John in Fairfax County, Virginia, on a grant of land made to them by King James 1st. This grant of land was called "Payne's Manor," and comprised many thousand acres. It is said that the King gave this munificent grant to placate these young and ambitious sprigs of nobility to get them to the new world, because he feared their power and influence in their native land.

William Payne, son of Sir John Payne, was born in Fairfax County, Virginia, August 10, 1671. He married for his second wife Anna Jennings, and their children were Edward, William, and Sandford. The eldest son, Edward, married Lady Ann Holland Congers, who was related to Lord Holland (Duke of Richmond). Elizabeth Payne, our great-grandmother, was the eldest daughter of the above-named parents. They were married in Fairfax County, Virginia, October 27, 1773.

Colonel Thomas Lewis, our great-grandfather, was commissioned Second Lieutenant of the Fifteenth Virginia Regiment of the Continental Army, November 21, 1776. He was made First Lieutenant March 20, 1777. His regiment was consolidated and numbered Eleventh Virginia on September 14, 1777. He retired from the army a Colonel, February, 1781. For all of this military career see "Historical Register of Officers of the Continental Army," page 263.

Colonel Thomas Lewis removed to Fayette County, Kentucky, in 1780 with his lovely young wife and their children, and settled on a large farm three miles northwest of Lexington, where he spent the remainder of his life, and raised to be grown a family of eleven children. When he came to Kentucky he possessed considerable means, consisting of money, slaves, and live stock. He made extensive investments in land, and very soon became one of the most influential and wealthy men in this State. He served his district in the convention which met at Danville and formed the first Constitution of Kentucky in 1792, and was a member of the first State Senate of Kentucky, which met in the same year. He filled other positions of honor and trust, and he and his wife were for many years honored members of the Old Baptist Church. Thomas Lewis died at the age of sixty years, in September, 1809, at the Olympian Springs, in what is now Bath County, Kentucky, having gone that far on his intended journey to Virginia on horseback, attended only by his body-servant. His body was returned and buried in the family graveyard on his farm. His grave with that of his devoted wife is still to be seen, marked with a monument with suitable inscription.

Hector P. Lewis, the eldest son, was left executor of his father's large estate, and guardian of the minor children. He was a man of commanding and striking appearance, dressed with scrupulous neatness in the finest of broadcloth and ruffled shirts. He was an aristocrat to the "manner born." He owned one of the finest landed estates in Fayette County. He possessed great force of character, intelligence, and high sense of honor; was fitted to occupy a position in the first ranks of politics if he had been so inclined. He was an intimate friend and associate of Henry Clay and other statesmen, but never held a political office. He never gave his note or any other written obligation for money, but adhered strictly to the cash system throughout his life. He was on the staff of his brother-in-law, General Green Clay, with the rank of Colonel in the War of 1812–13, and participated very efficiently in helping to raise the seige of Fort Meigs. Immediately after the British were driven from that post he was intrusted with a large detachment from this army to go to the rescue of General Dudley's army, which had just been defeated and was in great danger of capture or destruction. In this defeated army his younger brother, Asa K. Lewis, participated with the rank of Major. Colonel Hector gave timely and successful assistance and rescued them from a perilous situation.

Major Asa K. Lewis was the second son of Colonel Thomas Lewis, a man of more than ordinary talent and ability, a graduate of Princeton, both in college and law; a gentleman with very refined and polished manners. He practiced law a few years, and was Judge of the County Court of Clark County for several years, but after this retired to his farm in Clark County, and could not be induced to hold any political office, contending that he was disgusted with political affairs and professional business. He served in the War of 1812–13 as Major with distinction, and achieved an enviable reputation for skill and bravery. At the time of his death he was one of the highest Masons in the State, and had held the highest office of that fraternity.

I will revert to the early ancestry of Colonel Thomas Lewis, our great-grandfather. He was the son of Stephen Lewis and Elizabeth Offutt, his wife, both of Fairfax County, Virginia. Stephen Lewis died young, leaving this only son. His mother married Colonel William Douglas, and by this marriage raised several daughters and one son. Her youngest child, General Hugh Douglas, became quite distinguished in both military and political affairs.

Stephen Lewis was the son of General Robert Lewis, who was a noted officer in the British Army. After he retired from the army he emigrated early in 1700 and settled in Gloucester County, Virginia, where he spent the remainder of his life. General Robert, as well as his son, Colonel Robert, and grandson, Colonel Fielding Lewis — who married, first, General Washington's cousin, Mary, and after her death married the General's sister, Betty Washington — were all three active and influential members of the established Church of England. (See Bishop Mead's "Church and Families of Virginia.") General Robert Lewis was a son of Sir Samuel Lewis, who was one of the three brothers who fled from France immediately after the revocation of the Edict of Nantes in 1685.

Sir Samuel settled in Wales, William settled in the north of Ireland, and their brother John remained for a while in England, but finally settled in Portugal. (See Smiles' History of the Huguenots.) These three brothers were sons of Lord John Louis, of France.

Our father, Ben Franklin Van Meter, is the son of Isaac Van Meter and his wife, Rebecca, daughter of Captain Isaac Cunningham and his wife, Sarah Harness, both natives of Hardy County, Virginia (now West Virginia), but removed to Clark County, Kentucky, in 1802, soon after birth of their daughter Rebecca, and settled on a farm in that county, where they spent their lives.

Sarah Harness was the daughter of John Harness, who emigrated to the valley of the Potomac from Pennsylvania with his wife, Eunice Pettice, who was a native of the Island of Jersey. They came to Virginia early in 1744.

Captain Isaac Cunningham was of Scotch-Irish origin. The Cunningham family, as far back as we can trace them, were of the nobility of Scotland, and in the sixteenth and seventeenth centuries intermarried with the most noted families of that country. John Campbell, the seventh Duke of Argyle Inverness Castle, County of Argyle, married Annie Cunningham, of Craig's End. Thomas Wallace, of Cairn Hill, a noted merchant of Glasgow, married, in 1710, Lilias, a daughter of William Cunningham, the second son of Alexander, the first Earl of Glencairn. This ancient family gained their titles and renown by the clashing of glittering steel and helmets, when clan met clan in deadly conflict on the moors and glens of old Scotland, and ever since then it appears that the very first tocsin of war has ever made a Cunningham's sabre leap from its scabbard.

Captain Isaac Cunningham, our great-grandfather, commanded a company in the War of 1812–13 ; participated in some very severe campaigning on the shores of the lakes during the winter, "making his bed on the brush piles and covering with the snow." At the head of his gallant company of Clark and Bourbon County volunteers he did some desperate fighting against the British and Indians at the Battle of the River Raisin and other conflicts. He took a very lively and active interest in political affairs, and wielded as much influence as any man of his day in his section of the State ; while he had no aspirations for political preferment, he was ever ready to let his voice and influence be as potent as possible in the selection of the representatives of his district and of his State in the councils of the nation. Therefore he had many intimate acquaintances among the most prominent statesmen of his day; notably among them were Governor Clark, who resided in Clark County ; Honorable Richard H. Menifee, and the "Sage of Ashland." These and other politicians made him frequent visits, especially in times of great political excitement. He represented his county and district frequently in both houses of the Kentucky Legislature. For many years it was considered impossible to obtain the majority vote of Clark County against the expressed wish of Captain Cunningham.

His wife, Mrs. Sarah Harness Cunningham, possessed great force of character, energy, and determination, with practical common sense. Many persons attributed their great financial success fully as much to her capacity as his. One thing was obvious to those who were intimate at their home, that in a quiet way she exerted a great influence over her husband, and he seldom transacted any important business without consulting her. She invariably "had the casting vote." She was a very active member of the Presbyterian Church, and perhaps the most liberal con- tributor to its support in the county. It was during her life that the struggle came up between the old and new school factions of this denomination, and it was perhaps more through her influence than any other one person that the church in Clark County held fast to the faith and principles of the old school.

Captain Isaac Cunningham was the son of John Cunningham and his wife, Elizabeth, who came from Ireland and settled on the south branch of the Potomac River in Hardy County, (now) West Virginia, in about 1755. We find in "Historical Register of Officers of the Continental Army," page 142, John Cunningham made Ensign of the Seventh Virginia on the 8th of May, 1776, and William Cunningham (no doubt his brother, we know he had one of that name) was also made Ensign on the same day in the Revolutionary Army of Virginia, and we imagine that no more suitable men than Cunninghams could have been found to flaunt the Star-Spangled Banner in the faces of the British or any other foe.

John Cunningham left a fine estate to a family of seven chil- dren, of whom Captain Isaac was the youngest son. Some of the descendants of John Cunningham, who lived in Virginia less than forty years ago, could trace their ancestry, giving the names of the parents of each generation, through Ireland and back to Scotland to Sir William, but we have no records of this at hand.

The ancestors of Isaac Van Meter, our grandfather, who married Rebecca Cunningham, emigrated from Brommell in South Holland, and landed at New Amsterdam (since New York City) in 1663, when that village belonged to the Dutch—Jans Gysbertsin Van Meteren, a widower, and his son, then about ten years of age, named Kryn Jansen Van Meteren. This father and son located in New Ultricht in Jersey. The father married Miss Van Clief, and the son married a niece of his step-mother, named Nellie Van Clief. The above facts as well as the following are of record in "Bergin's Kings County," pages 345 and 346, but as we are more personally interested in the son, we will confine our statements to the records concerning him.

Nellie Van Cleif and Kryn Jansen Van Meteren were married at New Ultricht, September 9, 1683. He is on the assessment roll of New Ultricht from 1675 to 1709. He was elected a deacon in the Dutch Protestant Church in 1699 ; he was on Dongon's patent of 1686, and took the oath of allegiance to the British Crown in that town in 1687.

He was assessed on forty-six acres of land in New Ultricht in 1701, and in 1709 he removed to Middletown, Monmouth County, New Jersey. His eldest child, Jan or John, was baptized April 24, 1686. They had nine children born to them, their names and the time they were baptized being on church records there. This eldest son, Jan or John (as he afterwards wrote his name), became a noted Indian trader. He removed to the State of New York with his family, but he was of a roving disposition and spent much of his time from home in trading with friendly Indians. On one occasion he went in command of a band of Cough Indians on a trading expedition to Virginia in 1739, and on this excursion he explored the country then almost unknown to white people, the valley of the south branch of the Potomac, known then by the Indian name of Wapatonica.

This man soon became sufficiently Americanized to spell his name John instead of Jans, and to leave the "n" off of Van Metren, and the name was handed down several generations spelling the name Van Metre instead of Van Meter, as we of the present generation do.

When he returned home he urged his sons to lose no time in possessing that land, declaring that it was most beautiful and very fertile. Four of his sons emigrated to Virginia in 1744, viz: Abraham, Isaac, Jacob, and John. Abraham and John settled in Berkeley County, on the east side of the Allegheny Mountains. Jacob settled and built his fort at the lower end of the south branch valley, and Isaac settled and built his fort much further up "the beautiful and fertile valley" at a place known as the "Indian Old Fields." His fort he named Fort Pleasant, in what is now Hardy County, West Virginia.

John and Isaac had procured a grant of 40,000 acres of land through Governor Gooch from the British Crown. They sold one half of the grant to Joist Hite, which left them about 10,000 acres each, which they settled upon as here stated ; but as we are more personally interested in Isaac, we will confine our remarks to him and Fort Pleasant.

Isaac Van Metre with his wife and four children removed to Fort Pleasant in 1744. The father had come out four years before this and laid what was called a "tomahawk claim" on these lands. These facts as to the removal of the Van Metre brothers to Virginia, their location, their settlement, their adventures with the Indians, and the protection their forts furnished to the surrounding settlers, can be found in "Kirchevel's History of the Valley," "Foote's Sketches of Virginia," and other histories of the early settlement of that country.

Isaac Van Metre, the founder of Fort Pleasant, was killed and scalped by the savages in 1757, just a short distance outside his fort, when he was a very old man. He left a widow and four children, two sons and two daughters. The sons were Garrett and Henry. We are more personally interested in Garrett, the eldest son, who was born in the State of New York, February, 1732. He married Mrs. Ann Sibley (whose maiden name was Markee) in 1756. He inherited from his father's estate Fort Pleasant with a considerable part of the surrounding lands. General Washington had his rendezvous at Fort Pleasant when he was a Colonel in the Colonial Army of Virginia during the French and Indian War against the British Colonies. Years before the Revolution the acquaintance and friendship was formed between General Washington and Colonel Garrett Van Meter which continued through their lives. Garrett Van Meter was a Colonel in command of militia, and took a prominent part in the struggle for independence. He and his wife were among the foremost supporters of religion among the pioneers in their day. They lived and died at old Fort Pleasant as full of honor as of years. No man has ever commanded more respect or extended a greater influence over the entire South Branch Valley than he. These parents left two sons and one daughter to survive them, viz: Isaac, Jacob, and Ann. These two sons inherited the large landed estate which surrounded Fort Pleasant ; Jacob, in whom we are more personally interested, inherited the old fort and homestead where he was born. May 18, 1764, he married Tabitha, daughter of Joseph Inskeep and his wife, Hanna McCullock, who was a daughter of the most famous scout and Indian fighter of whom Virginia history gives account. McCullock was finally killed by the savages, when they cut out his heart—while it was still warm—saying, they ate it to be brave "like Cullock."

Colonel Jacob Van Meter and his wife, Tabitha, raised a family of five daughters and three sons. The eldest son, Isaac, married

Rebecca, the only child of Captain Isaac Cunningham, of Clark County, Kentucky, as previously stated, and our father, B. F. Van Meter, is the fifth son of these parents. This last named Isaac Van Meter spent his life from early manhood in Clark County, and died in 1854 at the age of sixty years. He was one of the most prominent, enterprising, and successful farmers in Kentucky. He owned a large landed estate; was for many years an exemplary elder in the Presbyterian Church, and during his life gave very liberally to the causes of religion, charity, and education.

Some years since a lady descendant from this Van Meter family, Mrs. A. L. Thompson, while traveling in Europe, spent some time in Holland, and while there tried to learn what she could of the ancestry of the emigrant, Jans Gysbertsin Van Meteren. She procured a copy of an old book written and published by Emanuel Van Meteren in 1582, which threw some light upon the early history and genealogy of this family.

Emanuel Van Meteren was born in Antwerp, Belgium, in 1535. He was the son of Jacob Van Meteren, who was born in Brecht, not far from Antwerp, who married Ortillia Ortell, a daughter of William Ortell, of Augsberg, Bavaria, Germany. Emanuel was twice married, his second wife being Esther Vanden Corbet, and they reared three sons and three daughters.

I now give a literal translation from this old Dutch book: "Jacob Van Meteren was a man of great learning. In his youth he learned the rare and noble art of type-setting, and later in collaboration with Miles Coverdale he translated and printed the first entire English Bible to the great forwarding of the Kingdom of Jesus Christ in England." And of him and his wife: "They were devoted followers of the light which had shined into the darkness and were sorely persecuted therefor."

Again, just a short while before the birth of Emanuel, while his father was absent from home, the Roman Church sent emissaries to search his house for the "forbidden books and papers." The mother prayed that they might not be found, and although the intruders had their hands on the chest which contained the treasured books and papers, they were not discovered; hence the name of the son—Emanuel, signifying "God is with us." They lived in the crucial days of the Spanish inquisition and withstood that persecution for years, but were finally compelled to flee for shelter and safety under the government of King Edward 6th of England, and taking ship for that country the vessel went down from a shot from a belligerent foe, and they found a watery grave, where they sleep in the ocean, in the sure hope that "in that day the sea shall also give up its dead."

The son, Emanuel, finally took up his abode in London. In 1582 he published this book, and in 1583 he was made Consul for the Dutch in London, and died there in 1612 at the age of seventy-seven years.

In conclusion, then, we find that our ancestry, whether Huguenot, Scotch-Irish, or of the sturdy old Knickerbocker, each vied with the other in support of civil and religious liberty and to establish the independence of our Republic, and, better still than all, we can point with joyous pride to the long unbroken chains of ancestry who have been for so many generations enlisted under the banner of the "King of Kings," which we women, as well as men, are permitted to bear aloft and march onward conquering and to conquer.

## THOMAS C. VAN METER.

Thomas C., sixth son of Isaac and Rebecca Van Meter, was born in Clark County, Kentucky, October 29, 1835. Married Orpha Campbell, of Mercer County, Kentucky, daughter of Whitaker Hill Campbell, of that county, and his wife, Parmelia Perkins. W. H. Campbell was a son of James Campbell, and his mother was a Miss Lewis, who descended from the same branch of the Lewis family as ex-Judge Lewis, of the Kentucky Court of Appeals, as given in this book. Parmelia Perkins' mother was a Miss Bowman.

Thomas C. Van Meter lived for many years on a fine farm in Clark County, Kentucky, and then removed with his wife to Eminence, Kentucky, where they now reside. They raised one daughter named Kate, who married Mr. Crabb, a prominent man of Eminence, Kentucky, who is cashier of a bank there and has other business affairs in that city.

Eliza Caroline, sixth daughter of Isaac and Rebecca, was born September 15, 1837, and died of scarlet fever when about four years of age.

## ABRAM VAN METER.

Abram Van Meter, seventh son of Isaac and his wife, Rebecca C. Van Meter, was born in Clark County, Kentucky, May 20, 1839. Married Anna Elizabeth, daughter of Jonas Marks Kleiser and his wife, Malita Stapp, who was born in Bourbon County, Kentucky, September 13, 1839. They were married October 26, 1859. They resided in Clark County, Kentucky, for seventeen years after their marriage, and then removed to Cook County, Texas, where they now reside. Jonas M. Kleiser, sixth son of Joseph Kleiser and his wife, Elizabeth Lyter, was born in Kentucky, July 28, 1805. Jonas M. Kleiser's wife, Malita Stapp, was born September 23, 1816, and was the second daughter of Achilles Stapp and his wife, Ann Millbanks. Joseph Kleiser was born in Switzerland, Europe, December 25, 1763, and as his oldest brother inherited the landed estate by the laws of that country, he left his native land at the age of sixteen years and went to London, England, about 1780, and served an apprenticeship under his uncle, John Kleiser, a clock-maker, after which he emigrated to Virginia, and in 1788 he married Elizabeth Lyter, who was born August 6, 1765, and was a daughter of Henry and Catherine Lyter, who were married and lived near Romney, now West Virginia.

Both the Lyter and Kleiser families removed with their families to Bourbon County, Kentucky, about 1793, and years afterward assisted in building old Hopewell Church, where for more than one generation their children were baptized.

Ten children were born to Joseph and Elizabeth Kleiser, and all lived to be grown.

Achilles Stapp was born in Albemarle County, Virginia, December 22, 1755, of English parents who had emigrated to that country at a very early period. He enlisted as a private in Captain Joseph Spencer's Company of Seventh Virginia Regiment, commanded by Colonel Alexander McClenachan, on March 2, 1776, and served through the War of the Revolution ; was in the battles of Brandy-wine, Germantown, and many others. He married Margaret Vanter in Virginia and removed to Scott County, Kentucky, where his wife died, leaving him with eight children, and after this wife's death he married, in 1812, Mrs. Ann Millbanks Delph, widow of John Delph, who died in Virginia and left this widow with four sons, viz : William, Jerry, Millbanks, and John.

Ann Millbanks, daughter of John and Mary Millbanks, was born in Culpeper County, Virginia, September 22, 1785.

John Millbanks was born in London in 1750, and was a tailor by trade ; emigrated to Virginia and married Mary Barlo, and after raising their family in that State, and after they were quite old, they removed to Scott County, Kentucky, near Stamping Ground.

To Achilles and Ann Stapp were born four daughters, viz : Eliza, Malita, Martha, and Margaret. Achilles Stapp died at the age of ninety-four years, in September, 1849, and his widow died in 1856 at the age of seventy-one years. John and Mary Millbanks lived to be more than eighty years of age. Joseph Kleiser lived to the age of eighty-four years. Elizabeth Lyter Kleiser was seventy-three. Jonas Markey Kleiser removed to Humbolt County, California, and died at the age of fifty-seven years.

The parents of Anna E. Kleiser, wife of Abram Van Meter, viz : Jonas M. Kleiser and his wife, Malita Stapp, had three children born to them, all of whom are still living, viz : Ann Elizabeth, Mary Kate, and Joseph Maxey.

Abram Van Meter and his wife, Ann Elizabeth, had eight children born to them, and six of these are still living, viz : Leta Mary, born in Bourbon County, Kentucky, October 8, 1860, married Thomas Brown, of Texas ; Jonas K., born in Clark County, Kentucky, September 17, 1862 ; Walter M., born in Clark County, Kentucky, May 17, 1865 ; Isaac, born in Clark County, Kentucky, October 5, 1867 ; Elizabeth K., born in Clark County, Kentucky, September 17, 1870 ; Anna Rebecca, born in Clark County, Kentucky, January 17, 1873 ; Thomas M., born in Cook County, Texas, June 4, 1882.

Abram Van Meter was a very successful and prominent breeder of short-horn cattle and other blooded stock in Kentucky for a number of years. He is now a prominent farmer in Texas and an elder in the Presbyterian Church there.

## LOUIS MARSHALL VAN METER.

Louis Marshall, eighth son of Isaac and Rebecca, was born February 8, 1841 ; educated at Transylvania, Lexington, Kentucky ; served three years in the Southern Army ; entered the army as First Lieutenant in Captain W. C. P. Breckinridge's company, and when Breckinridge was promoted, took command of the company, which he held to the close of the war ; married Nannie Moore, of Clark County, Kentucky ; resided in that county until 1889, when they removed to Shelby County, Kentucky, where they now reside. They have eight children, viz : Maria B., John D., Louis M., jr., Evaline B., Thomas Matthew, Nannie, Sallie M., and Benjamin.

### L. M. VAN METER'S WAR EXPERIENCE,

As he recalls it after more than thirty-five years have passed : I went out with General John H. Morgan in company with four other boys when he made his first great raid into Kentucky. We joined him about the first of July, the day after he fought the battle at Cynthiana. W. C. P. Breckinridge joined him at the same time and place, and each of us had four men which formed a nucleus for a company, which grew to be a large company before we left the State. General Morgan appointed Breckinridge captain of this company and me first lieutenant. We met Morgan's command just after it left Paris, on the road to Winchester, near the Sam Clay farm, about sunrise. We marched through Winchester that day, crossed the Kentucky River at Boonesborough, marched through Richmond late in the evening, and camped my first night several miles beyond Richmond on the road to Crab Orchard. Early the next day we captured a large quantity of supplies and military equipments, wagons, and stores of all kinds, and what we could not appropriate or carry out we burned or destroyed. We camped at Crab Orchard that night, and the next day we marched to Somerset, where we captured another large quantity of military stores and supplies, and from there we went out of the State over some ridge and through a gap west of Cumberland Gap ; there I was ordered to get the cannon which had been captured at Cynthiana over that ridge, which was very steep and made desperate heavy work, but we succeeded. We went through this gap into Tennessee and to Sparta, where General Morgan made his headquarters and recruited his horses, drilled and organized his brigade, which he had so largely increased on this raid.

A finer lot of men and horses that he had there and then—for the number of them—would have been hard to get together. There was no serious fighting on this raid after the battle at Cynthiana ; a few volleys from the advance guard drove the enemy in confusion wherever we found them, as they were few and readily demoralized.

After organizing his men and drilling them for two weeks, General Morgan began operating in the rear of the Federal Army from Nashville, north toward Louisville on the L. & N. Railroad, which was the main source of supplies and communication of the Federal Army of the West.

From the time this command left Sparta, in the latter part of July, until the end of that year there was lively and frequently thrilling campaigning, and not less than 15,000 prisoners were captured, and millions of dollars' worth of military supplies captured and destroyed. One of the most severe engagements of this campaign was at Gallatin, Tennessee, where twelve companies of picked Federal cavalry were sent to surprise and capture us, but we killed about 175 of them, wounded many more, and captured about 300 of them. In that engagement I saw the most splendid cavalry charge that I witnessed during the war. It was two companies of Texans commanded by Major Gano. The Federals were formed in a double line in a thin woodland on a ridge between the Scottsville and Louisville pikes, near their intersection, and as General Morgan's command came up from Gallatin to the intersection of these two roads, he would place each company or battalion into the fight. As our battalion came up, consisting of about 400 men, he ordered us to dismount and deploy to the right, thus forming his right wing in a cornfield of standing corn (in the month of August), and we moved to the front at a double-quick. My company being on the left of the line and I on the left of my company, commanding the second platoon, gave me the opportunity of advancing on the side of turnpike road, instead of in the cornfield, so that I and one other man (Hugh Rogers) advanced along the side of the pike with all of our command advancing through the standing corn. I had thus a good view of the battle from the right wing to the left, and Hugh Rogers and I did all the shooting that was done by our battalion during the advance through the cornfield.

When we had gotten some 250 yards or more from our horses and near half way of the cornfield and about 500 yards from the enemy, I looked back and to the left I saw the Texans under Gano coming and forming a line of battle as they came in a gallop, and by the time they got opposite to me they had formed a perfect line, when Gano immediately ordered a charge. Then instantly every man was out of sight on the left side of his horse, and you could see nothing but a right foot and a right arm with a double-barreled shotgun loaded with buckshot swinging on the right side of each horse. They swept by me in a perfect line like a cyclone, Gano, the only man in sight, riding erect and at the very top of his speed. I saw the end of his long black plume, which he wore in his hat, float off in the breeze from a shot that did not touch him ; they swept on like a hurricane until within about forty yards of the enemy, when Gano gave the order to fire, and instantly the entire line popped up erect in their saddles and unloaded both barrels of their shotguns with terrific effect, and then dropping their guns fastened to a belt at their sides, each man had a pair of six shooters with which they went to work with all possible energy, and for a very few minutes it was like a canebrake on fire, until the enemy's line in front of them, which was the center, was nearly destroyed and completely routed, and by the time all this had occurred, our battalion had reached the end of the cornfield nearest the enemy and delivered a few volleys into their left, when they fled in great confusion and as fast as their horses could carry them.

As soon as our horses could be brought up we began to pursue them. If I ever did much execution with my rifle during the war, it was in that fight. Hugh Rogers and I were firing on the enemy as they came in column down the road, and at the nearest point to us they would go right and left to form in line, and we shooting at the column. There were a good many dead horses and men in the road right there. Gano's cavalry charge on this occasion was the most perfect and beautiful military maneuver that I ever witnessed.

I made two narrow escapes from being killed that I know of. One was when I was on detached service and had six men with me in the mountains of Tennessee above Sparta, and we had taken possession of an old deserted two-story log house for the night and had a nice lot of provisions, and the boys were in for a good time. The horses were picketed close to the house. Two of the boys were cooking us some ham and eggs and chickens, etc., while the others were patting and dancing, and I was sitting on a bag of corn near the middle of the room smoking my pipe and enjoying the antics of the boys, when, without any warning, bang went a gun through the open door, and three bullets were buried in a log of the house, almost exactly in line with my head, where I sat on the corn. I must have moved my head suddenly and just at the right time in laughing at some of the boys' antics. The bullets were fired from an old-fashioned smooth-bore gun, and not more than thirty yards distant, as you could have covered all three of the holes they made in the log with a half-dollar. Not long before this occurred we had been talking of old Tinker Dave, a noted Yankee bushwhacker who frequented that section of the mountains, and who neither gave nor asked any quarters, and when that gun cracked, we all supposed it was him. I never left my pistols off when I was awake, and frequently slept with them. The boys were not allowed to keep their guns loaded when marching or in camp. The muzzle-loader, percussion-cap gun would be jarred off by a rough trotting horse or in some other accidental way, and do great mischief. At the crack of that gun I sprang to the corner of the room, and, with a pistol in each hand, guarding the door (which had no shutter to it and no windows to the house), ordered the boys up stairs. They grabbed their guns, and for about a minute there was a great rattle of old iron ramrods. I expected every minute to receive a charge from old Tinker Dave and his posse, but the boys very quickly commenced to come down the stairway, and as we received no charge from without, we soon determined to sally out and hunt the enemy. We found our horses all right, and, after a thorough reconnoisance, concluded that it was one of old Dave's scouts who was sniping around, and concluded to take a crack at me and make his escape.

Another time that I know of I was singled out for a shot was near Macon, Georgia, when Sherman evacuated Atlanta and started towards Savannah. Our company was ordered out of a thick woods, dismounted and in column on a road with orders not to fire on the enemy if they approached and we could avoid it, but make them form a line of battle and then fall back. We marched out on the road some four hundred yards or more, and could see the enemy approaching in column, and when they got within about nine hundred yards they began to throw out a skirmish line, and thus forming a line, and having fulfilled the orders I received, I ordered a counter-march, which placed me on the right and rear of our company, and I was closely watching the movements of the enemy, with Lieutenant Ed. Hines walking a few yards in front of me and directly in line with me, when I saw a cavalryman dash down the road toward us until he was closer than one hundred yards to us ; he dismounted and leveled his carbine, and I saw it was pointed directly at me, and I instantly spoke sharp and quick, "look out, Ed.," and bowed low to the ground, when Ed. did the same thing with military precision and just in time for that fellow's bullet to pass over both of us and lodge in a large black-jack tree only a few yards in front of us. I admired that fellow's bravery, but not his discretion, and but for the orders I had received not to fire, his carcass would have been food for worms. We had some excellent shots in our company. The prayers of godly parents and friends made the enemies' bullets harmless to me, fulfilling the Scripture of the 91st Psalm : "I will give mine angels charge over thee to keep thee. Thou shalt not be afraid of the arrow that flyeth by day nor the destruction that wasteth at noonday." I often thought of many such passages of Scripture as this while in battle and other dangerous places. I came near being captured the fall after Bragg went out of Kentucky. After we reached Tennessee I was taken quite ill, and was sent with a few others to Hartsville, a little town east of Gallatin, to the house of a Mr. Alaxander, where I was quite sick for two weeks and so weak that I was compelled to lie down nearly all the time, but at the end of about two weeks could go about the house a little. My horse (Old Ned), the best horse in the army, was badly worn down and needed recruiting nearly as much as I did, but while I was sick he improved rapidly and became quite coltish. About the time I could begin to walk around the place a runner came suddenly to inform us that the enemy were crossing the Cumberland River some three or four miles off, and would try to surprise and capture us. I saddled and mounted Ned, though hardly able to ride — this was about two o'clock in the afternoon. I rode up the river toward a little town called Rone, and when I got there I saw the enemy on the other side of the river preparing to cross, so I went up the river still a few miles further toward the little town of Carthage, but night came on and I was exhausted with fatigue, and asked to stay all night at a house on the side of the road, where I was kindly taken in. The landlord proved to be one of Zollicoffer's men, who had been wounded, and we talked awhile after supper, but I soon went up stairs to bed and slept well all night, waking in the morning just before day, and very soon heard talking for a while, and finally the door closed and immediately my host came running up the steps and told me the road in front of the house was full of Yankee cavalry. I jumped out of bed and into my clothes. Meantime his little son, nine or ten years old, came up, when I asked him : "Can you get my horse and saddle him and throw some old blanket over my saddle and get on him as though you would take him to water, and ride him back of the house?"

Ned was in a stable right in among the Yankees on the side of the road. He said he would do his best, and vanished toward the stable. When I got dressed I went out at a back door and peeped around the corner of the house, and could see them twenty yards away hitching their horses and preparing to cook breakfast and feed their horses, for they had been riding all night, and were tired and hungry and sleepy. What I first heard was when they came to the house for fire to cook with, and it was the advance guard.

After I got out of the house I saw at a glance that if I could get to the top of a steep ridge which terminated near the back yard of this dwelling and get on my horse up there I would be comparatively safe; so, keeping the house between me and the enemy, I made for the hill, and by keeping on the side of the ridge best concealed, by hard scrambling I made the top and fell down behind a log to rest, and very soon I heard the tramp of my horse, which the faithful and sprightly lad came riding up to me. He had watched my movements and knew where to find me. I asked the lad where there was a ford of the river close by, and he said he would show me one, so he sat back and I swung myself into my saddle. The road lay close along the river bank. I kept the ridge between me and the enemy until I struck the main road some distance in front of the enemy's column, and then rode down the pike a quarter of a mile, following the boy's guidance, until I struck the river at the ford, when he slid off, and I tried to express my thanks and gratitude to him, when I very soon put both ridge and river between me and the Yankees, and soon joined my command at Beard's Mills. After crossing the river and riding a mile or two, I stopped at Mr. Roland's and got my breakfast. He had a son at home wounded from a shot in the leg, and when I saw him afterwards he told me the negroes had told the enemy of me, and they had been trying hard to find me, but I had gotten a sufficient start to elude them.

One of the most amusing incidents that I remember occurred the last winter before the war closed, while we were in South Carolina, near Savannah, and on very short rations. We were marching along one evening, and we had a man in our company by the name of Louis Green, who would have something good to eat by hook or by crook.

As we were passing a farm house, all of the family at home, consisting of mother and daughters, were sitting on the porch, and a short distance beyond the house was quite a flock of geese. I saw Green gallop off in front of his place until he came to the geese, when he rode very slowly through them, while he dropped a grain of corn to a goose of his selection with baited hook with a strong cord attached. Very soon he struck out in a gallop with a goose hard after him with outstretched neck and wings, and the entire family in the porch wondering why the old goose was running a soldier. He soon passed around a bend of the road out of sight, when he drew the goose up, declaring that he would allow no goose to run him out of the command.

I saw a very amusing fight between two soldiers of our company, which occurred while we were camped at Dixon Spring and preparing to make a raid into Kentucky. These two fellows, whom I will call C and D, were good fighters in battle and at any time, but they were so filthy and rough that the other men would not mess with them or sleep with them, and when the weather was cold they were compelled to splice blankets and sleep together and mess together. But they very frequently quarreled, and there was little attention paid to that by the balance of the command. While we were all cooking rations and preparing to march, these two "wharf rats," as we called them, were cooking and having their accustomed quarrel. C was stooping over a fire made of small limbs and brush, and was frying some meat, while D was standing behind him and mixing some dough. The lie had passed once or twice between them, when C in a loud tone gave D the damn lie without ever looking up, still stooping over his meat and fire, and I saw D throw all of his dough into his left hand, and with his right fist gave C a hard jolt at the back of the head, which sent him forward on to his hands and knees and on to the fire; but C sprang immediately to his feet with a fire brand in each hand, with about a foot of live coals and ashes on the end of each stick, and with these he instantly made at his assailant, dealing him rapid blows with first one and then the other over the head and neck, as he ducked his head to dodge the blows, which left abundant room for the live coals and hot ashes to go down between his shirt and his body, and soon brought forth the most unearthly yells of agony.

This instantly threw C into the most uncontrollable convulsions of laughter as he rolled over and over on the ground, laughing about as loud as the other fellow was yelling with agony as he rapidly hulled out of his clothes. The uproar was so great that it soon brought the camp guard, who arrested both men and took them to the colonel's headquarters, who heard their statements and immediately ordered them to strip and fight it out. D was furious and running over full of fight, but C just laughed him clear out of a fight, saying all the time he had enough, thus furnishing intense amusement to all except D.

L. M. Van Meter was offered a major's commission when Captain W. C. P. Breckinridge received a colonel's commission, but declined with thanks, saying he preferred to remain with the boys, and did not wish to assume any more responsibility than he knew he could perform well. He did not receive even a captain's commission after Captain Breckinridge left the company, but performed the duties of that office for this company to the close of the war, and occasionally he had two or three companies under his command temporarily for some special purpose.

### How a Stampede was Averted at the Battle of Missionary Ridge.

Lieutenant L. M. Van Meter, of Breckinridge's Regiment, tells the story.

Governor Bradley has received a letter from L. M. Van Meter, a well-known Shelby County farmer, which gives a bit of history of the Civil War heretofore unpublished. Mr. Van Meter was a lieutenant of the Ninth Kentucky Cavalry, under Colonel W. C. P. Breckinridge, at the battles of Chickamauga and Missionary Ridge, and commanded the company that stopped the Confederate stampede from the latter place. He now recalls the incident through the announcement of the Governor that he would take fifty Kentuckians with him to this famous battle-ground in November to attend the unvailing ceremonies at the Kentucky monument.

His account of the stampede is as follows:

CHRISTIANSBURG, KENTUCKY, September 17, 1898.

*Governor Bradley:*

Honorable Sir: Some time since I saw in the papers that in November you, with a delegation of Kentuckians, would unvail a monument at Chickamauga Park to Kentucky for the part she played at the battles of Chickamauga and Missionary Ridge. At the latter I figured a little, and there has never been a report made.

On that day I was ordered by Colonel W. C. P. Breckinridge for Provost Marshal and to take my company (Company E of his regiment) and patrol in the rear of our line, which was on the northwest brow of the ridge, to see that every thing was in order and to take any stragglers to the front. I received the order early in the morning of the day of the battle of Missionary Ridge. I took my company from Chickamauga Station, where the regiment was camped, and proceeded from the center to the right of the line and found every thing in perfect order.

Wagons were all packed in the rear of each division with teamsters and cooks. I started back to go to the left of our line, and had not proceeded far when it sounded over the ridge as if a skirmish had sprung up, and, as I proceeded toward the center, it increased in volume of sound until I got in the rear of the center, when it amounted to a roar. I halted my company half way up the mountain side, opposite the bridge that supplied our line across Chickamauga from the station, and ordered them to hold horses. I had not proceeded more than twenty steps, when all at once the roar of battle ceased, and immediately after I saw our men coming over the ridge to the right and left as far as I could see in the woods and brush. My orders were to stop straggling, but I think this was not part of the programme. However, I had to think and act quickly. At the foot of the ridge was the bridge, and I thought they would make for that point, and there I could stop them and herd them, so I ordered my men to mount, and galloped them to the bridge, dismounted them on the opposite side and formed a double line, with loaded rifles, across the bridge before the first arrived ; and soon had the two brigades that gave way halted. I was kept busy from that time until sundown passing wounded and organized bodies and holding back the disorganized. Just about sundown I opened my lines to let a squad of cavalry through, I thought, and just after they had gotten over the bridge a colonel that was wounded and was sitting on an abutment of the bridge called to me to ask General Bragg, who had just passed, what to do with the two disorganized brigades, which I did, and he ordered me to march them to Chickamauga Station.

I told the wounded colonel to take command of them. He ordered them to fall in, and he would take them where they could rest and draw rations, which they did with alacrity. I mounted my men and proceeded ahead of them to the station, where I was ordered immediately with my company to picket the roads and fords on Chickamauga and prepare to fell trees to blockade the same, which was done by chopping trees almost down so that two or three strokes would fell them, and so they would cross each other. This I did, and about midnight I was recalled to join the regiment that was in the rear of the army, which was falling back toward Dalton. The next morning, at Ringold Gap, the Kentucky brigade and a Tennessee brigade gave General Grant such a severe repulse that he followed us no farther. They started a large grave-yard there in about five minutes with little or no loss to us.

This is the first written report I ever made, and for three or four years after events were transpiring so rapidly that one event crowded another out of mind, or I did not take time to make much of a report, except a short verbal one. You have never seen in any history who stopped the stampede from Missionary Ridge. This is a true account.

LIEUTENANT L. M. VAN METER,
*Ninth Cavalry.*


## HORATIO W. BRUCE,

of Louisville, Kentucky, lawyer, admitted to the bar in 1851, was elected Commonwealth's Attorney of the Tenth Judicial District of Kentucky, which office he held until 1858. In 1862 he was elected a representative from Kentucky to the Confederate Congress, and served in that body until it was dissolved by the fortunes of war. At the close of the war he returned to Kentucky and resumed the practice of law in Louisville. In 1868 he was elected Circuit Judge of the Ninth Judicial District, and in 1873 became Chancellor of the Louisville Chancery Court by appointment, and was soon afterward elected to that office to fill out an unexpired term, and in 1874 was re-elected for a full term of six years. He was married in 1856 to Elizabeth Hardin Helm, a daughter of John L. and Lucinda Barber Helm, of "Helm Place," Hardin County, Kentucky.

This Bruce family are from a noted and worthy old Scotch ancestry, and the Helm family are among the most noted of the early settlers of Kentucky. Children: Helm Bruce, Elizabeth Barber Bruce, Maria Preston Pope Bruce; Mary Bruce, married Thomas Floyd Smith; V. Alexander Bruce, married Sallie Moore Van Meter, daughter of Louis Marshall Van Meter, of Shelbyville, Kentucky.

## L. M. VAN METER.

As before stated, L. M. Van Meter, Sr., married Nannie Moore, a daughter of Thomas H. Moore and his wife, Mariah Bright.

Thomas H. Moore was a son of Thomas R. Moore and his wife, Evaline W. Hockaday.

T. R. Moore was a son of William Moore and his wife, Hannah Ransdall.

William Moore was born in Fauquier County, Virginia, March 5, 1753; was a soldier in the Revolutionary war, and married, as above stated, January 2, 1779, and died in Kentucky in 1817. William Moore and his wife, Hannah, had born to them eight sons and three daughters, viz: William H., Wharton R., Hindley, Thomas R., John W., Mary C., Charles C., Betsy, Sterin, Samuel T., and Ann C.

Hannah R. Moore, a woman of considerable note, was a sister of William, and was born in Fauquier County, Virginia, October 22, 1758, and died in Kentucky, October, 1810.

Thomas R. Moore and his wife, Evaline Hockaday, had born to them five sons and five daughters, viz: William Irvine, born November 9, 1817, and died March 14, 1819; Emily J., born October 27, 1819, married —— Bright, left a family of children, and died February 24, 1885; Thomas H., born July 22, 1821, married Mariah Bright, of Tennessee, and died March 19, 1879; Ann E., born October 14, 1823, married James R. Wornal and raised a family of children, and died January 9, 1896; Isaac I., born October 8, 1825, married Miss ——, and died June 2, 1879; John H., born September 12, 1829, died April 9, 1901; Margaret H., born April 6, 1832, married (Judge) Charles Stephen French, raised a family of children, and she and her husband are still living in Winchester, Ky.; Pattie F., born June 28, 1835, and died unmarried, November 9, 1876; Sallie C., born September 19, 1837, married J. Levi Wheeler, October 10, 1865, and raised two children (named John M., and Kate D., both of whom are still living). Sallie C. died October 27, 1886, and J. L. Wheeler died in 189—; Charles C., the youngest child of this family, was born September 18, 1841, and died unmarried, August 14, 1863.

Thomas H. Moore, eldest son of the above-named parents, and, as above stated, married Mariah Bright (a sister of Hon. John

Bright, of Tennessee, who was for many years a Congressman from that State), descended from an aristocratic English ancestry. Their children were: Nancy, who married Louis Marshall Van Meter; Mathew; Amelia, who married Andrew H. Hampton; Kate, who married Charles F. Exum; Pattie, and Thomas H., Jr., who married Miss Hulett.

After earnest solicitation, I am favored with a short sketch of Thomas R. Moore, written by his son-in-law, Judge C. Stephen French, who married Margaret H. Moore, sixth child and third daughter of Major Thomas R. Moore, which is given in full from his pen as follows:

Among the prominent citizens of Clark County in the past generation, no one is probably more worthy of mention than Major Thomas R. Moore. He was born in Fauquier County, Virginia, in the year 1786. While at a very young and tender age, his parents, William and Hannah Moore, left Virginia and came to Kentucky and settled in that part of Fayette County known as the Russel's Cave neighborhood. Their choice of a home was most fortunate. The land was rich, in the central part of the famous bluegrass section, the neighbors intelligent and kind, consisting chiefly of families who, like themselves, emigrated from Virginia. Educational facilities at that time in Kentucky were somewhat limited, which circumstance, together with the necessities of a large family, consisting, with himself, of nine children, confined the opportunities of young Moore for instruction to the course of study usually taught by the average country school. He, however, eagerly availed himself of these opportunities, and by close application acquired a good English education, with some knowledge of the classics. Having a decided literary taste, and wishing more thoroughly to appropriate what he had learned, his first venture in business for himself was teaching a country school. In after years he often alluded to his experience as a teacher. He oftentimes referred specially to one of his pupils, Robert J. Breckinridge, who afterwards became widely known and distinguished as scholar, theologian, and divine. He was not unmindful of the genius of his pupil, nor surprised at his rising fame. "He marked him as a far off Alp, and loved to watch the sun rising on his ample brow." After attaining manhood's estate, he cast about in his mind for choice of a lifework, and among the many avenues opening before him, none seemed more attractive than the profession of law. Accordingly he applied to

Hon. John Breckinridge, the great ancestor of the Breckinridges, for assistance, who generously superintended his course of study and gave him the advantages of his library. Soon, however, his dreams of forensic honors were disturbed by war's rude alarums.

England's piratical crusade upon American commerce, impressing sailors on board of American vessels, regardless of national citizenship or allegiance, seizing and confiscating American merchantmen as lawful prizes for pretended violation of mere paper blockades, to say nothing of insult to national honor, impelled Congress, after long and patient endurance of these outrages upon the high seas, to declare war against the British Government. It is known in history as the War of 1812.

A call having been made for volunteers to protect the Northwestern frontier from invasion by British soldiery and Indians, their savage allies, young Thomas R. Moore and his brother, Chilton C. Moore, still younger than himself, and many other brave Kentuckians promptly offered their services to the Government as soldiers.

After many hardships and privations in camp, and on the march, which led through a densely wooded country covered for the most part with swamps and marshes, they finally reached the scene of conflict. The action in which they were engaged was the Battle of the River Raisin. It was disastrous in the extreme to American arms, nearly the entire army having been either killed, wounded, or taken prisoners. Among the prisoners were the two young Moores, Thomas and his brother Chilton.

Captured as prisoners of war, they expected and had right to expect that they would be treated upon terms customary among all civilized nations, and that they would be protected from violence and insult. Had these terms been observed, it would have been creditable to the victorious army. But it has been recorded in history, shameful as it may be to British arms and British honor, these terms were recklessly disregarded.

After the defeated army surrendered themselves and their arms into the hands of the British officer in command, only a short time elapsed before a large force of Indians rushed in upon them and began the work of indiscriminate and fiendish slaughter. Crowded into a small enclosure from which it was impossible to escape, the tomahawk and scalping-knife were used upon them in most shocking and wanton cruelty. The strongest and most gallant in appearance were made the first victims, the feeble and wounded reserved for an after-play of ghoulish delight. It was a wild, barbaric frenzy, a carnival of crime, impossible of description.

In the midst of this awful scene of savage sport and heartrending cruelty, young Thomas R. Moore accosted General Proctor, the British officer supreme in command, and said to him in words of mingled pathos and indignation :

"Are you, sir, a man of woman born, and do you make the slaughter of your fellow-man a pastime ?"

"Who is it," said the General, "that thus dares address a British officer ?"

"A Kentucky volunteer," replied the gallant young soldier.

Stung by the rebuke and feigning surprise at the announcement of the massacre, he falteringly replied :

"I am unable to control the Indians."

"Restore to us our arms, then, and we will defend ourselves," said the brave Kentuckian.

It is a significant fact that shortly after this thrillingly dramatic episode the slaughtering ceased.

> Ah ! it was a word most fitly spoken,
> Of knightly manhood the grandest token;
> With gallant spirit it was bravely said,
> A word for the living and for the dead.

At the expiration of their terms of service as soldiers the two brothers returned to Kentucky. The health of Thomas having been much impaired during the campaign, he abandoned all idea of practicing his chosen profession. He first went to Greenupsburg and began the mercantile business, but not being pleased with the situation, came to Winchester, Clark County, Kentucky. At the latter place he recommenced the mercantile business in connection with his brother Chilton as partner. His efforts at this point were prosperous to a degree which probably exceeded his most sanguine expectations.

Meanwhile he was united in marriage to Miss Evaline W. Hockaday, of Clark County, whose family relations were numerous and influential and of Virginia ancestry. He continued the mercantile business for about fifteen years, when he and his brother dissolved their partnership and he retired to the country. With his share of the money accumulated during his business as merchant, he bought and paid for a beautiful farm of about four hundred acres. It is situated about two miles from Winchester, and on it may be seen traces of the fort mentioned in accounts of the Indian wars in Kentucky as Strode's Station.

His removal to the country was in hearty accord with his tastes. He loved the country, its freshness, its freedom, its groves, its meadow lands and its golden-crowned harvest fields. How rapidly and aptly he grasped his new field of enterprise may readily be inferred from the success which attended his efforts. His neighboring farmers and friends, and among the rest Captain Isaac Cunningham, a prince of farmers and of men, and Mr. Isaac Van Meter, ranking close beside him in enterprise and dignity of character, greeted him cordially on his advent into their circle, and gave him advice and every needed assistance in their power. It soon developed, however, that Major Moore, as he was generally called, was equal to the situation.

His manner of farming was quiet, practical, and systematic. At the beginning of each year he forecast his plans, and under ordinary conditions wrought them out successfully. He did not exhibit the restless energy, hurry, and strain characteristic of many who achieve success in that business. He was careful and vigilant, and had the confidence of sound judgment. Besides, he indulged his literary tastes. Many hours were spent by him in delightful communion with his favorite authors, of which he had a choice collection. Shakespeare, Burns, Goldsmith, Scott, and Dickens were to him cherished companions and guests of whom he never tired.

In the midst of this quiet and ease, this literary pastime interwoven as a golden thread through the tangled web of each day's business life, he added acre to acre and farm to farm, until he became the owner of one of the largest and finest farms in Central Kentucky.

In disposition he was eminently social, and was at home in every circle. He had a rich vein of humor, and told an anecdote with fine effect ; his home was distinguished for its hospitality. The poor had warm and generous welcome ; the cultivated and refined found there an atmosphere genial and inspiring. In politics he was a Whig, an ardent friend and supporter of Mr. Clay. At the solicitation of his party, he at one time became a candidate to represent Clark County in the legislature, and was elected by a flattering majority, but declined a re-election. He preferred the simple graces and dignity of country gentlemen to the empty honors of official rank and station. Had he lived to a ripe old age, his success in business could not well be overestimated. But just at the time fortune seemed most propitious and his hopes were ripening into richest earthly fruition, he was stricken down by disease. On the 24th day of April, 1844, he was seized with violent paroxysms of pain. Medical aid was promptly summoned, but in vain. The grim reaper had come, and on the following day he was cut down by death in the fifty-ninth year of his age. He left a widow surviving and nine children, each of whom esteemed his personal worth and honest fame their richest legacy. He was buried at the homestead he loved so well. In a quiet place in the garden where in the early spring the humble violet lifts its head and decks a mouldering heap, and the apple-bloom shed its sweet perfume, may be seen a modest white shaft pointing to the stars. On it there is a brief inscription. These simple memorials mark his last resting-place. And it is well ; it is full enough.

The boast of heraldry, the blazonry of monumental pile seek in vain to preserve man's fleeting memory. Earthly tablets soon decay, kingly mausoleums crumble into dust. Yet there are memories that will live beyond the rolling spheres when earth has grown dim with age. There are names that will never die. They do not need the engraver's art, nor richly sculptured marble to show their honors to the world. The story of their lives is graven by a hand divine on pillars of celestial glory, which will endure undimmed by cloud or flood of years, as the ages move on in endless succession.

As Judge French here relates, Major Moore and Captain Isaac Cunningham were near neighbors and very intimate friends, and an occurrence took place, after the death of ex-Governor Clark, which illustrates the character of these two men. They were very warm personal and political friends of Governor Clark, who lived in Winchester, and had all been life-long Whigs and worked together in many political campaigns. When Governor Clark died, it was very soon currently reported that his estate would not pay his debts. These two men with a very few others met and discussed the matter, and determined that his estate should pay his debts and have something left besides for the family, and had the sale of his effects made on twelve months' time. Then Cunningham and Moore bid against each other and against all others besides, so that the property realized the most extravagant prices that had ever been known in that country. The estate paid all debts and left a snug balance for the family, but it required several days to distribute the property and ascertain the purchasers of the different parcels and stock.

Evaline W. Hockaday, wife of Major T. R. Moore, was a daughter of Isaac and Amelia (Fields) Hockaday. She survived her husband many years, and died at a ripe old age.


## DEATH OF COLONEL JOHN H. MOORE.

The following was taken from the Winchester Sun :

With Christ, in the light of a glorified life, the beautiful and gracious spirit of our fellow-citizen and fellow-laborer, Colonel John H. Moore, rests from labor, and his works do follow him. Colonel Moore was a native of Clark County, and lived among the scenes he so well loved for seventy-two years. The son of Major Thomas R. Moore, he was the last survivor, but one, of nine children.

The early years of his life were devoted to farming. For many years Colonel Moore was an elder in the Presbyterian church of this city.

Faithful, gentle, and large-hearted, he wrought a blessed work among us, which shall abide. He was enthroned in the affections of the entire community, and every one delighted to do him honor.

Bible distribution and colportage work had a special fascination for him, and his fitness for such work has seldom been equaled. Throughout many sections of the mountains his name is a household word, from which, in the years to come, many noble men and women will draw inspiration for holier and better living. "Brother Moore," as he was familiarly called, was to them and to us a demonstration of the high principles of the Christian religion.

His death occurred Tuesday night, April 9, 1901, at the residence of his niece, Mrs. Ernest Bean.

His sister, Mrs. C. S. French, is now the sole survivor of a large family.

The Sun extends to her and all the friends and relatives the condolence of the community.

## RESOLUTIONS ON THE DEATH OF COLONEL JOHN H. MOORE.

WHEREAS, It has pleased God, in His mysterious providence, to remove from our number Colonel John H. Moore, who, on the 9th day of April, 1901, ceased from his earthly labors and entered into rest ; therefore, be it

*Resolved,* That the Presbyterian Church has, in the death of this good man, lost one of her most honored and useful members.

His Christian life was a worthy example to all those who seek to follow in the footsteps of the "meek and lowly Jesus."

He devoted many of the latter years of his life almost exclusively to the Master's work, and as he was strongly averse to any thing that had the appearance of ostentation of his Christian labors, his ministrations were largely among the poor of our own community and throughout the mountains of Eastern Kentucky. He served his God faithfully and conscientiously.

2d. That as the Session of our Church, we hereby express our appreciation of the fellowship and co-operation we have enjoyed with him during the time he has been Elder of our church, and we hereby tender to his bereaved relatives the assurance of our sympathy in their sorrow, and we commend them all to the Word of God and to the comfort of the Holy Spirit.

3d. That a copy of these resolutions be handed to the family and another copy be furnished to the city newspapers for publication.

WM. T. McELROY,
*Moderator.*

J. D. SIMPSON,
*Clerk.*


## THOMAS MATHEW VAN METER.

Thomas Mathew, son of L. M. Van Meter, Sr., married Clifford Louise, daughter of James N. West and his wife, Isabella Atchison. She was born in Fayette County, Kentucky, March 30, 1874, and married September 19, 1899, in Lexington, Kentucky. Her grandparents were Dr. Charles William West and his wife, Hannah Sharp, who resided in St. John's Parish (now McEntosh County), Georgia. Her next ancestor was Charles West, who married and moved from Charlestown, South Carolina, to St. John's Parish in Georgia, and raised four children ; was born May 20, 1720 ; was an officer in the Colonial Army. He possessed large grants of land, and was a wealthy man. The four children were named Elizabeth, Samuel, Charles, and William. Samuel and Charles died unmarried. Her next ancestors, the parents of this Charles, were Samuel West and Sarah, his wife. This Samuel was a member of the first Colonial Parliament which was "held under treaties ; a Constitution and Commissioner in the Grand Council." This Samuel West's ancestor landed in Charlestown, South Carolina, in 1669, on the good ship "Carolina," one of a fleet of three vessels, and commanded by Captain Joseph West, and this Captain Joseph West succeeded Governor Sole as Governor of the Colony, and was afterward elected twice by the people to the office of Governor.

Isabella Atchison, mother of Clifford Louise, was a daughter of Hamilton Atchison and his wife, Sarah Rossiter ; same family of Atchisons as the Pettits descended from, as recorded in this book.

Sarah Evalyn Nephew, wife of Dr. C. W. West, traces back through a long and distinguished ancestry to 1685, when her ancestor, a French Huguenot, Count Jacques de la Sauvier, came over soon after the revocation of the Edict of Nantes and settled in the Southern Colony.

Thomas Mathew Van Meter has purchased a farm in Oklahoma and removed there, to engage in stock-raising and farming.

John S. Hanna, who married Evaline, daughter of L. M. Van Meter, as his second wife, was born in 1847, was a son of William Chenoworth Hanna and his wife, Margaret Smith, which wife was the mother of all of his children, although after her death he married for his second wife Miss Morrison, of Central Kentucky. Thomas Hanna's parents were Protestant Irish emigrants who came to Philadelphia at an early day and thence to Kentucky. They were among the early Presbyterian settlers of Kentucky. John S. Hanna's first wife was Mary Elizabeth Gay, a daughter of John T. Gay and his wife, Sarah, of Woodford County, Kentucky, and from this marriage he raised three daughters and one son, viz : Sallie Jane, Agnes Wilson, John Gay, and Maria Louise.

The mother of John S. Hanna, Agnes Morton, was a daughter of William Quin Morton and his wife, Elizabeth Venable, she a daughter of Judge James Venable. This Morton family came to Kentucky from Prince Edward County, Virginia, and descended from Huguenot refugees who came to Virginia soon after the revocation of the Edict of Nantes. The Venable family also came from Virginia to Kentucky.

## JOHN MILTON VAN METER.

John Milton, ninth son and youngest child of Isaac Van Meter and his wife, Rebecca, was born June 21, 1842; graduated at Center College, Danville, Kentucky; enlisted in the Southern Army in 1862, and served to the close of the war in Captain Nicholas' company of Colonel Cluke's regiment of General Morgan's command; was surrendered by Morgan and Cluke, and taken prisoner on the famous Ohio raid, and remained in prison eighteen months.

After the close of the war he married Alice Yerkes, of Danville, Kentucky, in March, 1866, and has four daughters, viz: Amanda Yerkes, Susan Allan, Elizabeth S., and Alice.

After the war he also graduated in law, and practiced for a few years in Lexington, Kentucky, but soon returned to his farm and followed that occupation since. For more than ten years he lived on a fine farm in Woodford County, Kentucky, but has since and to the present time resided on a farm three miles from Danville, in Boyle County, Kentucky. Is a prominent farmer and a useful and efficient elder of the Presbyterian Church.

John M. Van Meter enlisted in the Confederate Army when Generals Bragg and Kirby Smith invaded Kentucky in 1862, in Company E, Eighth Kentucky Cavalry. His first service was in Eastern Kentucky with General John H. Morgan, trying to prevent the escape of Federal General George Morgan from Cumberland Gap to Ohio, hoping to co-operate with General John S. Williams' command in its advance from West Virginia for the same purpose, but General George Morgan eluded both armies through the mountains and made his escape to Ohio. General John Morgan's command then returned to Central Kentucky, and a day or two after the Perryville battle it skirmished with the advance guard of General Buell on the Clark farm, near Danville, Kentucky, but finally after maneuvering on the flank and rear of the Federal Army, Morgan's command fell back through Cumberland Gap into East Tennessee; thence through Kingston and over the mountains to Murfreesboro into Middle Tennessee, and made a brilliant fight at Hartsville, where Morgan with 1,100 men surprised and captured 2,400 Federals.

The next important move was the Christmas raid of General Morgan on the Louisville & Nashville Railway into Kentucky, when the road was torn up as far as to Elizabethtown. Then after falling back into Tennessee, John M. Van Meter went with his regiment, detached and under command of Colonel R. S. Cluke, and made a raid into Central and Eastern Kentucky, thus returning for the first time to his home and native county and giving a great surprise to friend and foe. Colonel Cluke made a very successful raid, taking many more Federal prisoners than he commanded of Confederates, with immense quantity of army stores, wagons, mules, etc. He could only parole the soldiers, burn the stores and wagons, and take the drove of mules and horses out with him. This was in the months of January and February, 1863, and he finally fell back to Monticello with very few casualties, but with very hard, laborious marching, and plenty of excitement to prevent any despondency or lack of courage.

The next movement of importance was the Ohio raid in July, 1863, and that was almost a continuous daily skirmish from the time he crossed the Tennessee line into Kentucky until General Morgan surrendered in Ohio, up near the Pennsylvania line. John M. Van Meter surrendered on the last day of that raid with Colonel Cluke and General Morgan ; was kept in prisons Camp Chase and Camp Douglas until 1865, more than eighteen months, when finally he was paroled, sent around for exchange to Richmond, Virginia ; was never exchanged, but was near Appomattox when General Lee surrendered. They were to have been declared exchanged at a certain time, and had promised to not take up arms until they were exchanged, but before the time arrived General Lee surrendered.

J. M. Van Meter relates thus : During this interval our command, just from prison, was sent up on the railroad between Lynchburg and Abingdon to be fed wherever we could get persons to keep us. We remained for a few weeks at Salem, Virginia, but after the surrender at Appomattox I left with five or six others to go toward the Mississippi River, and on this trip we spent the night near Doublin Station, in Pulaski County, Virginia, at the home of Mr. Alexander Mathews, who was away from home with his only son. During the conversation with the family, Mrs. Mathews learned that I was a son of Rebecca Cunningham, who had been a special friend and perhaps a schoolmate in former years. So, when we left next morning she called me back, after the others had gotten beyond ear-shot, and gave me $11.00 in silver and gold.

Elias Campbell, Jessie Spencer, John "Street" Van Meter, a young Smith, and a young Veal, and perhaps a few others, whose names I do not recall, were in our party. We came to Knoxville,

Tennessee, where we were arrested and required to take the oath of allegiance to the Federal Government. We were kept in camp there for a few days, and during that time I determined to see if I could not get some money from home through the banks. I saw the cashier of a national bank there, and he agreed to cash my check for $1,000.00, with $25.00 discount, if I would have $1,000.00 put to my credit in the bank of D. A. Sayre & Co., in Lexington, Kentucky, by wire. I. C. Van Meter put the money there with very little delay, and I gave the national bank in Knoxville my check for $1,000.00, and he paid me $975.00 in greenbacks. I reserved enough to get me home comfortably, and divided the balance among the boys, giving each one only what was really needed to get. him home. In a short time all that I had distributed was paid back to me, and a large interest was paid in gratitude. When we arrived at Nashville we got good clothes, bathed and barbered, rode on freight cars to Louisville, and thence to Lexington. When we got to Knoxville we had much trouble in getting entertainment, even of the poorest kind ; but finally were allowed to sleep on some man's kitchen floor, and while we were there the family learned that one of the men who were sleeping on the floor had cashed a check on a Lexington bank for $1,000.00, and then the family sent a basket of good things to us to atone for their treatment. There was much persecution of Southern sympathizers then at Knoxville by the Federal authorities. So that I did not blame the people for the treatment we received.

Soon after my return home I sent a shorthorn calf to Mrs. A. Mathews, of Pulaski County, Virginia, who had so generously given me the $11.00 in specie, and named the calf Token. I could think of nothing that would be of more real benefit to that naturally great cattle country, to rebuild the interest there, than a pure bred shorthorn bull, and years afterward I heard with great satisfaction of the benefit he had been to Mr. Mathews and that country in the improvement of cattle stock.

### WEDDING OF MISS ELIZABETH VAN METER AND MR. JOHN WOODFORD.

[Taken from the Danville Advocate.]

Mr. John Woodford, of Bourbon County, and Miss Elizabeth Van Meter were married this afternoon at one o'clock at the First Presbyterian Church (October 24. 1900).

It was a white and green wedding, and one of the prettiest of the year. The pulpit, banked with palms and ferns and studded with a huge cluster of immense white chrysanthemums, made a beautiful background for the wedding tableau.

At one o'clock the bridal party entered the crowded church, while Mr. Zeigler played Mendelssohn's march. The ushers came first, two by two, through the front doors, crossed and took opposite positions on either side of the pulpit. The four bridesmaids followed, in like order, and stood just in front of the ushers. The bride and groom came in together from the right door, and were met at the pulpit by the ministers.

The ceremony was pronounced by Rev. J. S. Van Meter, an uncle of the bride, from Clinton, Missouri, assisted by Dr. E. M. Green. During the ceremony, which was impressively worded, the organist rendered the beautiful "Call Me Thine Own."

No prettier bride was ever wedded in this old church. She was handsomely gowned in white mousseline de soie over white taffeta, trimmed in orange blossoms. Her veil was caught up with orange blossoms and held in place by a pearl pin which was worn at her mother's wedding. She carried a larger shower bouquet of white rosebuds and lilies of the valley.

The bridesmaids — Misses Martha Clay and Elizabeth Woodford, of Paris, Alice Van Meter and Amelia Yerkes—were attired in white organdie and carried white chrysanthemums. The ushers were Messrs. Samuel Woodford, Brooks Clay, Ford Brent, and Duncan Bell, all of Paris.

After the ceremony the bridal party went to the home of Hon. John W. Yerkes, an uncle of the bride, where an elegant luncheon was spread, and at four o'clock this afternoon Mr. and Mrs. Woodford left for a bridal trip East. On their return they will be at home on the groom's farm, near Paris.

Mr. Woodford is the son of Mr. Buckner Woodford, cashier of the Bourbon Bank, at Paris, and is one of the most popular and successful young men of his county. His bride is a daughter of Mr. and Mrs. John M. Van Meter, of this county. She has been a general favorite in Danville society, not only because of her brightness of mind and her amiability, but also on account of her goodness of heart and depth of character. Mr. Woodford is indeed to be congratulated.

Alice, the wife of John Milton Van Meter, was the daughter of Rev. Stephen Yerkes, D. D., and his wife, Amanda Lovell. Dr. Yerkes was born at Hatborough, a suburb of Philadelphia, Pennsylvania, June 27, 1817. He was the son of Stephen Yerkes, Sr., and his wife, Alice Watson. Stephen Yerkes, Sr., was one of the active movers in suppressing the whisky rebellion in Pennsylvania during Washington's administration. His ancestors came from Saxony and received deeds for lands from William Penn. Alice Watson was the daughter of John Watson and his wife, a Miss Yerkes, whose six brothers were Presbyterian elders, and were among the founders of the "Log College," which afterward became Princeton College. Rev. Stephen Yerkes, D. D., graduated from Yale College at the age of twenty years, in 1837, and soon after this located in Baltimore and engaged in teaching, thus becoming allied with the educational interests of that city. In 1851 he was called to a professorship at Transylvania University in Lexington, Kentucky, and later was elected to the chair of Hebrew and Oriental languages in the Danville, Kentucky, Presbyterian Theological Seminary, and was identified with this institution for the balance of his life.

Dr. Yerkes was twice married; first, as above stated, to Amanda Lovell, daughter of William Lovell, of Baltimore, and from this union were born six children, four of whom survived their father, namely, Professor William L. Yerkes, of Paris, Kentucky; Honorable John W. Yerkes, until very recently of Danville, Kentucky, but now, by appointment of President McKinley to Commissioner of Internal Revenue, he resides in Washington City, after having made a very active and exciting race as candidate of the Republican party for Governor of Kentucky; Alice, wife of John M. Van Meter, as before stated, and Elizabeth, wife of Rev. John Stonestreet Van Meter, of Missouri.

After the death of Dr. Yerkes' first wife, in 1872, he married, in 1875, Mrs. Amelia Rodes Anderson. Dr. Stephen Yerkes died March 28, 1896, and his last wife survived him only a few years. Dr. Yerkes was a classical and thorough scholar with extraordinary attainments, and he walked with God through a long and useful life.

Isaac Van Meter and his wife, Rebecca, the above named parents, were for many years consistent and influential members of the Presbyterian Church ; the former being an elder and one of the chief pillars of the Winchester Church, besides being a regular contributor to the support of two other churches in the country for many years, and up to the time of his death, which occurred October 8, 1854, at the age of sixty years and fourteen days. His widow, our beloved mother, survived him some ten years, and died in 1864, while two of her sons and one of her grandsons were in the Southern army. She passed through many hardships and severe trials during the last years of her life, but endured all with great Christian fortitude.

Solomon Van Meter, second son of Colonel Jacob and his wife, Tabitha, was born April 3, 1796, and died at twenty-one years of age. Joseph Inskeep Van Meter, their third son, and Benjamin Franklin Van Meter, their fourth son, both died in youth, in January, 1805.

Abram Van Meter, their fifth son, was born September 24, 1804 ; married Elizabeth Ann, daughter of David and Hannah Van Meter, June 21, 1827. She was born February 19, 1810. They resided for about ten years after their marriage in their native county of Hardy, in Virginia, on a part of the old Fort Pleasant landed estate of their ancestry, and then removed, in 1837 or 1838, to the farm in Fayette County, Kentucky, about four miles north-west of Lexington, where Colonel Thomas Lewis had lived and died. They purchased this farm and spent the balance of their lives on it. They had ten children born to them ; seven lived to be grown, and six are now living. John, their eldest son, was born March 21, 1828, and died when about fifteen years of age.

Jacob, their second son, was born August 4, 1829 ; married Elizabeth McDaniel, of Canonsburg, Pennsylvania, March 2, 1852, and raised two children, a son, named John, who lived to be grown, but died unmarried ; and a daughter named Mary, who is still living and married to Mr. Russell.

## ABRAM VAN METER.

Abram Van Meter, fifth son of Jacob and his wife, Tabitha, was born September 24, 1804 ; married Elizabeth Ann, daughter of David Van Meter and his wife, Hannah, both before mentioned. She was born February 19, 1810. They resided for about ten years after their marriage on a part of the old Fort Pleasant landed estate of their ancestry, and then removed in 1837 or 1838 to the farm in Fayette County, Kentucky, about four miles northwest of Lexington, where Colonel Thomas Lewis had lived and died. They purchased this farm and spent the balance of their lives upon it. They had ten children born to them ; seven lived to be grown, and six are now living. John, their eldest son, was born March 21, 1828, and died when about fifteen years of age. Jacob, their second son, was born August 4, 1829 ; was educated at college in Canonsburg, Pennsylvania, where he married Elizabeth McDaniel, March 2, 1852, and raised two children. a son named John, who lived to be grown, but died unmarried ; and a daughter named Mary, who is still living, and married to Mr. Russell, of Seattle, of the State of Washington. Jacob Van Meter and his wife lived in Illinois for several years, but he died in Fayette County, Kentucky, in 1862. His widow has since married Colonel Shallenberger, and is now living near Washington City, D. C.

James, their fourth son, was born June 14, 1832 ; married Fannie Lewis, October 28, 1858. They had eight children born to them, four of whom are still living. Fannie, his wife, died June 27, 1880. Their living children are named Clara, Amelia, James, and Abram. They resided in Lexington, Kentucky, until recently, when they removed to Frankfort, Kentucky.

Samuel, their fifth son, was born April 10, 1834 ; married Mary Whitney, of Canonsburg, Pennsylvania, and they are living in Mattoon, Illinois. They have no children.

William C., their sixth son, was born February 29, 1836 ; married Mary, the only daughter of Thomas G. Sudduth, Esq., of Clark County, Kentucky, and they raised three daughters named Alice, Ella, and Mary. The wife died in 187–. Alice married Mr. Bell Rash, and they reside in Shelby County, Kentucky. Ella married Bryan Prewitt, of Fayette County, Kentucky, where they now reside. Mary, the youngest child, married Mr. Willie Miller, and he is now dead and left no children ; Mary resides in Winchester, Kentucky. William C. Van Meter resides in Shelby County, Kentucky.

Hannah T., the oldest daughter of Abram Van Meter, was born February 1, 1841 ; married Charles C. McDaniel, of Canonsburg, Pennsylvania, December 5, 1860. They reside in Terre Haute, Indiana. Have no children.

Elizabeth Ann ("Bettie Skip"), youngest child of Abram Van Meter, was born November 10, 1849; married J. C. Galbraith, and they are now living in Parsons, Kansas. Have no children.

Abram Van Meter and his wife, Elizabeth Ann, were influential members of the Presbyterian Church. He was chosen an elder of the first church in Lexington soon after he came to Fayette County, and he took a very active part in religious affairs up to the time of his death, which occurred in 1864. His widow survived him only a short time, dying in the same year.

## GARRETT VAN METER.

Garrett Van Meter, sixth son of Colonel Jacob and his wife, Tabitha, was born near old Fort Pleasant, April 20, 1806, and inherited a part of the old Fort Pleasant tract of land handed down to him from his father's estate. He married Miss Elizabeth Cunningham, of Hardy County, Virginia (now West Virginia), and reared a worthy family of nine children. He died August 10, 1865, having lived to the age of fifty-nine years, and left a widow and nine children to survive him. He spent his life on a part of the estate where he was born. He was a quiet, unassuming, honest farmer; for many years a worthy member of the Methodist Church, and lived and died a Christian gentleman. After his death the Virginia homestead was sold, and the widow with most of her family removed to a large and very valuable tract of several thousand acres of land in Piatt County, Illinois, near Mansfield, of which his estate was possessed at the time of his death. There the widow died in 1892, leaving nine children to survive her.

The children of Garrett and his wife, Elizabeth, were: Solomon, who married Miss Jemima J. Parsons, of West Virginia; Jacob, who married Miss Anna Harness, of West Virginia; William C., who married Miss Margaret Chambers, of West Virginia; Rebecca, who married Rev. Mr. Crews, a Methodist minister; Isaac Newton; Tabitha; Charles W.; Sallie, who married Mr. Cunningham, of West Virginia; and Garrett. Nearly all of the above-named sons who were old enough for military service at the time of the last war were soldiers in the Southern army; nearly all bear honorable scars received in that unpleasantness, but all yet survive, and are all farmers in West Virginia or in the West.

Solomon, eldest child of Garrett Van Meter and his wife, Elizabeth I. (Cunningham), was born in Hardy County, West Virginia, as before stated, February 19, 1833 ; was reared to manhood on a part of the lands which his father inherited of the Fort Pleasant tract which had come down in an unbroken line since the grant purchased through Governor Gooch from King George 3d by Isaac Van Meter when he built the fort in 1744. Solomon was educated at the best schools of that vicinity at that time. When the Civil War began to threaten he joined Company B, Fourteenth Virginia Militia, Captain Isaac Stickley and Colonel William H. Harness in command of the regiment, but Colonel Harness resigned this command and raised a cavalry company, March 10, 1862.

Solomon joined the Confederate Army April 20, 1861, Company B, Sixty-second Virginia Infantry, which was regularly organized October 25, 1862, at Monterey, Highland County, Virginia, John J. Chipley, Captain. Solomon had a severe attack of typhoid fever in March, 1862, and was placed in care of Dr. Higgins, at Wardinsville, Virginia, and was taken a prisoner when he had nearly recovered from his illness, on the 29th of March, 1862, by twenty-five Yankee cavalry called Union Guards from Pennsylvania and Maryland, who were led by a Union man named Anderson. He was taken first to Winchester (David Pearce Van Meter was taken a prisoner at the same time), and there delivered to the Provost Marshal, who took a critical description of them, and they were then placed in jail, but were soon taken to General Shields' headquarters, asked a few questions, and then returned to jail, where they were fed on crackers and rice for three days ; after which the ladies of the town found this out and brought them plenty of good food.

General Shields offered to give them their liberty if they would take the oath of allegiance, which was declined. April 1st they were taken to Baltimore and placed in jail there, and on April 2d were taken on board the "Henry W. Gaw" to Fort Delaware, where they remained four months, and then taken by the ocean route to Fortress Monroe, and thence up the James River, August 5th, to Akins Landing, and there exchanged. On this trip they saw where the "Congress" and the "Cumberland" had been sunk by the "Merrimac." They went from there to Richmond, and soon joined their regiment. Solomon was in a very severe battle at New Market, May 15, 1864 — his regiment and brigade. The battle

was fought by General John C. Breckinridge, of Kentucky.  The
battle continued from twelve until dusk.   He says : '' Our regiment
went into this battle with five hundred and twenty effective men,
and came out of it with two hundred and eighty, all the others
killed or wounded.   We routed the enemy under General Sigel,
and drove them several miles from the battlefield and captured
five pieces of artillery.   We camped the night after the battle on
Roods Hill, near Mt. Jackson.   The roll of each company of the
Sixty-second Regiment was called, and a list of the killed and
wounded was taken.   Our loss was two hundred and forty men,
according to General Imboden's report.   Our flag was completely
cut into fragments.   July 19, 1864, we were engaged in a severe
fight at Berry's Ferry, which lasted nearly three hours.   The Federals charged us, but we held our position and finally drove them
across the river with considerable loss to the enemy.   In the fight
we had one man instantly killed and several wounded.   General
John S. Mosby aided us greatly by attacking the enemy just on the
other side of the mountain from us, thus drawing off their force so
that we could drive them.   We were engaged in a lively fight at
Charlestown, Jefferson County, October 18, 1864, where we captured five hundred prisoners, some horses, arms, and ammunition,
with a considerable wagon train.   We fought and fell back in good
order to Berryville, bringing our prisoners and booty safely with us.
We were engaged in a lively skirmish for nearly an hour at Bunker
Hill, September 3, 1864, where we captured some New York
cavalry.   The enemy nearly surrounded us, but we made our
escape down a steep hollow, with the enemy on both sides and our
rear, and brought our prisoners with us.   On July 3, 1863, our
command was within about six miles of the furious battle of Gettysburg and could hear its roar, but did not participate directly in it.
We were in the battle of Cold Harbor, June 3, 1864.   The Yankees
charged our fortifications, three columns deep, with great fury, but
we drove them back and forced them to the timber with great
slaughter, and on the 5th of the same month, at the same place,
the enemy made another determined attack on our rifle-pits and
were repulsed with severe loss.

   '' October 15, 1864, I was on guard with strict orders to not let
officers or privates pass without a written order from General
Imboden.   I called five times to a staff officer of General Lomax
to halt, which he entirely disregarded until I shot and barely missed

his face.   He reported me to Lomax, who came to me and said :
'Allow me to compliment you for doing your duty ; shoot again if
it is needed, and I will stand between you and danger.'

I was in the seven days' fight below Richmond, and we saw warm
service there.   April 4, 1865, while at home on a furlough to get a
fresh horse, I heard that General Lee had surrendered, which was
untrue, as he did not surrender until the 9th.   I bought a horse,
and with my captain (Chipley) and two others of our company
started for Staunton to join our command, but had only passed Mt.
Solar a few miles when we met Colonel White, of the Twenty-
third Virginia Cavalry, who informed us that the Federals had
possession of Staunton, and my captain, after complimenting me
upon having always done my duty as a soldier, told me to go home
and take the first opportunity to secure a furlough, which I did, at
New Creek (now Kyser), a few days after this."

Solomon Van Meter moved to Illinois in 1867, but returned to
West Virginia and was married, December 31, 1867, to Jemima J.
Parsons, daughter of David Parsons and his wife, Mildred Mullidy.
The Parsons and the Mullidy families were both of reputable old
Virginia stock.   Solomon and his bride returned immediately to
their new home in Illinois, where they have resided since.   They
are now living in Mansfield, Piatt County, Illinois, with two living
children, viz: William Thompson, born October 31, 1872, and
Lelia Vernon, born October 13, 1875, all consistent members of the
Presbyterian Church.   I have heard an amusing story told of an
occurrence which took place when this Solomon was making some
hard forced marches and fighting hard in the mean time, perhaps
under General John C. Breckinridge.   There was another Solomon
Van Meter, much older than this one and from the same valley and
neighborhood, a son of David Van Meter, and whose business it
was to supply this division of the army with beef cattle and other
meat, as it could be had.   The two Solomons, who had not seen
each other for some time, met on a hot, dusty road, and this one
tired and well worn from forced marching and hard service.   Each
one saluted the other with, "How are you, Cousin Sol?" and this
one enquired very particularly about all the folks at home, and then
the elder Solomon asked this one how he was standing the service,
and received the reply : "Well, I can tell you, Cousin Sol, this is
a mighty hard way to serve the Lord," and they bade each other
good-bye.

## WILLIAM C. VAN METER.

William C. Van Meter, third son of Garrett Van Meter, was born at his father's homestead in the Old Fields of Hardy County, and educated along with his brothers at the best schools of that vicinity.

He says: "When the war came on I enlisted early under Captain J. C. B. Mullen, who was very soon taken prisoner, and we then had for our Captain, William McCoy, of Pendleton County, who died with typhoid fever the first autumn after the war commenced, and after his death we elected for our Captain, Edd Boggs, of Pendleton County, who finally resigned, and Lieutenant John Johnson was made Captain. I belonged to Company E, Twenty-fifth Regiment of Virginia Infantry, General Johnson's Brigade, Ewell's division of Jackson's corps.

"The greater part of my army life was spent in a corps of 20,-000 to 30,000 infantry, and unlike the cavalry, we made no dashing raids or performed any great feat single handed. I was in twenty-seven engagements, the most important of which were: Battle of Rich Mountain, Allegheny Mountain, McDowell, Winchester, Gaines Mill, Malvern Hill, Cedar Mountain, second battle of Manasses, Sharpsburg, Fredericksburg, Gettysburg, three days in the Wilderness, and Spottsylvania Court-house.

"I was wounded through the right shoulder at the battle of Rich Mountain, and struck in the side in the second day's battle in the Wilderness; was taken a prisoner at the battle of Sharpsburg, having been left by order of our Brigade Commander to take charge of the wounded who could not be moved."

William C. appears to have not thought a wound in his hand of sufficient consequence to even mention it in his letter to me, but as I have it authentic, I will give it anyway. While he was leaning against a tree with his hands in his pockets, conversing with an officer and waiting for orders, a spent ball or piece of shell struck his hand in his pocket and gave it a bruise, which left him only one hand fit for service for some time.

There are very few men hale and hearty to-day as is William C. Van Meter, who experienced as much severe and dangerous military service as he did. He followed Stonewall Jackson as long as he lived through the war, and then followed his successor to the close of the struggle.

He is now a successful farmer of Grant County, West Virginia; married in 1868, Margaret Chambers, daughter of Dr. Jacob Kenny Chambers, of Grant County, West Virginia, and has raised to be grown three daughters and two son, viz : Norah, who married Howard Cunningham ; Kenny ; Tabitha Vernon, who married John Harness, Jr., of Hardy County, West Virginia ; Virginia Seymour, and William C., Jr., "the child of his old age."

Dr. J. K. Chambers and his wife were from a prominent family who came from Ireland and settled near Staunton, now West Virginia, and Dr. Chambers removed from there to Petersburg, Grant County, at the upper end of the South Branch Valley, where he was a prominent physician for many years.

## CHARLES WASHINGTON VAN METER.

Charles Washington, fourth son of Garrett and Elizabeth C. Van Meter, was born at his father's homestead in Hardy County, now West Virginia, December 5, 1837, and was educated in the best schools of that vicinity until 1857, when he and his older brother, Jacob, removed to Missouri and commenced farming on quite a large scale until the war between the States began in 1861.

He joined a volunteer company in that State and served one day under Colonel Marmaduke, to assist in capturing some boats loaded with arms for the Union forces in Kansas. This company disbanded, and about this time Virginia seceded, and he lost no time in getting back to his native State, and joined a company in Moorefield, Virginia, commanded by Captain Hays, July 1, 1861. This company was consolidated with a Hampshire company very soon after this, and was commanded by Captain Sheets, and was connected with Colonel Turner Ashby's cavalry regiment. He enlisted in this regiment for one year, and at the expiration of that time, when he was called on to enlist, he and a large majority of his company re-enlisted for "forty-five years, or during the war," and this company furnished their own arms and horses.

This regiment operated principally in the South Branch Valley and the Shenandoah Valley for the first eighteen months or two years, and had many skirmishes and picket fights, and occasionally one more severe, such as Slone's Cross-roads, Capon Bridge, Martinsburg, Charlestown, Moorefield, Harper's Ferry, and others. They were in the Kirnstown Battle, March 23, 1861, and with Jackson in the Banks race down the valley to the Potomac, and the Strasburg Battle, and Cross Keys, and Port Republic, and Cedar Mountain against Banks, August 9th.

Having kept no diary, Charles W. can give few dates after thirty-five years have elapsed since all this occurred. He was in the Battle of Harper's Ferry when Jackson took in Miles with 11,000 men, and was in the great Gettysburg Battle of July 1st to the 3rd, and he was taken a prisoner between Boonesborough and Funkstown in a hand-to-hand fight with the Eighth Regulars, while covering the retreat of the Confederate Army after that great battle. Was taken to Frederick City, Maryland, for a few days, thence to Fort McHenry, Baltimore, for about a week, and then to Fort Delaware, where he remained for two months, then removed to Port Lookout, Maryland, finishing out ten months in prison, and was then exchanged with a load of sick, and landed at Aiken's Landing, near Richmond, in May, 1864. After a short furlough at home he returned to the command, which he found at Petersburg, near Richmond, and a few days after he joined his command it made the famous raid to the rear of Grant's Army, under General Wade Hampton with three brigades of cavalry, where they captured quite a number of Federal Cavalry armed with sixteen-shooters, and brought out about 2,800 good fat beeves.

Here his cousin, Milton Van Meter, was killed, but Charles brought his remains out with the command, and the body was finally interred in the family cemetery. After this his service with his regiment was with General Lee's Army around Richmond, until the close of the war, April 9, 1865, when Lee surrendered at Appomattox. Charles W. says: "When we learned of Lee's intention to surrender, a committee from the companies and regiments waited on Major-General Rosser, commanding our wing of the cavalry, and informed him that they did not intend to surrender with the army, and if the officers were through with them, as they owned their horses and arms, they proposed to ride out or die in the attempt. General Rosser sent word back to his officers to keep their men together and he would take them out in a body, then cutting loose from all extra baggage they prepared for the ride and were soon off in a fast trot and lope to Leesburg, distant about twenty miles, ready for any thing that might turn up, but to their great surprise they were not required to fire a shot. Meeting no enemy, they camped for the night at Leesburg, and the next morning were drawn up in line and disbanded to return home, with the understanding that we were to meet General Rosser within ten days at Staunton, to go south and join General Joseph E. Johnson's Army."

The Van Meters, viz., Bell, David, " Big Isaac," and Charles W., went home together and met four or five of the old Van Meters (their fathers and others) at the junction of the lane with the main Moorefield Road, where a consultation was held, and it was finally settled that they might go South if they went in a body, with an officer in command. They went to the Shenandoah Valley with eight or ten others a few days after this and found that General Johnson had surrendered, so they returned home and gave up the fight, without a parole or surrender in it, and so it is to this date.

Charles went to farming and stuck to it until about eight years ago, when he with his sister, Tabitha, and his brothers, Isaac and Garrett, none of whom have ever married, built a nice mansion in Mansfield, Illinois, where they now all reside together.

Their father died a few years after the close of the war and left an estate of several thousand acres of land near to this city, and these four with their brothers, Jacob and Solomon (this last named having been noticed before in this volume), inherited these lands and still own their farms, though they all reside in the city. Jacob, as before mentioned, married Ann Harness and removed to Missouri before the war, and after the death of his father removed to and took possession of his portion of the Illinois estate, where he still resides.

Garrett, the youngest child, born in 1849, was not in the army, and is a thrifty farmer and bachelor.

Isaac Newton, here above mentioned, was in the army along with his brothers, and participated in nearly all of the battles which either of them have mentioned.

Sarah Inskeep (Sallie), youngest child of Colonel Jacob Van Meter and his wife, Tabitha Inskeep, was born September 26, 1810 ; married William Streit Cunningham, of Hardy County, now West Virginia, and lived for nearly all their lives on a farm near Petersburg, at the upper end of the South Branch Valley, very near to where the Cunningham family settled when they came from Ireland to this valley, and where they reared a family of seven children, six of whom are still living

After Mr. Cunningham's health became impaired, they removed to Moorefield, West Virginia, where he spent the remnant of his days. This husband and wife were for many years influential members of the Methodist Church, and left the following named children: John, who married Mary Virginia Fout, of Frederick County, Maryland; Jacob, who married Emma Grove, of Maryland; Susan, who married Judge John M. Van Meter, of Chillicothe, Ohio; Rebecca Lanck, who married Edward A. Alexander, of Moorefield, West Virginia; Anna, who married Colonel Henry M. Trueheart, of Galveston, Texas; William Streit, who married Henrietta Austin, of Tom Green County, Texas; and Joseph, who married Emma McMeekin, of Moorefield, West Virginia.

We have more in this volume in regard to W. Streit Cunningham under the head of the Cunningham Family. John, above mentioned, who married Mary Virginia Fout, raised two children, who are still living, viz., Virgie, a daughter, who married Dr. S. D. Van Meter, and they are living in Denver, Colorado, and Wilber E., a son grown and in the mercantile business.

Mary Virginia, here named, was a daughter of Greenberry Fout and his wife, Ann Eliza Grove, of Maryland. Mary Virginia, wife of John Cunningham, died June 13, 1894.

Jacob Cunningham, here above named, married Emma Grove, of Maryland, and they reside in or near Washington City.

Susan T. and her husband, Judge John Marshall Van Meter, reside in Chillicothe, Ohio, and have two living children by this marriage. She is his second wife, and more is given of him under the head of Van Meters.

Rebecca L., who married Edgar Alexander, lived and died in Moorefield, West Virginia, and raised two children, named Bernard C. and Mary; the latter married Major John Johnston, and they are the parents of Mary Johnston, the now noted authoress. She is their oldest child.

Annie V., who married Colonel H. M. Trueheart, has five children, viz: Sallie C., who married Albert Sidney Williams; Henry M., Jr., Annie V., Rebecca, and Elvira. Colonel Trueheart resides in Galveston, Texas; was a gallant and daring soldier in McNeill's Rangers during the late unpleasantness; is a banker and extensive capitalist, and influential member of the church and worker in the Sabbath-school.

Joseph I., who married Emma McMeekin, raised two children, named William Streit and Mary. They reside in Moorefield, West Virginia.

William Streit, Jr., youngest child of William Streit and his wife, Sallie V., and who married Henrietta Austin, and who resides in Tom Green County, Texas, has raised five children, viz : Austin, Sarah, William, Hal, and Valeria Hebert.

William S. Cunningham, here mentioned, enlisted in the United States Army for the war against Spain ; was made a Lieutenant of a company in the Thirty-third Texas Volunteers, and after the bloody battle of San Jacinto, where Major Logan was killed, he was made Captain. He is now in the army in the Philippines ; was with the battalion which captured Aguinaldo's wife and mother, and did the best military service yet reported from there, and appears to be maintaining the reputation achieved by the Cunninghams, centuries before he was born, away back in the bloody glens of old Scotland, where with glittering steel and helmet they gained military fame, and which has been fully maintained from that day to this.

For the following the author is indebted to Mrs. Anna L. Thompson, of Clinton, Iowa :

John first of Berkeley, as he has been called to distinguish him from other Johns, was a son of John Van Meter, the Indian trader, and brother to Isaac, of Old Fields, Fort Pleasant.

Owing to the fact that many old county documents were burned at Martinsburg, Virginia, during the Civil War, the records of his descendants can not be given with the fullness and accuracy that might otherwise be possible. The names of the children of John first of Berkeley are taken from his will, which was probated in 1745 at Winchester, (now) Frederic County. The will distributed John's share of the original grant of 40,000 acres of land.

According to records in possession of some of his descendants, the father was married first to Sarah Berdine or Bertine, a name that appears among the early Huguenot exiles of New Amsterdam ; and afterwards to a Margaret, whose family cognomen is lost, but whose baptismal name has been faithfully kept in every generation even unto the present. The children were : Abraham, Isaac, Henry, Jacob, Sarah, Mary, Rebecca, Elizabeth, Magdalena, Rachel, and Joanese or John.

This Joanese had a son Johan, who had the distinction of being the first white child born west of the Blue Ridge Mountains, and the yet greater honor of being a member of Washington's staff. He was a "mighty hunter," and died of pneumonia contracted by throwing himself upon the wet ground when heated from the chase.

Elizabeth married Thomas Shepherd, for whom Shepherdstown is named. It is built upon land inherited by his wife. Shepherd was one of the executors of her father's will.

Abraham, son of John first of Berkeley, married Ruth Hedges, and after her death Mrs. Martha Wheeler, *nee* Roberts. His children were: Joseph, Rebecca, Jacob, Mary, Abraham, Isaac, Ruth, Hannah, Daniel, and John, the last four being children of the second marriage.

The Hedges are a family with a history of romantic interest. The American branch, so the story goes, descends from Joseph, son of Sir Charles, Secretary of State under Queen Anne of England, and a very great man in general. One version has it that Joseph married some "daughter of a hundred Earls," or at least of higher degree than himself. This estranged the lady's family and high-born friends, and, finding herself a stranger to her own, desired to leave England, and they fled to Maryland in 1734, whence their descendants radiate toward all points of the compass. There was a tradition that at the end of a hundred years an enormous fortune would be divided among the surviving heirs. The century ended about the close of the first quarter of last. For many years a large "Hedges Association" existed for the purpose of recovering the estate, which, alas, has not been accomplished.

It was doubtless the John of this family who, one day when he was at a neighbor's breaking flax, heard the report of guns, and looking toward his home saw that it had been attacked by a band of Indians. They burned his house and murdered his wife, daughter, and two small sons. Three older boys, Abram, Isaac, and John, were working in a field, and they were carried away. Two of them afterwards escaped, but John, the youngest, grew up with his captors and married a young Indian girl. He sometimes visited his relatives, but could not be persuaded to abandon the free life of the forest. Hannah, the daughter who was murdered, was at a spring washing. She had on a sunbonnet that concealed her face. One of the savages sank a tomahawk into her head, but when they saw that she was young and beautiful they lamented the act, saying that "she would have made a pretty squaw."

The story of this massacre was told by the notorious Simon Girty, who took part in it, and is taken from a book of notes on the settlement of Western Virginia and Pennsylvania. The tragedy occurred in the vicinity of Fort Van Meter, to which the family was accustomed to flee in times of danger.

Joseph Van Meter, son of Abraham, was born about the year 1743. He married his first cousin, Margaret Morgan. Their children were: Morgan, Joseph, William, Abram, Ibba, and Isaac.

Margaret Morgan is reported to have been nearly related to General Daniel Morgan of Revolutionary fame; the proofs of this, however, are not at present available.

Joseph was lost from a hunting party in the year 1778. He was last seen with a Mr. Hite attempting to cross the Ohio River in a canoe during a high wind. Whether they were drowned or captured by lurking Indians was never known. No trace of the boat was found; but forty years after, one summer when the water was unusually low, some boys playing about a sandbar discovered a gun-barrel that was easily identified as having belonged to Joseph's gun. It is narrated in a local history that a blacksmith undertook to heat the iron for some purpose, when the charge put into it by Joseph's hand forty years before exploded. Joseph held a commission in Washington's army, and it was on his part of the old grant that Fort Van Metre stood, the scene of many stirring events, witness of many tragedies. It was here that Major Sam McColloch, one of the greatest Indian fighters of history, spent his last heroic days, as Commandant, and here his mutilated body was buried.

It is told in the local chronicles of the place that the Indians, who were anxious to take him alive, because they believed that if they should eat his heart while it was yet warm with his life-blood they would become "brave like Collaca," once had him surrounded on three sides, while on the fourth was a cliff descending almost perpendicularly for nearly a hundred feet. He plunged down the precipice that his enemies had taken no pains to guard, swam the river, and reached the gates of the fort. The men inside, alive to the danger of opening them, hesitated; a woman—and a Van Metre woman, too—ran to the gates and let him in. Not long after this McColloch, accompanied by his brother, left the fort to reconnoiter. Impressed by a premonition of disaster, the Major returned and left his watch and a message for his wife. Two miles out he was ambushed and shot, the savages having abandoned all hope of being able to take him alive. They cut his warm heart from his body and devoured it, and hung the rest of the viscera upon the branch of a tree. Mrs. Vincent Van Metre, who lives in the vicinity of the old Colonial fort, describes the tree as still standing near her home.

Besides the John Van Metre before referred to as having lost his home and family, there was another of the name who one day left the shelter of the stockade to plough in an adjoining field. He took several of his children with him, as the savages were not thought to be in the region at that time, but as always, he carried his gun. Suddenly he perceived Indians moving in the timber. He knew there was no chance of reaching the fort with the little people if he ran. He placed himself between them and their enemies, and told them to run for their lives. He succeeded in holding the red men in check until a bullet found his heart just as the children were clambering over a fence that stood between them and the fort. All got over except the youngest, a little fellow who fell back after reaching the top. He was seized and carried away. There is a tradition that years afterward his identity was discovered in a curious way. When he was sober he had apparently no recollection of who he was, but being overfond of "strong waters," he was sometimes intoxicated. Then he would say, "John Van Metre." This coming to the knowledge of the old men, they followed up the clue and found that it was indeed their brother. He was persuaded to return to them, but always when the "hunting moon" came round he would for a time abandon civilization for the haunts and habits of the red men.

Isaac, son of Joseph, disposed of his ancestral acres and servants, and with two or three of his brothers migrated to Bourbon County, Kentucky. He married Mary Caldwell, daughter of William and Mary (McCune) Caldwell, of Scotch-Irish extraction. She is said by those who knew her to have been a woman of a fine mind, finely trained, and a sweet Christian character. Isaac and Mary were married March 9, 1797. Their children were : Margaret, born May 29, 1798 ; Joseph, March 13, 1800 ; William, June 24, 1802 ; Agnes, April 4, 1804 ; Morgan, May 3, 1806 ; Sarah, June 14, 1808 ; Elizabeth, February 18, 1811 ; Isaac, January 2, 1813 ; Mary Ann, April 2, 1815.

Margaret married James W. Brown in 1821, and died in 1835.

Joseph married Nancy Diltse in 1821.

William married Elizabeth McNeil ; died 1835.

Agnes married Dr. William Burr.

Morgan married Mary Pierce. He died October 13, 18—.

Sarah married Samuel Brown.

Elizabeth married George Brown.

Isaac married Judah Crype.

Mary married Greenbury Nolan. She died 1890.

Isaac crossed the Ohio into Indiana, and his children, with the exception of Margaret, were born there, on his farm near Anderson. The whole place is one of exceptional beauty, with woodland and river and open, smiling fields. Aside from the beauty of the landscape, the farm is interesting from the fact that in one of its woodlets are still to be seen several tunnels left to us by the ancient Mound Builders. Curiously enough, a few miles away at Middleton, Mr. Cyrus Van Metre in draining a marsh came upon a queer object nearly the size of a bushel measure. Experts of Smithsonian Institute pronounced it to be part of the tooth of a mammoth. That two pre-historic relics of so much significance should be found so near together and in the domains of the same family is unusual.

In the autumn of 1834 Isaac had a severe attack of brain fever, which appears to have produced a lesion, for although he fairly recovered bodily health, he became subject to fits of melancholy that soon developed into suicidal mania, and on July 4, 1835, he finally accomplished his purpose of self-destruction. He was a man of deeply religious nature, as well as one concerned in the welfare of his community and the country in general. He held a position of public trust at the time of his death.

The husbands of three of Isaac's daughters were three brothers, a singular case of inter-family relationship.

Margaret, daughter of Isaac, was born May 29, 1798. She married James W. Brown in 1821, and died in 1835. It is thought her death was mainly due to her father's tragic fate a month before. Two newborn children were buried with her. Besides these and her first child, a boy who died soon after his birth, her children were : Mary, born in 1822 ; Isaac Van Metre, July 12, 1826; William Josephus, in 1828 ; Sarah, in 1830, and Samuel Lafayette, in 1832.

James W. Brown, husband of Margaret Van Metre, was a son of
Thomas Brown, of County Donegal, Ireland.   It is said in the
family tradition that he left the old country on account of the sudden
troubles between the Catholic party and the Orangemen, of whom
he was one ; abandoning a fine property for the sake of peace of
mind.   He married an English woman named Blake.   Their son
James was born at Carlisle, Pennsylvania.   His later home was in
Indiana, near Margaret's, and there they were married ; he had been
trained to be a builder, but seems to have turned to speculating in
real estate and mines.   In the year 1843 he went to the State of
Texas, investing in or locating mines at Houston and at Dallas.
He is supposed to have been murdered for money on his attempted
return home a few years later.   In Indiana he held commission as
Major of Militia.

Isaac Van Metre Brown, son of Margaret Van Metre, was
born at Chesterfield, Indiana, July 12, 1826.   Losing his mother
by death and his father by absence, he grew up in the family
of his mother's sister and his father's brother.   In 1846 he
married Elizabeth Drummond Carrl, or Carroll.   Their children
were : James W., born in 1847, died 1847 ; Anna Louise, born January 9, 1849 ; Mary Eleanor, born August 15, 1851, died October,
1853.   Isaac was trained for an architect, but later, following his
own inclinations, he entered the ministry of the Christian Church.
Hence it goes without saying that as he received but little inherit-
ance, he passed his short life a comparatively poor man.   Yet never
did helplessness and poverty find in any one a more ready or generous
friend than he.   He entered the Federal army at Waterloo, Iowa,
in 1863, going out under Lincoln's call for "six hundred thousand
more."   He shared in common with others of his race a disinclina-
tion for distinction that had not been earned by service.   In this
spirit he put aside a proffered office and entered as a private soldier.
He had a presentiment that he should fall in battle, and asked that
he might be buried on the field.   He died May 15, 1863, at Fort
Pillow Terin, before his regiment had been called into its brilliant
career of thirty-eight engagements.   His only remaining brother
died in the army the same year.   All of his cousins, so far as known,
and all of his nephews old enough to bear arms, enlisted, but few of
them returned alive, and none of them unscathed.

Elizabeth, wife and widow of Isaac, died in June of 1866.   She
was a granddaughter of Loudon Carll, a soldier of the Revolution,

who migrated from New Jersey to Bourbon County, Kentucky, at the close of the war. He seems to have been a man of affairs; for besides managing a considerable property in farms, tanneries, stock, etc., he was a "circuit rider" for the Methodist Church, and held continuously political office. He met a tragic death in 1834. An anecdote is told of him that seems characteristic. Being urged by some pension agent to apply for the provision the Government had made for its soldiers, he replied that he thought that he could take care of himself and his family without the help of the United States.

Anna Louise Thompson, daughter of Isaac Van Metre Brown, was born at Logansport, Indiana, January 9, 1849. She was married to Watson Thompson, of Syracuse, New York, in 1874. Their two children, Ralph Watson and Eleanor Foster, died in infancy at their home in Clinton, Iowa.

Mr. Thompson was a quiet Christian gentleman, much loved by his friends. A whole city mourned his untimely death, which occurred accidentally, November 28, 1891. His widow survives him.

Of this branch of the Van Metre family it may be said in general that they are an unassuming, self-respecting people, never seeking the upper room at feasts, never lacking in dignity where dignity is required; open-hearted, open-handed, with little striving for riches or for political preferment.

Apparently they prosper best as agriculturists and in the professions; the Christian ministry and medicine claiming a large proportion of them: preachers and teachers and doctors. They do not appear to have much taste for commerce, nor to succeed particularly well in that direction. But in every movement in the great life of the country, from the far-off storming of Louisburg through the Revolution to Lewis' and Clarke's famous expedition into the far West, to its great Civil War, to the knightly undertaking of making Cuba free, they have been unostentatiously but effectively present.

When the Civil War came on, for every man in gray that mustered under the new flag a man in blue hastened to the defense of the old, until practically the entire clan was clad in blue or gray. Sometimes the sons of one household faced each other on the field; but one need not fear contradiction when he says that in gray or in blue the Van Metres bore themselves with courage and with honor. It would seem to be a family trait to desire to begin in the ranks and "work up" along the path of glory, and many instances are recorded of individual daring.

In common with all the Van Metres, this branch inherits the strong religious tendency begotten in the stormy days of the Reformation and its attendant persecution. It is rarely indeed that one meets one of them who is not an active worker in some church ; and in every mission field they have labored and died for the Cross.

Physically the children of John first of Berkeley as a rule are tall and not inclined to flesh until later life. Another persistent feature is known as "the gray-blue eye of the Van Meters."

### MEETING IN REUNION AGAIN.

[Copied from Freeport Daily Democrat of August 17, 1900.]

The unsettled weather of the week which has interfered so much with the program at the Freeport Driving Park and the Camp Meetings at Lena and Oakdale, also interfered somewhat with the attendance at the reunion of the Van Metre family at Lathrop's grove yesterday. However threatening the clouds may have been in the forenoon, they cleared a little about noon, and by 1:30 o'clock nearly five hundred members of this historic family and quite a number of invited friends had gathered to greet each other once more in happy reunion, to relate again the experiences of the past and enjoy the program which had been arranged, and which, though unintentionally short, was nevertheless interesting. The brevity of the program was due to the absence of two of the principal speakers —Dr. Byers, of Monroe, and Dr. Naramore, of Lena, the former on account of sickness.

Some two hundred people had ventured to the grove in face of the threatening clouds by 12 o'clock, when J. W. Van Metre, of Orangeville, introduced Judge W. N. Cronkrite, of Freeport.

"Since I am not a member of the Van Metre family," began Judge Cronkrite, "I must naturally speak as a rank outsider. It would be useless for me to try to trace the history of this family. Some of these older heads could tell the story of the struggle of those pioneers with much more accuracy and interest than I could. You meet here to extend the hand of friendship, to renew old times, and to keep in touch with each other as members of the same great and illustrious family.

" I want to tell what a stranger thinks of the Van Metre family, whose connection with the history of this community dates with its earliest colonization. Members of this great family have been recognized as leaders in agricultural pursuits, in the production of fine stock, in politics, and in the educational and religious movements which have marked the progress of this section of this great Commonwealth. The Van Metre family has placed its mark upon the history of this community. By your fruits are you known. Not every hero makes his mark as a president or a professor. Members of this family were heroes in the pioneer life and in the humbler walks in life, but were heroes nevertheless. The community regards this family with pride, and well it may.

"As for myself, you always make it pleasant for me when I am with you, and I assure you it has been a pleasure for me to have been with you upon this occasion."

Judge Cronkrite's address was followed by music by the Winslow band, and then preparations were made for dinner. By the time this interesting feature was over nearly five hundred people had gathered.

The president again called the meeting to order, and, after more music by the band, introduced Honorable T. J. Van Metre, of Fayette, Wisconsin. The gentleman related in an interesting manner how he and his brothers went fishing once in an early day, and upon returning home, Joe, one of the brothers, went to wash the milk utensils preparatory for use next day. Mrs. Van Metre had made some tallow candles, and had left an incomplete mass of tallow in a kettle in which Joe would do the washing. She thought of this after Joe had gone, and hastened to tell him not to spoil her tallow, but she was too late. The result was that Joe, from that time to this day, was called "Greasy Joe." Mr. Van Metre used this story as an illustration of how the tobacco or liquor habit will fasten itself upon one and cling to him tenaciously, as did the name of "Greasy Joe." He urged upon those members of the Van Metre family who are rearing families to prevent, if possible, the formation of a habit or habits by their boys that will cling to them through life.

Mr. Van Metre related some reminiscences in a happy manner, all of which were much enjoyed.

Nathan Kelly Van Metre, of Mineral Point, Wisconsin, was then introduced, and began by saying that he was not a public speaker, neither was he a preacher or a politician. His mind was carried back to 1850 when some of the boys often sought to come back to the Pecatonica, or "Picky," as they facetiously called the stream, to fish.    All the older folks of that time are gone, he said, and new generations are coming on.    Then he reminded those raising families that they have a great responsibility resting upon them in the proper development of their children.    He, too, urged upon parents the duty of teaching temperance to their children.

There was a vocal solo by Mrs. M. G. Wirsing, of Orangeville, and City Attorney Bruce Mitchell, of Freeport, was then presented to the audience, and he made an address that was very kindly received. He said he felt it an honor to enjoy the hospitality of the Van Metre family as he had on this occasion—a family that had been so closely identified with the growth and development of Northern Illinois and Southern Wisconsin.    He declared that the early Van Metres as pioneers were proud of the principles which underlie the foundation of our government, and it was very evident that it had always been their endeavor to maintain them.

Attorney L. H. Burrell, of Freeport, was then introduced.    Mr. Burrell said that this assembly of Van Metres is one of the foundations of society.    In union there is strength, and as this family stands together by these picnics it preserves that unity which is so necessary in society.    He then referred to the unity of action of the English and the Americans in 1849 and 1853 in Chinese waters, where they brought about a peaceful solution of a very difficult problem.    This unity of family relations of the Van Metre family is preserved by these family picnics.

A duett was rendered by the Misses Howe, of Cadiz, and later Miss Clare Howe, of Freeport, gave a recitation, which was greatly enjoyed.

Some of the younger generation indulged in dancing, but at this time the sun was shining brightly, and the dancers found it too warm to prolong their vigorous exercise.

And thus ended the fifth, one of the pleasantest reunions of the Van Metre family, the members of which are held in the highest esteem in a community they did so much to build up.

The officers will continue the same, and the next reunion will be held at the same place on August 16, 1901.

While there were in attendance some 500 people, this gathering was marked by the presence of more members of the family from Wisconsin than had ever attended before at any time.    Those present from Wisconsin were : Nathan K. Van Metre, Mineral Point ;

EMANUEL VAN METREN,
Of Holland and London.

Thomas Van Metre, wife and daughter, Fayette; Joseph Van Metre, Blanchardville; W. I. Van Metre, Wiota; Andrew Van Metre, Wayne; Abe Compton and Frank Compton, Fayette; George Compton and wife, Waldwick; Aaron Denio, wife and daughter, Fayette; and Mary Carter, Jonesdale. J. L. Van Metre, Elgin; Mrs. Willard Van Metre, Chicago, and W. Battin, Spencer, Ia., were also present from a distance.

The attendance was also marked by the presence of John Alexander, who is a resident of California, going there in 1850. This is his first visit since he went West.

## MEMORANDUM.

Emanuel Van Meteren, author of "Historie van de Oorlogen en Geschiedenissen der Nederlanderen," born at Antwerp, 1535; was a grandson of William Ortels, of Augsburg, and first cousin of the historian, Abraham Ortelius. He lived in England as merchant and Dutch consul until 1612, the year of his death.

Emanuel Van Meteren's history was originally published in Latin at Amsterdam, 1597. He translated the work into Flemish, and published it in 1599; then continued it in the same language up to 1612, in which shape it was republished after his death at Arnhem in 1614. French editions of the work appeared in 1618 and 1670, and a German one at Frankfort in 1669.—"Narrative and Critical History of America." Published by Houghton, Mifflin & Co., Boston and New York, Vol. IV, page 424, and Notes 1 and 2.

[Translated from the old Dutch book.]

LIFE AND DEATH OF THE VENERABLE, PIOUS, AND RENOWNED
EMANUEL VAN METEREN, BRIEFLY DESCRIBED BY
HIS LOYAL FRIEND, SIMEON RUYTINCK.

Among the writings of our venerable friend, E. Van Meteren, we have found his accurate and elaborate notes on the main occurrences of his own and his family's life, interspersed with many fine quotations taken from the Scriptures, from our ancestors, from poets and philosophers. These were written down for the recreation of his soul and as an admonition for his children, to whom he left them as a sure pledge of his piety and love. We have extracted from them the most noteworthy items to adorn his book therewith, in order that the name of the excellent man may forever be honored ; whose virtuous and wise old age we have always respected. Emanuel Van Meteren, who with great diligence and discretion compiled this book, was born in Antwerp, June 9, 1535. His father's name was Jacob Van Meteren, of Breda, son of Cornelius Van Meteren. His mother was named Ottilia Ortels, daughter of William Ortels, of Ausburch (Augsburg), who was the grandfather of the world-famous geographer, Abraham Ortel (or Ortelius). His (Emanuel's) father had learned in his youth the noble art of type-setting ; was gifted with the knowledge of many languages and other useful sciences. He knew how to distinguish light from darkness in his age (he had accepted the new—reformed—creed), and showed fine enthusiasm in defraying the expenses of the translation and print-ing of the English Bible at Antwerp, for which he availed himself of the services of a learned scholar, Miles Coverdale (Couerdal) by name, much to the furtherance of the kingdom of our Savior in England.

His mother was a God-fearing and blithesome lady who also had accepted the knowledge of truth (*i. e.*, the reformation of the Church), and, together with her husband, had suffered much for it.

Now it happened while her husband was in England on his business and she was pregnant with her son, that the authorities sent men to search her house in order to arrest Leonard Ortels, her uncle (who used to stay there, for religious reasons), and at the same time to see whether any forbidden books were to be found. The cruelty of this searching party caused the good woman to en-treat the Lord that they might fail to find the papers ; and it so happened, although they several times laid hands on the box which contained the books, they failed to get them. Recognizing in this God's merciful aid and protection, she made a vow, if she gave birth to a son, to call him Emanuel, *i. e.*, "God with us." This vow she fulfilled. Hence Emanuel, when he grew up to be a man, took cause generally to add to his name, "*Quis contra nos?*" *i. e.*, "If God be with us, who is against us?" in order bet-ter to remember the Lord's mercy previously shown, and to trust in him in all danger.

These God-fearing and zealous parents sent their son to school early in youth to be instructed in languages and all good learning, taking these to be the most useful and safest possessions. His first school was at Antwerpen, his second at Doornick, the third at

Deiffeln, where, to the joy of his parents, he made great progress in Latin. They summoned him home to see this gratifying improvement in 1549. As described by Cornelius Grapheus : Emanuel's father having gone to England on business, called his son thither in 1550, and made him understand that since he was now fifteen years old, it was befitting that he should consider what he would like best to engage in, commerce or study. If he preferred studying, he would send him to the renowned Emanuel Tremelins, who had arrived in the company of other excellent men from Germany and stood high in the favor of King Edward the 6th. He answered his father that he was inclined to be apprenticed to a merchant to learn commerce, and in this way make a living in the course of time.

Thus he was turned over for a period of ten years to the business house of Sebatian Daukkearts, of Antwerp, who, in 1552 (in the year of King Edward's death), removed from London to Antwerpen. And since persecutions on account of religion increased daily in their country, Jacob Van Meteren and his wife, Ottilia, undertook the voyage to London to enjoy there a peaceful life under Edward the 6th, the pious prince, but it did not please the Lord that they should reach this shore, where persecution was also to come. But it happened since there was a heated war going on between Charles the 5th and Henry the 2d, that a French man-of-war shot fire into (*i. e.*, set on fire by a shot) the powder of the ship that they were in. Thus they were called hence by the Lord on the sea, in the firm belief that "the sea, too, will give up its dead on that day." Emanuel, having thus lost his God-fearing parents, or, much rather, having found them again (in the Lord), settled down faithfully to his tedious service. His patience was rewarded by God's manifold blessing. During his time of service he went on two voyages, viz., in 1556 and 1558, to England, and saw there the great cruelty which, under the reign of Mary, was used against the reform church, as he often told me. When he was in London his master died in Antwerp ; thence he gave the remaining years of his bond-service to his master's widow, after which he settled in London, received commissions of many excellent merchants, and behaved with great prudence. And, seeing that wedlock is the haven of youth, he asked the Lord for a pious and suitable wife ; also took advice with Mr. J. B. Bartelotti. The latter pointed out to him Miss Van Loobroeck. This lady had been a prisoner in

Antwerpen a short while ago because she had attended the sermon
at Hoboken.   But she had become miraculously rescued through a
hole bored in the wall.   He took her for his wife, as sent to him by
the Lord, and became wedded to her in 1562 ; his age being twenty-
six and hers twenty-two.   When they began to keep house there
boarded with them a nobleman from Trenton, called James Acon-
tius, who had seen, done, heard, written, and suffered many things ;
had also been quite intimate with Emperor Maximilian.   Through
his conversation Emanuel learned many beautiful things.   And as
the Lord, to try our faith and patience, mixes our joy with sadness,
so it was that he took from Emanuel his dear wife on the 13th of
December, 1563, in which year (from pestilence as well as from
other illness) there died in London about twenty-three thousand
seven hundred and sixty persons.   Several months after this sad
occurrence (the pestilence ceasing) Emanuel tried to re-establish
himself by wedding a second wife.   When he had gone to Antwerpen
on business, he was introduced to the society of Miss Esther van
den Corput, daughter of Nicolaus van den Corput, secretary of
Breda, son of Johann (John) van den Corput, formerly mayor of
the same place.   And the Lord turned their hearts toward one
another, so that after a certain time, with the consent and congrat-
ulations of the parents, the marriage came to pass.   And he
returned to London together with his wife in 1564.   By this wife
(who is still living) the Lord enriched him with thirteen children,
of whom nine remain, viz : three sons and six daughters.   One of
the main difficulties which befell him during his married life was
his imprisonment at Antwerpen, where he had gone on business in
1565.   He describes it at length, while we only briefly mention it.
On the 2d of May, at noon, coming from the Exchange, he writes,
and going to my cousin's (Abraham Ortel's), where I was lodging,
I was arrested by a Spaniard, Julian de la Sierna by name, lieutenant in the service of Comergo, the Provost.   He came in company
with six or eight helbardiers, and arrested me in the name of the
Governor-General of the country.   They took hold of me as
though I were a disorderly person (disturber of the peace), binding
together my arms.   No questioning or parleying availed, but I was
taken to the Backers gate prison between two helbardiers, the
Spaniard preceding us.

I was much dismayed.   They took from me my letters and keys,
and asked if my home was not at Mr. Andreas' in Gallicia.   I told

them that they had the wrong man before them. Nevertheless they went straightway to my house and took all of my writings, books, and letters. I was much afraid, expecting the worst, viz : that they would torture me and put me to death. At night they locked us up in a small house, in which there were but three little holes as big as a fist that we got light through. On the next day an old woman came to us doing charity to the prisoners, and, seeing me, asked if I were Emanuel. I said yes, and found out then how she came to know me. She told me to have good courage, since many good friends, such as the Hoefuagets, Hufman, etc., were exerting themselves in my behalf (soliciting favor for me). This gave me some courage, and I took so much the more earnestly to praying. At supper the jailer said that a Spanish criminal was to die on the next day, and that a mass would be said for him, and that we were to attend it. This was a great discomfort to me. I remained in bed and ardently entreated the Lord to assist me with His Spirit.

The other prisoners told me at noon that the jailer had told everywhere I did not want to hear mass ; so when the occasion to do so recurred, I said to him that I did not care to attend mass because I was an Englishman ; that such acts were subject to a fine of one hundred marks (shillings) in England, etc. He took this statement and desisted from urging me. Two or three days I sat in perplexity, hearing and seeing nothing, only praying to God, and after considering how I could best make my defense, I was unable to make up my mind whether to defend myself as a citizen of Antwerpen or as an Englishman. While these thoughts were troubling me, the daughter of the assistant jailer came to my door stealthily and called through the key-hole : "Englishman ! Englishman !" I asked what she wanted. She said I was to defend myself as an Englishman ; that I was to be tried that day by Councillor Boone, but it would be all right, etc. This was good doings and gave me courage. I thanked God for this assistance. On the 7th of May in the afternoon Councillor Boone came, took me separately to the chamber where oaths were administered, had me sit down, had all my papers before him, charged me on my oath that I was to tell the truth in answering all questions. I remarked at length, highly commending at the same time his honesty and uprightness. But he asked me to follow his advice and I should do well. Thus perceiving that he favored me and had consulted with my friends, I yielded to him. He began taking down name, date of birth, and names of my friends; asked me if I knew certain people in London and Antwerp, Peter Luls, John Rademaker, John Niket, and others; also what I was doing with Eobanns Hess' psalms in Latin verse, and with a German pamphlet on the Dutch treaty of peace, and whether I did not know something concerning the last (recent) treason of Antwerp. He also asked what contributions were made by the Secret Council and the City of London to the Prince of Orange; whether I had persuaded any one from giving the King the assessed; what letters Daniel Rogers, Secretary of the English Ambassador, had handed me, etc. To all of this I gave (God be praised, who gave me strength) brief and cautious answer, referring him to Messrs. John Boyschot and Van Swevigem, who knew well how I had been employed in England in matters pertaining to international(?) communications and in the making out general decrees. All this he put down, and made me sign the statement. In the mean time the news of my imprisonment reached London, to the great afflictions of my wife and friends. Martin de la Faille received letters in my favor from Mr. Boyschot, Ambassador in England. John Rademaker obtained letters from Secretary Walsinghan to the English Court-Master(?) at Antwerp that I was to be treated as English. My good friend in Antwerp, in my name, submitted a petition to the Grand Commander; so that at last (after I had often thought of preparing for death), unexpectedly, Councillor Boone came again to see me, exactly when I had finished reading "De Immortalitate Animæ," by Lewis Vivis, which Al. Ortels had found a way of sending to me. The Councillor said that he had requested His Excellency to dismiss me, although he had great cause to proceed against me with rigor. He advised me to leave by the first ship, without, however, having any order to require me to do so or exile me. Hereupon I got ready my belongings in the prison and left on May 20, 1575, which day will ever be sacred to me. I thanked the Lord with all my heart, took leave of my good friend, who rejoiced with me, and reached London on May 30th, to the joy of my family and friends.

During the peace of Ghent some patriots, Emanuel's faithful friends, worked for him to promote him to some acceptable office, but Emanuel, seeing that all was built upon sand, showed little inclination for this.

The next paragraphs comment on Emanuel's interest in the history of his country and on his way of compiling the book before us.

In 1583 he was elected chief or council of the " College of Dutch Merchants in London."

Anthon Diest anagramatized the name Emanuel Van Meteren as " Een mael met Vreden," meaning " some time with peace." The first warning of approaching death came in the shape of a slackening of the vital (more especially secretory) functions. These premonitions caused him to prepare for death. He kindly took leave of the merchants and other friends who in great numbers came to see him, and thanked them for their comforting words. He also expressed a desire to see once more his medals, foreign coins, shells, and other rarities, in which he used to take delight in his leisure hours. Yet he said that all this was vanity. Therefore he took to praying steadily, also accepting, when he grew very weak, a minister's aid. He blessed his children, who surrounded his bed, and gave his soul into the hands of the Lord Jesus, who had cleansed it with His blood, in the seventy-seventh year of his age, on the 8th of April, 1612 (old calendar), in London.

# THE CUNNINGHAM FAMILY.

There was a Lord John Cunningham of Ireland, who lived there as late as 1850, and quite probably his descendants are living there now, and who descended from this old Scotch family.

Three sons and their aged father came from Ireland and settled at the upper end of the valley of the South Branch of the Potomac about 1750 to 1755. The aged father died and was buried in the garden at the homestead not many years after they settled there. William, Senior, and his sons Robert, John, and William, Jr. (nick-named "Irish Billy"); this last named William married Phoebe Scott and raised a family of children, who will be given later on. It is said this William has been known more than once to give the lineal descent of the family from recollection back in an unbroken line to Scotch titled ancestry, but no record of it can now be found. John and his wife, Elizabeth, were married in Ireland, and her maiden name is not known. His sons : John, William, Robert, and Isaac. Daughters : Nanny, who married William Grimes and lived in Kentucky ; Gemima, who married William Shobe, and Elizabeth, who married Samuel Scott and lived in Kentucky. Robert, who married (Mary) Polly Robinson and lived in Kentucky ; John, who married Rebecca Harness and lived and died in Hardy County, Virginia ; William, who married Jemima Harness and lived and died on the South Branch Valley, near to where the Cunninghams first settled Captain Isaac (the writer's grandfather), who married Sarah Harness (a twin sister of Hannah Harness, who married Hanry Hull), removed to Clark County, Kentucky, in 1802, and lived the remainder of his life there.

Of the Emigrant Robert, the brother of John and "Irish Billy," the writer of this can get little information, and has found no descendant from him.

The Emigrant William 2d ("Irish Billy") married Phoebe Scott, of Hardy County, Virginia, and lived and died there ; his grave is on the east side of the South Branch River and Valley, at the foot of a hill in the old Cunningham graveyard, marked by a plain stone slab, on the land where they settled when they came from Ireland to Virginia. His children : William 3d, married Jemima Harness ; Jesse, married Miss Hutten ; Hanna, died unmarried. Children of William Cunningham the 3d : William 4th, married Sallie Van Meter (daughter of Isaac Van Meter, of Old Fields, he a brother of Jacob and son of Garrett, of Old Fort Pleasant); John, married Rebecca Lanck, of Winchester, Virginia ; Solomon, married Kittie Seymour ; George, married Rebecca Seymour ; Hannah, married David Van Meter (son of Esquire Isaac Van Meter, father of Sallie above named); Sallie C., married Garrett Van Meter, a son of Esquire Isaac Van Meter, and brother of David here named.

The children of William Cunningham 4th, viz : Isaac, who married Catherine Harness ; Jesse, who married Betsy Ann Williams ; Lizzie, who married Garrett Van Meter, son of Colonel Jacob Van Meter, who owned and lived and died at Fort Pleasant (the grandfather of the writer of this); Jemima, who married J. Hanson McNeill, the famous Commander of McNeill's Rangers in the great unpleasantness ; Rebecca, who married Rev. N. Fish ; David, who married Lizzie Vance ; Mary, who married Rev. William Champion ; Hannah, who married A. J. Fisher ; Sallie, who married R. J. Silden ; others died young and unmarried.

Children of John Cunningham, the brother of this William 4th, above, viz : William Streit, who married Sallie Van Meter, youngest daughter of Colonel Jacob Van Meter, of Fort Pleasant (the writer's grandfather) ; Charles L., who married Mary Jane Welton ; Hannah, who married Andrew Dyer, of Pendleton County, Virginia ; Susan, who married George Shultz, of Winchester, Virginia.

Children of Solomon Cunningham (son of William 3d and brother of John here above), viz : George S., who married Jane Ann Harness ; Seymour, who married Martha McGreer ; William H., died unmarried ; Garrett, unmarried and living near the old Cunningham homestead where the old emigrant ancestry lived and died ; Jane, married Felix B. Welton ; Ann Jemima, married Charles Green ; Phoebe, died unmarried.

Children of Emigrant John Cunningham : Robert, who married Polly (Mary) Robinson, came to Kentucky about the year 1792, and settled in Clark County, on the banks of Johnson Creek, about four miles north of where Winchester was afterwards located. There he spent the balance of his life and raised quite a large family of children, viz : John, Isaac, Abner, and Jesse ; daughters, Elizabeth, Maria, Belinda, Mary, Lucinda, and Jemima. Of these, Lucinda and Jemima died unmarried ; Elizabeth married John Flournoy, of

Scott County, Kentucky; Maria married Mathew D. Hume, of Clark County, Kentucky; Belinda married Nimrod Hutchcraft, of Bourbon County; Mary died without issue; John, the eldest son, married Mary Bean, of Clark County, Kentucky, and raised a large family of children in Bourbon County, where he resided all of his life. He served a campaign in the War of 1812-13, volunteering for that service at the age of nineteen years. He served a hazardous and severe campaign under General Shelby, participating in the battle of the River Raisin and other severe engagements until victory was won and peace was made. He was with the Kentucky troops who crossed over into Canada and made the severe winter campaign, and was on British soil when peace was made. He represented Bourbon County in the legislature, and afterwards served that district in the State Senate. Isaac married Millie Donaldson, and lived and raised a family on a part of his father's estate in Clark County. Abner married Pamelia Clarkson, and lived and raised a family on a part of his father's landed estate. Jesse married a Miss Wood, and lived and raised a family on a part of his father's landed estate until late in life, when he removed to Missouri with his family and died there.

Isaac Cunningham and his sister Elizabeth also came to Kentucky. Elizabeth married Samuel Scott, of Virginia, and they lived in Bourbon County, Kentucky. Samuel Scott died leaving quite a family of young children, viz: Robert, Benjamin, Samuel, Cunningham, and one daughter named Amanda. These children were all young and uneducated at the time of their father's death, and were transferred to the care of Captain Isaac Cunningham, who was their mother's youngest brother, and who had one child. Under his care and their mother's they all grew up to be very intelligent, influential citizens in the community in which they lived.

## JOSEPH HELM CLAY.

Born October 22, 1803; married February 1, 1832, Amanda Fitz Allen Scott, daughter of Samuel D. Scott and his wife, Elizabeth Cunningham, who came from Virginia to Kentucky. This wife a sister of Captain Isaac Cunningham and his elder brother, Robert, who removed to Clark County, Kentucky, from Virginia.

This Samuel Delay Scott was a son of Benjamin Scott and his wife, Madam Delay, who was from Paris, France.

CAPTAIN ISAAC CUNNINGHAM,
Of Clark County, Kentucky.

## CAPTAIN ISAAC CUNNINGHAM.

Captain Isaac Cunningham was born in Hardy County, Virginia, December 7, 1778, and January 5, 1800, he married Sarah Harness, who was born in Virginia, December 2, 1783 (with a twin sister who married John Hull). He commenced his business life as a merchant in partnership with a man who went to Philadelphia to buy a stock of goods, taking all the firm's money along with him (the man was not heard of after for more than ten years), which left Captain Cunningham flat broke and with a few debts unpaid. His father squared his accounts for him, and his wife's father gave her about $7,000 worth of property, consisting of negroes, stock, and money, with which they came to Kentucky and settled on a farm about four miles northwest of Winchester, which he purchased of the estate of Mathew Patton in 1802, and then and there he commenced his business life again, to become one of the most successful and influential men that ever lived in Kentucky. He raised only one child of his own, Rebecca (my mother), who was born in Hardy County, Virginia, October 14, 1800, and married Isaac Van Meter, of Hardy County, Virginia, June 17, 1817.

While this was his only child, he nearly all the while had a house full of other people's children. He raised and educated nearly all of his sister's, Elizabeth Scott's, children. His wife's twin sister died quite young and left three daughters, whom he reared and cared for as long as he lived. He reared and educated George Grimes, a sister's son and orphan, who became quite a worthy and influential citizen of Bourbon County. He adopted and raised a child by the name of Thomas Landrum, and, being a member of the legislature at the time, he had the lad's name changed to Thomas L. Cunningham. He gave him a fine farm in Bourbon County, which he occupied to the time of his death, and some of his children still own it. Notwithstanding the general liberality of Captain Cunningham, by his extraordinary judgment, foresight, and skillful financiering he became one of the wealthiest men of the county. He was for many years a magistrate of Clark County, and, according to the law at the time, by seniority of rank as magistrate he became high Sheriff of the county.

After this he frequently represented the county in the State Legislature. He was a member of that body in 1823-24, and at other times, and was afterwards a member of the State Senate for more than one term.    He commanded a company in the War of 1812-13, and participated in some very severe campaigning on the shores of the lakes during that winter, "making his bed on the brush piles and covering up with the snow."    At the head of his company of Clark and Bourbon County Volunteers he did some desperate fighting against the British and Indians at the battle of the River Raisin and in other conflicts.    He was one of the most noted breeders of fine stock in the State.    He bred the finest of thoroughbred horses for some years, and became quite a noted breeder, and was, with his partner and son-in-law (my father), one of the few Kentucky stockholders in the Ohio Company, which made the famous importation of Shorthorn cattle in 1834, and they became the owners of three of the best cows and a bull imported by that company.    Previous to this importation he owned some of the best cattle which could be had in this country up to that time. They were a breed of cattle known as the Patton stock, and were of English origin, but derived their name from the fact that they had been brought to this State by Mathew Patton, the man from whose estate he had purchased his home farm.

Captain Cunningham took a very lively and active interest in political affairs, and wielded as much influence as any man of his day in his section of this State.    While he had no overweaning aspiration for political preferment, he was ever ready to let his voice and influence be as potent as possible in the selection of the representatives of his district and his State in the councils of the nation.    Therefore he had many intimate acquaintances among the most prominent statesmen of his day.    Notably among them were Governor Clark, who resided in Clark County ; Hon. Richard H. Menefee, and Henry Clay, the "Sage of Ashland."    These and other politicians made him frequent visits, especially in times of great political excitement.

I have been told by old men who have been conversant with these times that for many years it was impossible for any man to obtain the majority vote of Clark County against the expressed wishes of Captain Cunningham.

His wife, Sarah, was a daughter of Mikel Harness, of whom further notice is given elsewhere.    Mrs. Cunningham possessed great force of character, energy, and determination, with great practical common sense, and many persons attributed their great success as much to her capacity as to his.    One thing was very obvious to

SARAH (HARNESS) CUNNINGHAM,
Wife of Captain Isaac Cunningham, of Clark
County, Kentucky.

those who were intimate with them—that in a quiet way she exerted quite an influence, and he seldom transacted any important business without consulting her. She invariably had "the casting vote." She was a very active and influential member of the Presbyterian Church, and perhaps the most liberal contributor to its support in the country. It was during her life that the struggle came up between the old and new school factions of that denomination, and it was, perhaps, more through her influence than any other person that the denomination in Clark County held fast to the faith and principles of the old school. There was a very strenuous effort made by the new school faction to bring her to their views, and the Rev. Joseph C. Stiles, a very gifted and talented minister of the new school party, and to whom she was very much attached, made frequent visits to see her and brought his best efforts to bear, but in vain.

Captain Isaac Cunningham died at his residence in Clark County, November 7, 1842, aged 64 years. His widow survived him only a few years; she died April 12, 1845, aged about 62 years. They were buried in their garden, near their residence, and the remains of their only child (Rebecca) with her husband (Isaac Van Meter) and several of their children were afterward placed by their side, where their ashes now rest.

Captain Cunningham left his large estate (after providing bountifully for his daughter) to be equally divided between all of his grandchildren after the youngest one became of age. Meantime the lands were to be kept as nearly as practicable in blue grass, and the surplus money as it accrued from rent, etc., was to be invested in land. Consequently the larger part of the land was in grass nearly twenty years, and a very valuable landed estate was divided between eight grandchildren in 1865, immediately after the close of the late war, several of the heirs being in the Southern army until that time.

## THE HARNESS FAMILY,

who intermarried so frequently with the Cunninghams and Van Meters, all descended from Michael Harness and his wife, Elizabeth Jephebe, both natives of Pennsylvania, and both were children of Hollanders who had emigrated to Pennsylvania among the very early settlers. Michael Harness leased land of Lord Fairfax for ninety-nine years, and at the end of lease to buy it at one penny per acre. He and his wife, Elizabeth, removed from Pennsylvania and built his fort three and one half miles up the South Branch River from where Moorefield is now situated, in 1744, the same year and just before Isaac Van Meter built his Fort Pleasant, about nine miles down the river from him and on the opposite side. When they emigrated to Virginia, Elizabeth, the daughter of Michael Harness, went in advance of the wagon and helped to clear the road and blaze the way with punk-steel and tomahawk in hand, leading the way from Capon River across the mountains to the South Fork River, and kindled a fire for the camp by the time the men and wagons came up. Thus she was the first white woman that ever set foot on the valley of the south branch of the Potomac. This Harness family were not only enterprising, but a fearless, daring, and reckless family. Three of Michael's sons were scalped by the Indians, and the family had many reckless adventures and narrow escapes.

Michael Harness raised thirteen children to be grown, nine sons and four daughters : Elizabeth, the oldest child, married Phillip P. Youcum ; Rebecca, married Michael See ; Kate, married Andrew Trumbo and removed to Kentucky ; Dolly, married Samuel Hornback and removed to Kentucky ; John, the eldest son, married Elizabeth Youcum ; Adam's wife's name not known ; he was killed and scalped by the Indians ; Leonard, married a Miss Hatch and removed to Illinois ; Peter, married Susan —— and removed to Ohio ; Conrad, married —— and was killed and scalped by the Indians ; Jacob, married Unice Pettice ; after her death he married a Miss Roaber ; Michael, Jr., was killed and scalped by the Indians, and at the same time Leonard's only child, a daughter, was killed, and the body was found three years later and recognized by a silver chain she wore around her neck when killed ; two other sons, names not known.

Michael Harness, oldest son of John and his wife, Elizabeth Youcum, raised ten children, five sons and five daughters, viz : Jemima, married William Cunningham ; Elizabeth, married Michael Welton and removed to Missouri ; Rebecca, married John Cunningham ; Hannah, married Henry Hull ; Sarah (or Sallie), married Isaac Cunningham (the writer's grandfather) and removed to Kentucky ; George, married Rebecca Casey ; Joseph, married Rebecca Williams and removed to Ohio ; Adam, married Elizabeth Baker ;

Solomon, married Catherine Taps; John, married Hannah Inskeep and lived in Maryland.

Hannah married Henry Hull. Their children : Rebecca and Jemima, who were never married, and after the death of their parents lived with Captain Isaac Cunningham and his wife, the twin sister of their mother, as long as their aunt and uncle lived. Francis, the youngest daughter, married Isaac C. Van Meter, and after the death of their aunt, Mrs. I. Cunningham, then Rebecca and Jemima made their home with I. C. Van Meter and his wife, their youngest sister. Labin, married Martha Tucker and removed to Missouri. Peter, married Eliza Long, died young, and left one son named Richard and one daughter named Bettie ; she was never married, and died in 1896. Sarah (or Sallie), who married Captain Isaac Cunningham, raised one child to be grown, named Rebecca, who married Isaac Van Meter (the writer's father and mother), and for further particulars see "Van Meters." For Rebecca, see "William Cunningham." For Jemima, see "William Cunningham."

Elizabeth married Michael Welton ; removed first to Kentucky, and then, after a few years, removed to Missouri, and no trace can now be found of the family. No doubt descendants are now living in Missouri and the far West.

In response to an earnest request, the following letter in regard to McNeill's Rangers was received from Lieutenant Isaac S. Welton, of Petersburg, Grant County, West Virginia, dated March 9, 1901, as follows:

" When the war commenced in 1861 we had a company of riflemen in Petersburg which had been organized at the time of the John Brown insurrection, and John H. Everly was captain of it. We were ordered to report for duty May 1, 1861, and were all captured soon after this by McClellan, along with the Hardy Blues, near Beverly, in Randolph County, and were paroled and not exchanged for about ten months.

"In the mean time Captain J. Hanson McNeill had enlisted in the Southern army in Missouri, where he then resided, and in the battle had been captured and sent to prison ; had dug out and made his way back to this, his native land. Captain Everly died while we were paroled.

"Captain McNeill went to Richmond and obtained from the Secretary of War a commission to take command of our company and organize it into Partisan Rangers, which he did, and secured our exchange.

"You ask me to relate some of the most daring exploits of the Rangers. I think the most daring thing we ever did was attacking Milroy's wagon train in the Old Fields, about twelve o'clock in the day in the broad open fields, with a road full of the enemy, not less than 10,000 of them, and capturing sixty or seventy prisoners with as many horses, without firing a gun from our force and no shot from them until we were about a mile away with our booty, when they commenced to shell the woods on the mountain side.

"The attack was so bold, sudden, and reckless that they could not understand it. They saw us charging right at them and unhitch the horses from their wagons, and did not seem to realize that sixty or seventy men would do such a thing until we had the men and horses in the brush and out of harm's way.

"At another time, near the junction of the Moorefield and Romney pikes, with twenty-seven men we captured ninety-six prisoners and one hundred horses with good harness on each horse, and burned twenty-five new wagons loaded with hay. This wagon train was heavily guarded with cavalry and infantry. The cavalry ran to Romney and the infantry took to the brush, except those we captured and carried away on their horses, leaving the wagons and hay making a great fire.

"As for the man with the haversack full of apples, to which you refer in your letter : He had gotten them from Daniel R. McNeill's cellar, and the captain got him about seventy-five yards from the house. The balance of them—about twenty-five—ran with their horses into William C. Van Meter's barnyard, expecting to get through the fence and into the valley below the road and make their way back to Moorefield ; but we were on to them and captured every one before they could get out of the barnyard.

"I think our command captured nearly or quite 1,500 prisoners during the war. Captain McNeill was severely wounded at Meem's Bottom, near Mt. Jackson, Virginia, in a night attack battle, and then died from pneumonia in Harrisonburg after his wound had well nigh healed.

"It can never be definitely known whether he received this wound from friend or foe. He may have been shot accidentally in the dark, and in a hand-to-hand fight it is hard to tell friend from enemy.

"This was the only fight that he was ever in after he took command of the Rangers that I was not with him. I was this time left in charge of Company Q, composed of broken-down horses and sick and invalid soldiers. Yours very truly,

"Isaac S. Welton.

"P. S.—Roosevelt was not the first man who commanded the 'Rough Riders.' Missouri John Cunningham gave this name to McNeill's Rangers during the war."

The following is an extract taken from a letter written by Colonel H. M. Trueheart, of Galveston, Texas, who belonged to McNeill's Rangers, to the Galveston News, and dated Rockingham County, Virginia, October 10, 1864:

"I belong to McNeill's Partisan Rangers. Most of our time is spent far within the Yankee lines, operating on the Baltimore & Ohio Railroad, attacking scouting parties and wagon trains, destroying bridges, cutting communication, etc. Our field of operations is principally the Shenandoah and South Branch Valleys. McNeill's reputation may not as yet have reached Texas, but he stands deservedly high in Virginia. He is independent; subject only to the orders of the Secretary of War and the Commanding General of the Department.

"The gallant old captain now lies suffering from a severe wound received in an attack which we made with sixty men on one hundred Yankee cavalry in Sheridan's rear. Although with their horses saddled and bridled and ready at one moment's notice, we surprised and charged them before day, killing and wounding seventeen, and capturing forty-three, including a captain and a lieutenant and fifty-seven horses and equipments, with that number of small arms.

"Our captain was the only man wounded on our side. Not long since with eighty men he attacked by surprise upwards of one hundred of the enemy; result, five killed, six wounded, fifty-nine prisoners, two of these commissioned officers; one hundred splendid horses, equipments, etc.; no loss to us. This is his style.

"Report says Sheridan has ordered all of Mosby's and McNeill's men falling into his hands to be shot. If so, it will be a losing game for him. Since McNeill's organization two years ago he has lost in prisoners seventeen men, and captured nearly 1,400 Yankees, etc."

From Lieutenant Welton's letter which precedes this we learn that Captain McNeill died from pneumonia about the time he was recovering from this wound. Captain John Hanson McNeill was born and grew up to manhood in Hardy County (now West Virginia). He was a son of Strauther McNeill and his wife, a Miss Pugh, and descended from an old family who were among the very early settlers of the South Branch Valley; was from the same family as Daniel R. McNeill, who was one of the most influential men of the valley; lived to be quite old there, and owned a fine landed estate near Moorefield.

This family came, no doubt, from Ireland to Virginia among the early emigrants. Captain J. H. McNeill removed to Bourbon County, Kentucky, when quite a young man, but lived there only a few years, and then removed to Missouri, where he lived until the war came on, when he went early into it in Missouri, and was captured and sent to prison, but soon dug out and made his way in disguise to his native State, as has been already stated by Lieutenant Welton.

## McNEILL'S CAPTURE OF CROOK AND KELLEY.

After reciting the death of Captain John H. McNeill, who was accidentally killed at Mount Jackson, and stating that his son, Jesse C. McNeill, First Lieutenant of the Rangers, knew of his father's purpose to endeavor to capture Generals Crook and Kelley at Cumberland, General Imboden proceeds to describe this daring enterprise as follows:

General Kelley had his headquarters at the Barnum Hotel, and General Crook slept at the Revere House near by, in the heart of the city of Cumberland, then with a population of about eight thousand, and there were eight to ten thousand Federal troops in winter quarters in and around the city. Jesse McNeill had amongst his followers several young men who had lived in Cumberland. One of these, Jacob Gassman, had been a clerk in the hotel where General Crook slept, and another, Sergeant James Dailey, was a son of the landlord and a brother of Miss Mary Dailey, afterwards the wife of General Crook, and who was then probably engaged to him; and still another of his trusted followers was John B. Fay, a native of Cumberland, and so familiar with all its approaches and streets that McNeill had sent him a few days before the expedition, with a comrade, C. R. Haller, a mere boy, from Missouri, to ascertain and report the exact position of the troops quartered there, the locality of their outposts and pickets, and, in short, get all the information useful in carrying out such an enterprise. Fay performed his duty admirably, and reported to Captain McNeill en route on the night of February 21, 1865. Lieutenant Isaac S. Welton, fully the equal of McNeill in courage, ability, and intelligence, was second in command, and also entirely familiar with all the country round about and enjoying the entire confidence of the men.

There was snow on the ground and the night was cold. McNeill had set out to cross the river far enough west of Cumberland to make his way into the old National road and enter the city from the north, not likely to be closely guarded in that direction ; but as they approached the river the night had been so far spent that there would be no time left to accomplish so great a detour before daybreak. Finding this to be the case, McNeill called a halt and hastily consulted with Lieutenant I. C. Welton and Isaac Parsons, Sergeants Dailey, Vandiver, and Cunningham and Fay, and several privates, amongst them R. G. Lobb, Charles Nichols, and J. W. Kuykendall (Parsons and Kuykendall were volunteers from Rosser's Brigade), when it was decided to take the shortest route across and down the river to the city, and when challenged to answer, "Friends from New Creek," where a garrison was in quarters a few miles west of Cumberland, and then to ride rapidly upon the pickets and capture them, and, upon a threat of instant death, to extort the countersign.

This scheme was successful, and the countersign, "Bull Gap," for the night was obtained, and two or three successive outposts were passed, and the party rode into the city along its principal streets singing Yankee airs and songs and chaffing a few belated stragglers. Separating, a squad of ten went to each hotel. It was lacking then only an hour and a half until daybreak ; no time could be lost. Passing themselves off as a company of Ohio cavalry with "important information for the General," each squad had no difficulty in imposing on the sleepy guard in front of the hotels ; and making right for each General's room, roused him from his slumbers, and as he opened his door, it was to look into the muzzles of several cocked pistols and to receive the information : "General, you are a prisoner! Dress quickly and keep quiet if you value your life. Any attempt to give an alarm will compel us to kill you instantly. Keep quiet and go with us, and you will not be harmed."

Whilst this was going on at the hotels, Sergeant Fay with a squad of men were playing havoc with the telegraph instruments and wires. Along with General Kelley, his Adjutant General was captured. In detailing the circumstances of his capture and abduction, General Kelley told me in Philadelphia that he and General Crook were ordered to send to the stables for their best horses by an orderly or sergeant as if nothing more serious had happened than that they wished in person to make an early visit to the outposts to see that the officers and men were doing their duty. He said when he and Crook first met on the street they looked at each other with such an expression of bewildered astonishment that finally both almost simultaneously smiled, and would have laughed aloud but for a hint to keep quiet and ride "side by side" together with a Ranger on their flanks and a squad in front and rear, all with drawn pistols in their hands.

They went down the river, passing on the outskirts of a part of their army then sound asleep, and soon to a camp guard, and were challenged with, "Who comes there?" To which McNiell replied, "Company B, Third Ohio Cavalry, with the countersign, and we are in a hurry." Instead of requiring the countersign, the officer on duty inquired, "What's up?" McNiell responded, "Oh, old granny Kelley had a nightmare or bad dream that the Rebs are about to come down on him, and he is sending us out this bitter weather to scout the other side of the river. I sometimes wish they would catch him. Don't you think he is a regular old granny in his nervousness whenever he hears there are a few Johnnies across the river?" "Yes, I do! Every time I am put on outpost duty such weather." And away they went at a gallop. General Kelley told me that during this colloquy Crook, who was at his side, kept nudging him with his knee and chuckling at his expense.

A similar chat occurred at the last outpost they had to pass, where McNiell, still personating the Ohio Captain, said, "I wish that General Grant would remove Granny Kelley from Cumberland and put Crook in command," and in this wish the outpost officer concurred, when Crook laughed audibly and again punched Kelley's leg next to him, and from that time till they got to Richmond, Crook lost no opportunity to poke fun at him. But after they had crossed into Virginia, he said McNiell and all his followers treated them with the utmost courtesy and consideration, but compelled them to ride at breakneck speed to escape apprehended pursuit. The total distance ridden by the Rangers, from starting on the evening of February 20th, till camped in the mountains on the night of the 21st, was ninety miles, in about thirty hours.

Great was the consternation in Cumberland that day, and furiously rode pursuing cavalry, doomed to disappointment and thrown off the track by civilian friends of the young confederate rangers. As, for instance, at the farm-house where they dined and fed, not far from Moorefield, two hundred pursuers arrived not twenty minutes after they left, and the commanding officer inquired of the farmer: "How long since these men left your house?" "Only about an hour and a half ago." "Do you know how far it is to any rebel forces?" The farmer replied he had heard there were a good many about Petersburg (a village only a few miles distant). "Who is in command of them?" "A Mr. Smith was down with them at my place" (Colonel George H. Smith was then in command of my brigade). "When did you see them?" "They were down this way day before yesterday." "How many of them?" "I don't know, but I would think about a thousand." "A thousand! Did you count?" "Oh, no, I just saw them riding around and guessed at them." "Well, sir, look at my line and tell me how many men I have without counting them." "Well," said the farmer, "I should think you had about one hundred and fifty men." "How often does Mr. Smith come down here?" "He comes every other day." "And when did you say he was here last?" "Day before yesterday." "What time of day does he come?" "From one to two o'clock in the evening." (It was now after twelve o'clock.)

This interview seemed to convince the Colonel that he was needed at New Creek or Cumberland, and turned back thither. "Mister" Smith had but a handful of men anywhere near Moorefield, the rest of my old brigade being many miles further South wintering. This interview is given in a recent letter to Lieutenant L. N. Potts, acting adjutant of one of my old regiments, who vouches for its truth. It is a graphic illustration of the shrewdness under the guise of rural simplicity often shown by our non-combatant sympathizers during the war.

The only official reports of the affair on record are the following, which I give *verbatim :*

HEADQUARTERS ARMY OF NORTHERN VIRGINIA, February 24, 1865.

*Hon. John C. Breckinridge, Secretary of War :*

General Early reports that Lieutenant McNiell with thirty men, on the morning of the 21st, entered Cumberland, captured and brought out Generals Crook and Kelley, the Adjutant-General of the Department, two privates, and the headquarters' flags, without firing a gun, though a considerable force is stationed in the vicinity. Lieutenant McNeill and party deserve much credit for this bold exploit. Their prisoners will reach Staunton to-day.

R. E. LEE.

CUMBERLAND, MARYLAND, February 21, 1865.

*Major-General Sheridan, Winchester, Virginia :*

This morning about three o'clock a party of Rebel horsemen came up on the New Creek road, about sixty in number. They captured the picket, and quietly rode into town, went directly to the headquarters of Generals Crook and Kelley, sending a couple of men to each place to overpower the headquarters' guard, when they went directly to the room of General Crook, and without disturbing anybody else in the house, ordered him to dress and took him up on a horse already saddled and waiting. The same was done to General Kelley. Captain Melvin, A. A. G. to General Kelley, was also taken. While this was being done, a few of them without creating any disturbance opened one or two stores, but they left without waiting to take any thing. It was done so quietly that others of us who were sleeping in adjoining rooms to General Crook were not disturbed.

The alarm was given within ten minutes by a darky watchman at the hotel, who escaped from them, and within an hour we had a party of fifty cavalry after them. They tore up the telegraph lines, and it required almost an hour to get them in working order. As soon as New Creek could be called, I ordered a force to be sent to Romney, and it started without any unnecessary delay. A second force has gone from New Creek to Moorefield, and a regiment of infantry has gone to New Creek to supply the place of the cavalry. They rode good horses and left at a very rapid rate, evidently fearful of being overtaken. They did not remain in Cumberland over ten minutes.

From all information, I am inclined to believe that instead of Rosser's, it is McNiell's Company. Most of the men from that company are from this place. I will telegraph you fully any other information.

ROBERT P. KENNEDY,
*Major and Assistant Adjutant-General.*

This paper is indebted to Mr. Hunter Robinson and Mr. George Gassman for the copy of the above acccunt from the pen of General Imboden.—*Cumberland Alleghanian* of February 23, 1899.

ROLL FURNISHED BY LIEUTENANT ISAAC S. WELTON, OF MCNEILL'S COMMAND.

Those with * before name known to be dead.

*Captain John Hanson McNeill.
Lieutenant J. C. McNeill.
Lieutenant I. S. Welton.
*Lieutenant B. J. Dolan.
*Lieutenant A. A. Boggs.
*Sergeant H. Taylor.
Sergeant James Daley.
Sergeant David Hopkins.
*Sergeant Jos. Vandever.
*Sergeant Loyd Cleary.
Corporal Isaac Judy.
Corporal George Little.
*Corporal John Mace.

PRIVATES.

Jack Bobo.
Fred Bean.
George F. Cunningham.
*George S. Harness.
Sam Daugherty.
R. C. Davis.
Rev. Jeff W. Duffy.
John Harney.
Jont Hallerman.
William Burkemp.
John Acker.
A. L. Maupin.
Jesse Hevener.
William Hoy.
James H. Mason.
*Henry Ritter.
Samuel Shafer.
*John Smith.
Robert Fobb.
John Lynn.
John Markwood.
James Crawford.

John B. Fay.
*Sprig Leynn—killed in Cuba.
*Fred Stewart.
H. R. Duvall.
Payton Tabb.
John D. Mountz.
David Parsons.
M. S. Alexander.
David Judy.
Seymour Welton.
Henry Seymour.
John Cunningham.
H. M. Truehart.
George Markwood.
Thornton Neville.
*George Vandever.
Snyder Stickley.
Isaac Pennybacker.
Ervin Hill.
Joseph Triplett.
John Triplett.
William Houck.
John K. Long.
John Steel.
D. H. Showalter.
William Macgollis.
James Mitchell.
John Houseworth.
Mort O'Haver.
George M. Allen.
Jack Connelly.
George Grady.
James Hess.
Nathan Anderson.
St. Clare Gray.
Simon Miller.

*Isaac Ferebaugh.
Robin Dyer.
Charles White.
John Coakley.
Hiram Hord.
John Vanpelt.
Sam Jones.
Ben Richards.
Rader Miller.
James Miller.
Jack Cannon.
James Saunders.
George Blakemore.
William Robinson.
*Henry Kellerman.
P. E. Bacon.
*C. J. Dailey.
*Thad Clary.
*R. L. Clary.
*James Wilson.
*A. C. Hack.
*Charles Nichols.
*E. R. Browning.
*Sam Tucker.
*Lewis Frederick.
*V. O. Williams.
*John Johnson.
*Abel Seymour.
*S. L. Vallandingham.
*Harry Shores.
*Joe Coffman.
*Robert Ligget.
*Reuben Mills.
*Peter Devecmon.
*John B. Williamson.
*William Spaulding.
*Wallace Chisolm.

*Taylor Martin.
W. H. Maloney.
James McGinnis.
James A. Parker.
William Pool.
N. R. Paienter.
John Showalter.
William Seaman.
William W. Harness.
Harlan Tabb.
M. G. Trumbo.
E. Tucker.
James M. Temple.
Ben Wootring.
J. Ed Pennybacker.
James Welch.

Charles Miller.
John Carson.
Charles Johnson.
Newton Breathwate.
Jont Shipman.
John Clever.
*William Martin.
David Couger.
Tom Cain.
Jack Coleman.
Frank Davis.
Joseph Barnum.
Mark Westmoreland.
E. R. Haller.
John W. High.
William Athey.

*Charles Watkins.
*Van Cresop.
*William Miles.
*Wayne Cossner.
*Fisher Johnson.
*Robert Rosser.
*George Carrol.
*John Overman.
*John Harper.
*Isaac Michael.
*William Hopkins.
*Nelson Kericoffe.
*John Wilson.
*Jont Hutton.
*Henry Bennett.
William Shertager.

## MARY JOHNSTON.

Mary Johnston, which "To Have and To Hold" and other similar writings have placed in the very front rank of the authors of the present day, is a daughter of Major John Johnston, of Botetourt County, Virginia, and his wife, Bettie Alexander, of Moorefield, West Virginia. Bettie Alexander was a daughter of Edgar S. Alexander, of Moorefield (who lost an arm as a member of the Rockbridge Artillery at the battle of Fredericksburg), and his wife, Rebecca L. Cunningham, of Moorefield, West Virginia. Rebecca L. Cunningham was a daughter of William Streit Cunningham, of Hardy County, West Virginia, and his wife, "Sallie" Van Meter, of the same county and State. "Sallie" or Sarah Van Meter was the youngest daughter of Colonel Jacob Van Meter, of Fort Pleasant, Hardy County, West Virginia, etc., as written elsewhere in this book.

Major Johnston descended from a long line of honorable ancestry, originally Johnstones, who won their titles and note away back in 1400 and before this, in their native moors and glens of Scotland, during the bloody wars between that country and England, and before the days of gunpowder, when clan met clan with glittering cold steel and helmet, with spear and lance and saber. This family was early transplanted to the mountains and valleys of Virginia, where they held fast and true to their lineage through all of the wars, including the seven years' struggle for the liberties and independence of our country, and the bloody strife between the sections of this Union, where,i n the Southern cause, they added many fresh stars to the cluster which had never grown dim — still maintaining the sturdy and inflexible old Scotch character which fears God, honors the king, but must *have its own way or it is no go.*

Edgar S. Alexander was a son of Samuel Alexander, Sr., and his wife, Mary Lobb, of Moorefield, West Virginia. Samuel Alexander came to Moorefield when a very young man, and with very limited means, when that town was only a village, commenced busi-

n.

# ERRATA

### FOR

## Genealogies and Biographical Sketches
### By B. F. VAN METER

The fourth paragraph on first page—John Lewis born in France in 1768.

On page 60, in last paragraph, in statement concerning old kettle, 1774 should be 1744. Make 7, a 4.

On page 58 (since publication) we learn that some of "One-Eyed" Garrett Van Meter's descendants are living in Hardy county, W. Va.

On pages 139 and 140. The youngest son of Abram Van Meter and his wife Elizabeth Ann was left out, viz: David Van Meter, who married Julia, a daughter of Eli M. Kennedy of Bourbon county, Kentucky removed many years ago to Denton county, Texas, where he now resides and has raised a family of children.

On page 148, paragraph sixth—Miss Rebecca L. Alexander is not dead, as stated, but has been living at San Angelo, Texas, for the past fourteen years, with her two children. Bernard C. and Mary, the latter having married William A. Guthrie, of Texas, and not Mr. Johnson as stated in the book. The author was most grievously misinformed in regard to this family, and made the most serious error of any in the book.

On pages 182 and 183 (the last of this book)—In sketch of Mary Johnston is incorrect as to the families of Van Meter and Cunningham. The author was misinformed as to her parentage.

**If this slip is pasted on blank page opposite Preface, and then reference is made to it on the margin where these errors occur, this book can thus be materially corrected, as the author greatly desires it to be as nearly as possible free from errors.**

B. F. VAN METER.

www.ingramcontent.com/pod-product-compliance
Lightning Source LLC
Chambersburg PA
CBHW031122020426
42333CB00012B/188